Mastering Services
Pricing

PEARSON

At Pearson, we believe in learning – all kinds of learning for all kinds of people. Whether it's at home, in the classroom or in the workplace, learning is the key to improving our life chances.

That's why we're working with leading authors to bring you the latest thinking and best practices, so you can get better at the things that are important to you. You can learn on the page or on the move, and with content that's always crafted to help you understand quickly and apply what you've learned.

If you want to upgrade your personal skills or accelerate your career, become a more effective leader or more powerful communicator, discover new opportunities or simply find more inspiration, we can help you make progress in your work and life.

Pearson is the world's leading learning company. Our portfolio includes the Financial Times and our education business, Pearson International.

Every day our work helps learning flourish, and wherever learning flourishes, so do people.

To learn more, please visit us at **www.pearson.com/uk**

The Financial Times

With a worldwide network of highly respected journalists, *The Financial Times* provides global business news, insightful opinion and expert analysis of business, finance and politics. With over 500 journalists reporting from 50 countries worldwide, our in-depth coverage of international news is objectively reported and analysed from an independent, global perspective.

To find out more, visit **www.ft.com/pearsonoffer/**

PRAISE FOR *MASTERING SERVICES PRICING*

'Kevin is a highly engaging teacher. His innovative approach to Value Engineering shows service providers how to collaborate with their clients to positively shape the relationship and make it more valuable, thereby justifying higher prices and delighting the client at the same time.' *Heidi K. Gardner, PhD, Distinguished Scholar, The Center on the Legal Profession, Harvard Law School*

'This comprehensive guide to services pricing will help those in every size and type of practice develop effective strategies and tactics for negotiating and setting prices in the new market. Kevin's focus on strengthening the client relationship through the identification and provision of client value will prove especially important for those seeking to price their services fairly and effectively.' *Jordan Furlong, Principal, Edge International*

'Kevin Doolan has written a lively and practical guide to a problem that bedevils law firms: how they price their services. As important, the book will help lawyers get closer to their clients, the key task at every firm that plans to succeed in this difficult market.' *Aric Press, Partner, Bernero & Press and former editor-in-chief, The American Lawyer*

'Contains valuable new ideas and strategies that can be used by anyone looking to address the price versus value conflict: how exactly to price professional services so that they reflect the value that clients receive, and not just the time that has been taken. Above all, it is a practical and pragmatic guidebook which goes beyond just theory and into easily implementable steps that anyone can take to see real returns on their pricing strategy.' *Steven G. Manton, Strategic Pricing Leader, Debevoise & Plimpton LLP*

For Debbie and Kimberley,
who give my life meaning and value

Mastering Services Pricing

Designing pricing that works for you and for your clients

KEVIN DOOLAN

PEARSON

Harlow, England • London • New York • Boston • San Francisco • Toronto • Sydney
Auckland • Singapore • Hong Kong • Tokyo • Seoul • Taipei • New Delhi
Cape Town • São Paulo • Mexico City • Madrid • Amsterdam • Munich • Paris • Milan

Pearson Education Limited

Edinburgh Gate
Harlow CM20 2JE
United Kingdom
Tel: +44 (0)1279 623623
Web: www.pearson.com/uk

First published 2015 (print and electronic)

ISBN: 978-1-292-06336-2 (print)
         978-1-292-06338-6 (PDF)
         978-1-292-06337-9 (eText)
         978-1-292-06339-3 (ePub)

British Library Cataloguing-in-Publication Data
A catalogue record for the print edition is available from the British Library

Library of Congress Cataloging-in-Publication Data
Doolan, Kevin.
Mastering services pricing : designing pricing that works for you and for your clients / Kevin Doolan.
pages cm
Includes index.
ISBN 978-1-292-06336-2
1. Professional corporations.   2. Fees, Professional.   3. Customer services.
4. Service industries–Prices.   I. Title.
HD62.65.D66 2015
658.8'16–dc23
                                                                                          2015016981

10 9 8 7 6 5 4 3 2 1
19 18 17 16 15

Print edition typeset in 11.5/13.5pt Garamond 3 LT Std by 35
Print edition printed by Ashford Colour Press Ltd, Gosport

NOTE THAT ANY PAGE CROSS-REFERENCES REFER TO THE PRINT EDITION

Contents

About the author

Kevin Doolan is Managing Partner of the Møller Professional Service Firms Group based at Churchill College in the University of Cambridge and teaches pricing on the professional service firm leadership programme at Cambridge Judge Business School. In 2013 he wrote the Harvard Law School Case Study on Pricing and teaches there as visiting faculty.

After more than 25 years as a partner in a leading global firm, Doolan now consults into service firms throughout Europe and the United States, advising on pricing strategy and client attainment, running workshops to help partners and directors to create pricing that works both for them, and for their clients. The underlying principle behind his work is that pricing needs to be 'aligned' so that the service provider maximises their return while at the same time delivering best value to clients. The models that he uses were developed from research conducted as part of his MBA at Henley Management College.

A regular keynote speaker on the conference circuit, his aim is to move service firms away from a 'cost plus' culture, with prices based on the time taken plus a margin, and into one where the service itself has been designed to maximise its value to the client, irrespective of the time taken for delivery. Having had extensive experience over many years on the front line of pricing conversations with major international clients, he brings a wealth of practical experience to the topic, enabling readers to learn real-world techniques that deliver better prices and happier clients.

Publisher's acknowledgements

We are grateful to the following for permission to reproduce copyright material:

Figures

Figure 5.1 from Schlesinger, L.A. and Heskett, J.L., 1991. 'Leonard A. Schlesinger and James L. Heskett Respond', *Harvard Business Review*, November–December. Copyright © 1991 by the President and Fellows of Harvard College; all rights reserved.

In some instances we have been unable to trace the owners of copyright material, and we would appreciate any information that would enable us to do so.

Author's acknowledgements

The journey from research to publication has been a long one and I am massively indebted to my friends and colleagues who have given so much of their time and expertise.

I am particularly grateful to Moray McLaren who asked me to teach pricing on the Lawyers' Management Program at IE Business School in Madrid, to Professor Ashish Nanda at Harvard and Professor George Triantis at Stanford Law School who worked tirelessly with me to create the Harvard Law School Case Study on pricing, to my colleague Luke Warwick who worked with me in creating this book and to my editor at Pearson, Chris Cudmore, for his wise counsel (and his patience) and my Associate at Møller PSF Group, Alexis 'Casper' Caught, for his support on our pricing consulting projects and in creating the Harvard Law School Case Study on Business Development.

Preface

It was an unusually warm summer's day when I turned my car into the country house hotel where partners from a global law firm had gathered for their annual retreat. I was to deliver a keynote speech on the post-crisis pricing challenges for professionals, as they dealt with an unfamiliar growth in client power and were experiencing daily problems in winning and retaining work.

Gathering my thoughts as I drove along the impressively long avenue of trees leading to the house itself, I smiled as I remembered a long-forgotten conversation I had with a plumber who had told me that he priced 'by the driveway', which meant that the longer this was, the more he charged. 'Well they can afford it, can't they?' he had explained. His words stuck with me because didn't lawyers used to charge by the word, explaining the somewhat flowery language used in the past?

The theme of my talk that day was simply this: protected by regulatory restrictions on competition and by their own ability to limit numbers of new qualifiers, lawyers had been living inside a pricing bubble. This had largely allowed them to charge by the hour, independent of the outcomes (value) for clients and with most of the risks (overruns for instance) firmly placed on the client. That bubble had burst, and in doing so it was forcing partners to learn from real-world pricing practices and develop new strategies that were more sustainable and could benefit both them and their clients at the same time.

What happened after my speech, when I was alone in the auditorium and the partners had moved onto lunch, was something of an epiphany. George, the technician who had been running the audio-visual facilities, making sure that my radio mic was working and that my PowerPoints and videos appeared on cue, came over to talk to me. George said that he had really enjoyed my speech and that he had built up his business based very strongly on a core issue that I had discussed – the importance of human relationships both in developing a strong business and in creating successful pricing.

He went on to explain that in his line of work people tended to focus on technical skills but, as he explained, any number of his competitors could successfully run a conference such as this. Quite commonly, those who were technically strong could be weak when it came to building relationships. This was his strength. He personally knew the law firm partners for whom he worked, they had recommended him to others and he had built up a very successful and large firm as a result. 'There will always be cheaper competitors,' he added, 'but I beat them on relationships.'

This commonality of issues across services pricing, from plumbers to audio-visual technicians to accountants and lawyers, management consultants and investment banks, testing laboratories and publishing, through to partial services such as restaurants, hotels and airlines, is what makes the subject so extensive and fascinating. The joy of delivering services is that 'we haven't made it yet' so we have an amazing opportunity to change what we will deliver and to tailor it and shape it based on the clients' needs, but also what they're willing to pay for.

Given the breadth of service firms, it would have been possible in this book to refer to partner/manager/technician/scientist/ director, etc. However, in order to avoid that, I have defaulted to the expression 'partner' for the person who delivers the service and creates its pricing (even though others are commonly involved) and to 'client' rather than customer. My apologies to those who feel excluded by this naming convention, but it has substantially shortened the text!

Introduction

Providers of services come in many varieties. Many belong to the professions and receive considerable training in how to develop key skills for their chosen calling. With the rise in learning and development together with coaching, many partners are fortunate enough to have a continuous and lifelong opportunity to improve their skills. However, when it comes to agreeing a price for their services, the approach is rather more amateur. This is particularly unfortunate at a time when clients are becoming more sophisticated in negotiating price, are under pressure to reduce costs and are turning increasingly to procurement professionals to help them attack the prices charged by their service providers and advisers. Over the last 50 years we have seen manufacturers reinvent themselves as service companies: IBM becoming a solutions provider rather than just a manufacturer of computer equipment, Rolls-Royce offering aero engines as 'Power by the Hour' rather than as a one-off sale, and airlines developing and segmenting different parts of their market with very different pricing offers.

The purpose of this text is to describe a more professional approach to the pricing of services and to learn from other sectors of the economy more advanced in the field. To do so, I will help to unravel and demystify the client's purchasing decisions, complemented with techniques (developed, practised and honed over decades as a senior partner in a professional service firm) that will support you in getting the results that you want – better sales at better prices as well as more sustainable relationships with your clients. As we will see, this is not just a matter of increasing the price to the client. There are many ways of achieving a better return, including moving from time-based charging to fixed or project-based fees, better managing the team carrying out the work and changing the service being provided to one that is more valuable for the client.

Many traditional service providers have faced unusual challenges over the last few years. I have heard stories from my peers about an inability to increase charging rates, despite overheads starting to rise again, and about clients being ever more willing to challenge fee quotes and shop around or run highly competitive tender processes. From the client perspective, there is strong feeling that the providers of many services have had it too good for too long and now need to face up to reality. A surprising observation I have encountered from clients of many service providers is how easy it has been to negotiate ever bigger discounts or demand more and more added value, sometimes with just a single telephone conversation. Those working in procurement cannot believe their luck – here is an enormous area of spend with suppliers who seem wholly unprepared for negotiations.

Whatever the reason, one thing is clear: we have lost confidence in our prices. We find them difficult to defend or explain to our clients when challenged; many of them will be paying quite different amounts for very similar services for historic reasons or because of their negotiating power. This alone carries a great risk to the client relationship, with huge potential to instil distrust and therefore disloyalty.

With this text, it is my aim to teach you all I have learnt, often the hard way:

■ How clients choose between different firms, and more specifically between different individual advisers, so that you have a clear model for understanding client buying behaviour and their drivers of value.

■ Pricing models that bring method to the madness, aligning the price with the service being delivered and, as a result, bringing back confidence in your pricing. Aligned pricing delivers both the right profit for the firm, and meets the client's needs at a price they are happy to pay, therefore leading to a sustainable relationship.

Additionally, we will look at both the strategy and tactics of pricing a wide range of services to enable us to produce profitable growth with satisfied clients.

There is a considerable body of international expertise on pricing. Every business, whether manufacturers, retailers, logistics companies, computing services outsourcers or fashion houses – every conceivable type of business – needs to understand how to price their products and services if they are going to be successful. Even if you do everything else right, if your prices are wrong then your businesses will fail entirely, or at least fail to deliver the proper return. Much of the published research and advice about how to price is not wholly relevant to traditional services, particularly those from the professions. We can learn from it, but it will not provide the whole answer. Today, service providers require solutions that are grounded in the client relationship and built upon the special features of trust and expertise that are uniquely important in their field.

This book is based on a number of sources and experiences, which means its applicability spans across a broad range of service-focused organisations. At its core is a primary research project that I carried out as part of my MBA: a series of training courses run across the world to assist partners in pricing their services in my position as Head of Client Services at global law firm Eversheds, my consulting practice working with professional service firms in the United Kingdom and in the United States and also on the workshops and seminars delivered by me at IE Business School, Madrid, The Judge Business School, Cambridge, England and on the Executive Education Program at Harvard Law School in Cambridge, Massachusetts, where I teach as Guest Faculty, having developed their Case Study on Pricing (HLS 13–17) with Professor George Triantis of Stanford Law School.

After more than 25 years as a partner in an international service firm I have incorporated lessons learnt on the front line, particularly as the latter stages of my career have focussed entirely on business development and upon winning new work and new clients in which fully understanding pricing was crucial for success.

Chapter 1 – How clients buy services

This chapter aims to lay a strong foundation based upon a much clearer understanding of client buyer behaviour which can then be used to create and support much more *aligned pricing*. The term 'aligned pricing' means an ability for the service provider to earn a higher profit at the same time as maintaining or improving a client's level of satisfaction.

What is going through the mind of a client when they are faced with a choice of different service providers? It is not just about price, because we know from experience that clients don't always choose the cheapest firm or the lowest fee deal on offer. However, I'm sure that you have been involved in situations where the clients chose a cheaper firm, even though they had assured you that price was not the main issue.

Key point	The real breakthrough came when we understood that clients bought three very different types of services and the criteria they used to choose who to appoint were completely different in each case. This was a real 'eureka' moment.

It all became clear after an in-depth research project revealed that clients behave very differently, depending upon how they view the services that they are buying – which of three possible types of service they are seeking. These three types of services I call 'Rocket Science', 'Relationship Advice' and 'Routine Work'. By using this division of services, it becomes easier to predict the outcome, and also to tailor a firm's offering to give the very best chance of success. One of the most interesting discoveries I made was that at the Rocket Science end, most service providers tended to undercharge, compared to the value that they delivered to their clients. At the opposite end, Routine Work, it had long been settled that prices would be a fixed fee per matter. For Routine Work I had particularly wanted to understand what would drive a client to pay a higher fixed fee for one service when compared to another. I was reminded of a photograph I had seen of two men standing at a county fair. One was holding a sign saying 'Free Hugs', while the man next to him had a sign saying 'Deluxe Hugs $5'.

In the middle of these two extremes I found Relationship Advice, which typically generated the largest proportion, in terms of volume, of fees earned by a firm. It was here that clients had become most disillusioned with simple time-based billing. That method of billing appeared to make service providers rich and took no account of the actual value that the client received from the work carried out. Here, clients were looking for innovation in pricing and a much clearer link between the price charged and the value of services that the client believed that they had received.

Chapter 2 – Cost-plus pricing and beyond

Given the sophistication of some of the services being provided by service providers, which may involve coordinating hundreds of people across dozens of countries, it is perhaps surprising to find that the core of pricing decisions is often simple 'cost-plus' pricing. That means just calculating the total overhead costs of the firm (salaries, offices, infrastructure, etc.) and then adding to that the desired profit. This total of required income is then spread across the various levels of fee earner, based upon an assumption of how many hours and days they will work in the coming year. Cost-plus pricing does have a role, particularly for some work types and in calculating breakeven points, but it was largely labelled as not fit for purpose decades ago in the outside world and therefore abandoned. The main failure of a cost-plus system was that it was an internally focussed approach that took no account of demand levels for various types of service, or that increasing the price (because of an increase in overheads) might cause fewer hours to be sold. There was really no link between the cost of the service and the actual value that the client believed they had received.

In this chapter, I will look at the options available which will help to lead towards the idea of 'value pricing' and how you can use this to align the interests of the firm and of the client. I will also look at generic competitive strategies – why should a client choose your firm or service rather than the firm next door? Understanding this will really help you focus on how you are going to beat your competitors, and the actual role that price plays in the client's choice of service provider. From my experience, partners typically have a poor understanding of market positioning – theirs or others – yet this is a primary stage for determining the prices that a firm can charge. Positioning is about where you place yourself in the market compared to your most similar competitors, and then pricing your services to reflect this position.

Next I will examine the challenges faced by a firm that is launching a new service, where it has the opportunity to set the market price. Where do you start? How can you best position this service in the minds of potential clients who are faced with buying something entirely new?

Chapter 3 – Pitching for work

In this chapter I am going to look at how to approach competitive bidding, whether this is new work from an existing client or winning an entirely new client. There are special considerations here, particularly where the scope of the project cannot be well specified in advance, or where you have no real feeling for the price sensitivity of the client. The pricing risk here is twofold: you could frighten the client off by going in way too high, or you could price too low and so appear as if you haven't understood the importance of the work or the steps that are involved in getting it right. Either could result in the client turning elsewhere.

Choosing an opening offer is one of the most difficult situations faced by anyone trying to price work, but there are a series of practical steps that can be taken to make sure that the price is focussed on the key issues for that client. This will increase the chances of success and also show the client how much you understand their true needs. There are also some particular issues to think about when you are involved in a 'beauty parade', whether it is to join a client's panel of advisers or to hang onto a client who is retendering their work. This can be a time of high emotion as your team are personally invested in the success of the bid. Special attention is needed to make sure that the pricing involved in a proposal supports the chances of a win, rather than reducing them; and also to prevent partners from devoting their energy to formulating a 'How low can we go?' pricing strategy.

One of the key issues that is explored here is the way that clients choose between different advisers and the extent to which pricing is relevant at all. Generally speaking, partners think that price forms a greater part of the decision than it actually does, and that leads them to focus on price cutting as a way of winning clients – when it actually may have the opposite effect.

Chapter 4 – Negotiating price

Here I start to look at the issues around market segmentation and an understanding of how a firm might address different clients with quite different offers. I also introduce an alternative to the usual dichotomy of time-based charging or fixed fees. Called project-based costing, this approach seeks to tie the price to a defined and detailed scope of work, bringing greater certainty for the client while avoiding the typical problems that fixed fees bring to the service firm.

What about the long-standing client who is on unrealistically low rates? Should you risk losing the client by raising prices, or do you put up with a low profit for the long term? What do you do in a situation where you have one chance to put in a bid, and there will be no opportunity to negotiate this later on to create a win? Do you go in low and perhaps hope to increase the price later on?

With the increasing influence and sophistication of professional buyers and procurement there is an urgent, and growing, need for all service providers to learn how to negotiate fees (something for which they are surprisingly ill-equipped). Procurement is a profession; it involves study and real qualifications. You can study this at Master's degree level; any decent procurement director will have been thoroughly trained in negotiation skills. When they enter the room to negotiate, they are going to be well prepared and heavily armed. Unfortunately, a poorly prepared colleague once summed up his experience of dealing with procurement as though he had 'brought a knife into a gunfight'.

Chapter 5 – The pricing lever

The pricing lever effect is the term for how relatively small changes in the end price can have a dramatic effect on overall profitability, and this chapter aims to show this in practice. For example, it is quite typical for a 5% increase in price to create a 15% increase in actual profit, or for a 15% cut in price to reduce profits by 30% or more.

What tools do you have to analyse the effect of variations in price, and what tactics can you use to create sustainable increases both in the value delivered to the client and to the price that you charge? How do you avoid the most common mistakes made when pricing services? For example, failing to differentiate the price of partners with different experience or who operate in different sectors.

Finally, I examine the wide range of options available to a firm that wants to increase profit, from raising prices, cutting overheads or improving utilisation through to the (more risky) option of dropping prices to win more business.

Giving the client a 15% discount meant that profit was cut in half!	**Key point**

Chapter 6 – Alternative fees

More and more clients are asking their service providers and advisers to offer alternative fees, quite often without specifying what type of alternatives they are looking for, or even more often staying on traditional methods of billing even after alternatives are offered. Our basic model of buyer behaviour is of huge benefit here because it shows which different types of alternative fees are appropriate for different types of work. By understanding this, it is possible for the service provider to create an alternative fee which doesn't put at risk the quality or deliverables of the work, and truly to align with the client's interests.

This chapter provides details of specific offers that are relevant for each type of service. In particular it focusses upon the problems of simple time-based costing (hourly or daily rates) and the equally problematic fixed fee/flat fee. It then looks at how to introduce the much more successful project-based costing system, and then beyond that to look at success fees, contingent fees and other alternatives.

Chapter 7 – Pricing tactics

This chapter gives a selection of 20 of the best and most commonly used pricing tactics. They are no substitute for a good strategy, but they can assist when facing a difficult situation and will certainly help partners to make improvements along the way. As people are keen to learn about actions that they can start implementing immediately, somewhat frustratingly, on the training courses that I have run, this is always the part where everyone begins frantic scribbling of notes, diagrams and reminders to themselves.

Situations in which these tactics may help you: what to do, for example, if a good competitor lowballs and offers to carry out a project at 50% of your fee? What if you are unsure how to position your prices against your most direct competitors? How to find out what your competitors are charging and how to manage trophy clients so that they don't end up with unreasonably good terms.

Chapter 8 – Drivers of value

It's business sense to try to increase your prices. Do the same work with a higher price tag and you're happy, but done overnight and it's risky. This chapter provides you with ways of identifying the most reliable ways to increase your value to the client and, as a result, enable you to achieve a price increase. Understanding what clients value, and the activities that are not valued, makes a real difference to your ability to construct a winning pricing offer. How do you create a framework which enables you to identify what is important to your client? How do you avoid the more typical approach where different clients have negotiated quite different prices, yet all receive exactly the same level of service? How do you create differentiated offers so that you can address different segments of your potential market?

Chapter 9 – Learning from industry

What can service providers learn from the strategy and tactics adopted by various industries which enable them to segment their marketplace and charge different prices to different customers, bundle or unbundle variations on their services and maximise available profits in a sustainable way? Can you offer the equivalent of maintenance contracts, business class and economy services, loyalty cards and the like without cheapening your services or over-complicating them? Can you learn from great companies that have remodelled their businesses to sell services rather than products? There is a huge body of research on pricing, both business-to-business and business-to-consumer, which can provide you with new insights on how you might benefit from restructuring your offering to maximise profitability.

Chapter 10 – Saving clients money

It can be high risk to be reactive and wait for clients to raise issues around price. Are there ways that you can reduce a client's spend while maintaining your profitability? Can you change the way that you work with the client, to reduce the effort involved and there-fore the cost? Can you run a pilot project jointly with a willing client?

What about finding ways of reducing a client's total spend across all of their service firms? Or can you develop different approaches to the work which reduce spend and then take a share of the saving? If you can create real examples of how you have saved a client money, then similar clients will beat a path to your door. Learn how to swap really valuable benefits to you, in return for client savings, so that both sides benefit.

Chapter 11 – Pricing controls and capabilities

This chapter is about moving from theory to practice in a struc-tured and organised way. What simple tools can you use that will enable you to analyse the most important price problems you are facing so that you can prioritise action? How do you demonstrate the effects and gain partner buy-in? What are the different stages of pricing effectiveness, how do you identify your current position and build towards a pricing strategy that will support your business strategy and enable long-term profitable growth?

What simple steps can you take to analyse the returns from different clients and map how those differences have occurred using waterfall diagrams? How can you see at a glance, using scattergrams, whether clients' prices, compared to the volume of work that they supply, are logical and fair? What can you do to improve control of prices and reduce write-offs? What are the different strategies that you can use to retain the most valuable clients and improve returns on the problem ones?

The chapter ends with a review of how service firms can go about building real pricing capabilities. Moving away from ad hoc and distributed structures into treating pricing as a key skill for the firm, and giving it the resources and power to make a real difference to the overall success of the firm. Contributed by Robert Browne, a partner at KPMG who leads their pricing practice in the United Kingdom, this section shows the comparative benefits of different organisational structures that will position your firm for market-leading success in this most important business skill.

How clients buy services

The key question for this chapter is: *'What are the criteria that clients use when choosing a service firm for a project or for a panel appointment?'* Once you have a clear understanding of the decision-making process, you will have a better approach towards pricing your services.

My thinking in this area has been shaped by a research project in 2006 which built upon models that I developed when completing my MBA dissertation. By undertaking this research I had hoped to improve my firm's win rate on proposals for work. The better I understood the way that clients made these decisions, the more successful this task could be. In fact, I was able to produce substantial improvements in win rates, and in doing so I realised I had developed a model that was fundamentally important to the pricing of all services. Then came the recession of 2008 and clients' focus turned to cost savings and value for money. The result was that the importance of truly aligned pricing came to the fore – it was necessary to use the models developed in order to shape the services provided so that they better met clients' newly changed needs.

THE DATA

The primary data in my research project involved the analysis of more than 1100 formal pitch results and detailed feedback from clients on 700 of these pitches. I was looking through this data to uncover and understand the reasons clients had given, subjective as they may be, for their decision to appoint or to reject my firm. However, when I started tabulating these reasons it created something of a fog of results. Vague patterns were emerging: there were regular references to price, experience and chemistry (how the client felt about the team that had attended their offices to make a formal presentation). However, it was hard to see any strong correlation. Proposals made to clients who appeared very similar sometimes failed on price, sometimes were successful, with experience being mentioned but no reference to price. In other cases, where everything else seemed to be right, there was a comment on not being impressed with the presentation team. A breakthrough occurred when one of my business analysts aided me by grouping all of the results based upon work types. As I started to refine this, a startlingly strong picture emerged. In the end, I found that the best results came when I divided the work into three categories which I later termed 'Rocket Science', 'Relationship Advice' and 'Routine Work'. These three titles will be a constant feature in the rest of this book.

In a sense, there was nothing radical here. Many authors and researchers in services had come up with similar categorisations, for example: 'Expertise, Experience and Efficiency'. However, what surprised me was to find that whenever I spoke to colleagues in other service firms they, like me, had failed to understand how this division affected the buying decisions of their clients. In particular, it was crucial to understand that we all needed to use quite different language and evidence when seeking to win work from clients in these different categories, and to offer very different pricing options.

After analysing the data and conducting further face-to-face interviews with key clients, I ended up identifying five criteria that clients were using when buying each of these three work types. Using this understanding, I completely redesigned my firm's proposal process with quite startling results. On the highest value proposals, our win rate moved from 30% to 57% and on average across all proposals it increased from 31% to 49% and stayed there. This wasn't about clever marketing wording, but simply an improved understanding of the criteria needed to make successful proposals, irrespective of whether it was Rocket Science, Relationship Advice or Routine Work. Importantly, I also gained a much better understanding of whether my firm should actually even attempt proposals on particular pieces of work or panel appointments.

Key point — Using our new understanding of clients' buying criteria, we lifted the win rate on the highest value proposals from 30% to 57%.

As a first step, it is important to look at my definitions of work types (Figure 1.1).

Figure 1.1

Three types of advice

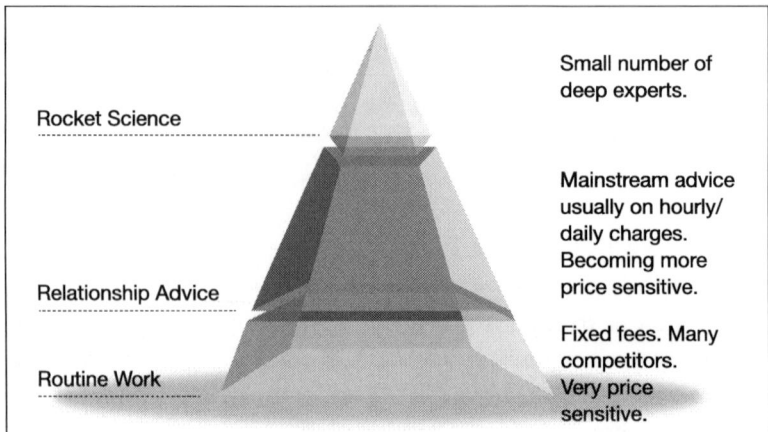

Rocket Science — Small number of deep experts.

Relationship Advice — Mainstream advice usually on hourly/daily charges. Becoming more price sensitive.

Routine Work — Fixed fees. Many competitors. Very price sensitive.

ROCKET SCIENCE

What does 'Rocket Science' mean? This is work which is of primary importance to the client either because of its size, its risk or its urgency. Importantly, it is the client that decides whether work is Rocket Science or not.

What are the key features of work that could be called Rocket Science?

■ It typically involves a director of the client company. If a director is worried then it is Rocket Science work (and incidentally there will be no issue over the cost).

■ The partner involved in the work might be a little arrogant (and I used to joke that much more commonly I would find that they were massively arrogant). This was important. The best analogy that I found was of the truly expert surgeon who had earned a leading reputation in a particular field, one recognised as particularly difficult, with life-and-death decisions being made on a daily basis. These surgeons would often have quite a distant air about them. They might not have a good bedside manner and in fact this different attitude could be comforting to the patient.

One FTSE 100 client that I interviewed described being in the boardroom when a hostile takeover had been launched for the company. She said, 'Two really arrogant partners arrived from [a major law firm], were quite abrupt but asked exactly the right questions and we felt really safe in their hands'.

In fact, from a client's point of view, this extreme confidence of the adviser is very reassuring, even though it might be described as arrogant. Rocket Science work, by definition, involves substantial risks or opportunities (or both) for the client and this is a time when an arrogant, 'I have seen this all before' attitude is really comforting. They are the Olympians of their specialist subjects.

■ The outcome of the project might be quite vague. It could be because this involves novel issues or great business uncertainty. Quite often clients may not be able to specify exactly what work is needed and it will be quite open-ended.

■ The Rocket Scientists may not be typical 'relationship' people. They may be strongly introverted and may not see that client again after the project finishes. Similarly, the client may have no wish to see them again. They will be excited by the intellectual challenge of each piece of work; they will perform at an extraordinarily high level, often working extremely long hours. One of the key pieces of understanding from my research was that where Rocket Science work was involved, the client chose based upon the *personal reputation of an individual, not upon the firm's reputation*. The primary criterion for clients when selecting a provider for Rocket Science work is the track record of the individual partner; pretty much everything else will be irrelevant. To continue the example of a surgeon, this will be comparable to a situation where you have been told that you need a difficult and complex operation which carries a serious risk of death. When choosing your surgeon, you need to know the comparative success rates of the alternative practitioners. How many of this surgeon's patients were still alive five years after the operation? You won't particularly care about which hospital the surgeon is using or whether or not they are pleasant to deal with. What matters is the end result. What is the individual surgeon's track record with the exact problem that you had? If they really are 'the best', they will be working in a hospital that is fine.

Key point	It was the partner's individual track record that mattered – it was nothing to do with the firm.

It was interesting to start thinking about how partners known for their Rocket Science work needed to market themselves, something which they almost universally hated doing. How does the client with some Rocket Science work find the right partner? I discovered that there were commonly two decision routes. The first one was through the client's existing 'Relationship Partner' at the firm. So, internal networking by Rocket Science partners was important and easily achieved. The second route was referrals from other clients. To an extent this depended upon the Rocket Scientist having a high enough profile within the business community, but this also could be helped through client partners offering existing clients meetings with Rocket Scientists for free, particularly to give expert talks and presentations (which they enjoyed doing).

It was also worth noticing that, if anything, Rocket Scientists would charge too little for their advice. This came about because the firms where they worked relied upon charging for them by the hour or the day just like everyone else, but that hardly reflected the value which they brought. These experts were the most likely to have a flash of inspiration and solve the client's problems in an extremely clever way. The best pricing practice that I came across for this area of work, resulting in clients who expressed the highest satisfaction with the price, was to create a safe budget. At the start, the Rocket Scientist talked to the client about the likely total cost. They put themselves on the side of the client by describing the total budget that was needed if the client was going to be safe. For example, a conversation might be: 'From my previous experience, I can tell you that this project will cost between £1.5 million and £2.5 million. So you are going to need a budget of £2.5 million and we will not exceed that.' The client was reassured because the worst thing is to create a budget that is too small, so that the client faces the embarrassment of having to request more funds from the board at a later date, which would involve an admission that they had underestimated the cost the first time around.

Once this overall budget had been established the partner would bill regularly, based upon hours worked, in the usual way. However, at the end of the matter the partner would see the client (face-to-face, not on the phone), and would discuss the work that had been done and *the outcome that had been achieved for the client.* The partner would then agree a final fee. If the results were particularly good, the fee would be at the higher end of the range. If, due to circumstances outside of that partner's control (not because the partner had failed in some way), the result was not great, then the fee would be at the lower end of the range (or even below it). The partner was seen to win or lose in the same way as the client, and in this way had worked towards 'value pricing' – asking for a fee that reflected the value the client considered they had received. In the pricing community, value pricing is considered the highest quality of pricing.

There was something else that was mentioned frequently by clients in this area of work. They were extremely loyal to the Rocket Scientist partner. I would often hear clients say, 'If that partner left their existing firm then I would follow the partner, I would not stay with the firm'. I didn't hear this in respect of the partners delivering Relationship Advice (which surprised me) or about Routine Work. This loyalty to the Rocket Scientist partner was understandable. A client who had been through a difficult, important, perhaps risky, situation with a particular partner understood the value that partner brought and would want to use them again if a similar situation arose.

It made me start thinking about the wording I used when talking to clients about particular Rocket Science partners. It was important to emphasise that the particular partner would be committed to the transaction and to promise that they would not take on other work which might cut across that commitment. The client was choosing to instruct my firm solely because of the track record and expertise of a specific partner, and it was important to understand that.

RELATIONSHIP ADVICE

This is the layer of work underneath Rocket Science. It could involve very substantial matters, but they are not seen as life or death and are typically of a repetitive nature. There was one area where I found possible disagreement between partners and clients about whether work was Rocket Science or Relationship Advice. This was where the client had a stream of high-value transactions. The partners handling such work (often correctly categorised as 'deal junkies') tended to think of themselves as Rocket Scientists, but for the client this was quite often seen as 'business as usual' work and so closer to Relationship Advice. The key features that I identified for Relationship Advice were as follows:

■ The stronger the actual relationship the partner established with a client, the more they were able to charge. The trust and depth of understanding of the client's situation developed its own value: so much so that it was clients who originally described this as 'relationship' work. By its nature, Relationship Advice is not typically about 'one-off' pieces of work where the client does not expect to see that partner again, but rather about important pieces of work that form part of a continuum.

■ Whereas in Rocket Science, clients had been reassured by the steely arrogance of their adviser, in Relationship Advice they were typically seeking a friendly and trustworthy 'bedside manner'. Clients choose people with whom they can have a pleasant working relationship. Interestingly, I came to the conclusion that clients chose advisers *that they liked!* This was because they could source Relationship Advice from many firms, so liking ('chemistry' was how it was often described) became a crucial differentiator as the core skill that they were buying was available from many firms, and so it cancelled out when the choice came to be made.

■ There was much more talk of 'the team', and a recognition by the client that the relevant partner would not be involved in every piece of work and certainly would not be delivering all of it personally.

■ The client did not focus so much on the individual track record of the partner, recognising that it is a team effort, and so was much more interested in hearing that the firm and the team had relevant experience. This was typically evidenced by the firm acting for other clients that this client would consider to be peers, or in the same division as them. What I found particularly interesting, and reinforced my view that this needed to be called 'Relationship Advice', was that clients said only some firms understood that creating a real relationship between the whole team and the client was important. A relationship means going beyond simply delivering the service that is required and actually starting to understand the client's business, spending time face-to-face with them off the clock, helping them to achieve their business and personal objectives, and helping to train and manage the client's whole internal team. This truly was the zone of *The Trusted Advisor* as described in the bestselling book of that name by David H. Maister, Robert Galford and Charles W. Green[1]. The most successful partners in this zone tend to be more people-focussed and less task-orientated, and displayed a genuine interest in the client's business rather than just delivering the services. They were less transactional and longer term in their approach. However, just as interestingly, the relationship-building skills which were so important in this area of work were not relevant (even though they may exist) in relation to either Rocket Science or Routine Work.

| Relationship Advice is the zone of *The Trusted Advisor*, as described in the bestselling book of that title. | **Key point** |

ROUTINE WORK

I found little dispute between clients and partners about what could be categorised as Routine Work. It typically arose in volumes, was almost always provided on a fixed fee basis (rather than on the uncertain hourly or daily based charge), and even the choice of external supplier was often delegated quite far down in the organisation. One possible area of contention was that to be truly Routine Work there had to be very low risk if the matter went wrong. It had to be a situation where problems could be resolved with relatively minor financial compensation. There was an inevitable desire by clients to talk of work as 'routine' as a method of requiring

[1] Maister, D. H., Galford, R. and Green, C. W. (2002) *The Trusted Advisor*, Free Press.

a lower price. If work was repetitive, but carried a real risk – for example, substantial adverse publicity for the client if something were to go wrong – then there would be grounds for inserting a Relationship Advice level overview of the work to protect against such risks. The typical features of Routine Work were as follows:

■ The actual work required, or the end result to be achieved, could be specified in considerable detail.

■ Even if the actual cost of carrying out each individual matter might vary, there were sufficiently large numbers for an averaging approach to be taken to produce a single fixed fee.

■ There were lots of potential providers and, subject only to a 'quality hurdle', the client didn't really care who carried out this work.

■ Price and performance would be under continual pressure, with the service firm expected to produce improvements year on year and to lower prices as well.

■ There was very low client loyalty and while clients recognised that some firms did actually deliver a much better service than others (particularly in terms of making the work easy for the client rather than causing them lots of additional administrative tasks), they will still play firms off against each other to achieve, the lowest price that they could, from the best provider available.

At first sight, this might appear somewhat depressing from a price and profit point of view. However, firms that were well set up to handle Routine Work could actually make very high returns with very low partner involvement. The effect of leverage meant that a partner running this type of work could often produce more profit for the firm (per partner) than the best of the Rocket Scientists. Partners involved in this work tended to be good at process and procedure (quite likely the opposite of a Rocket Scientist), and the best of them managed to integrate their processes with those of the clients so as to produce a higher cost of switching for the client. They would also introduce Key Performance Indicators (KPIs), which could be used to generate the data that would justify better prices for better performance.

THE FIVE CRITERIA

Having defined three separate work types, it became possible to analyse the data on wins and losses and to isolate the key criteria that clients used when choosing their service provider, and as a result, to understand the implications for firms in terms of their pricing and their approach to clients' buying decisions.

These criteria, which became the '5 Ps of Services Pricing', are as follows:

1. **Purchasing criteria** – how does the client decide which service firm to use?

2. **Proposal** – what evidence does the firm need to produce to convince the client?

3. **Pricing** – what is the best way for the firm to price its services to maximise profit and client satisfaction?

4. **Promotion** – what are the most effective ways that partners can use to market themselves?

5. **Procurement** – what is the role (if any) of procurement and how can the firm best deal with it?

This leads to a grid where the three work types are matched against the 5 Ps of Services Pricing and this is set out below.

	Rocket Science	Relationship Advice	Routine Work
Purchasing Criteria	Track record of the individual expert (best match).	Personal chemistry, track record of the team, price.	Price, track record of the firm, performance data.
Proposal	Facts of individual performance. Demonstrate best fit between experience and current issue.	Demonstrate team track record and meet the team. Innovation in price.	Facts, performance, similar clients.
Pricing	Confident budget given – actual fee linked to outcome (value billing).	Hourly; daily; project-based; value billing; annual retainers, caps with share of savings, innovation.	Fixed (flat) fees. Can link final fee to performance data to give uplift or reduction in a mechanical way.
Promotion	Books, articles, conferences. Network at 'C-Suite' (Board) level in the client and inside your own firm.	Network with primary buyer, peer group referrals, profile of firm.	Networking with business units and procurement.
Procurement	No.	Yes, but only a part of the decision. Rely on relationship.	Procurement may lead. Decision is data driven. Get data!

For now, I am going to focus on the pricing issues and look at these in turn against each of the three work types. An understanding of how clients use price as part of the buying decision underpins the selection process and forms a foundation for this text.

PRICING ROCKET SCIENCE

Price was not mentioned by clients as one of the criteria when they were choosing their adviser for Rocket Science matters. In addition, satisfaction with pricing for this type of work was found to be high. This seemed to be built upon the principle that nobody staggers into accident and emergency with a heart attack and starts asking the price of the various doctors. But importantly, it also didn't mean that it was entirely open season on price. Those working at this level in service firms jealously guarded their reputations, and it was important not only that they delivered to a very high standard, but also that the clients did not complain afterwards of having been 'ripped off' (although a client describing them as 'extremely good, but expensive' was considered something of a badge of honour).

On further investigation I found that the best of these people did not talk about the actual price at the beginning, but rather that they talked about the client needing to put in place a budget that was sufficient for the task in hand. As I mentioned previously, the best partners were seen to be *on the side of the client* in making sure that an appropriate sum was set aside by way of budget to deal with the issue, so that the client would not be left embarrassed at a later stage by having to ask for considerably more budget.

The best of the conversations contain the following elements:

- The Rocket Scientist referred to previous similar situations (reinforcing their specific expertise in the particular problem or transaction) and gave a range of possible costs. For example, the client might be told that the cost would 'not be less than £1 million, and could be as high as £2 million', so it would be sensible for the client to create a budget of £2 million and then the partner would make sure the budget was not exceeded.

- The basis of charging was clearly laid out so the client understood exactly how the ultimate charge would be calculated. In the best cases the partner kept the client up to date on a very regular basis to show how spend was comparing with the stated budget.

■ The actual total cost was the subject of a conversation at the end of the project at which the partner talked through what work had been done and in particular, and much more importantly, what had been achieved for the client. Should the outcome not have been fantastic (for reasons unconnected with the skills of the Rocket Scientist partner) then the fee would be reduced so there was an element of 'sharing in the pain'. Similarly, when a particularly good result had been achieved, a conversation which referred to '£1.2 million being on the clock, but in view of the spectacularly good result I propose to invoice £1.5 million' was seen as both acceptable and appropriate.

Among pricing specialists, the gold standard of pricing is described as *'value pricing'*. Similarly, it is widely accepted that this is extremely difficult to achieve. Value pricing occurs when the seller has been able to maximise their profit by focussing the service around what is most valuable to the client, and the client has been able to maximise their satisfaction, which includes the price paid. Value pricing implicitly accepts that there may be variations up and down depending upon outcomes. In my research, I found that even if the actual time taken had considerably exceeded the budget delivered at the outset, the Rocket Scientist partner was very likely to write off any excess, because to admit the budget had been wrong would reflect badly upon their supposed expertise. Exceptions could occur if a radical alteration had taken place part-way through the matter, which had been well flagged up and a revised budget agreed, but otherwise there was a matter of pride involved in keeping within the originally stated budget.

This also helped to explain why, when a group of partners discuss pricing strategy, some of them will be massively more bullish than the others. It is as if Rocket Scientists are immune to the ups and downs of pricing in the marketplace. When partners have positioned themselves as being in the Rocket Science part of the market, they place considerable pressure upon themselves in terms of the quality of advice and the perfection of delivery. They also understand, importantly, *that no amount of price cutting will lead to them winning more work.* Clients choose their adviser in Rocket Science situations based entirely upon their personal track record. The better that partner's track record meets the exact problem that the client is facing, the greater the chance that partner will be chosen. If the partner is not the right person, then cutting their price in half would not alter that at all. There was also a status issue involved. If a partner claimed to be delivering Rocket Science advice then the price (in terms of the quoted hourly rate or daily charge, as opposed to the final bill, which would be discussed) needed to be consistent with that position. It needed to be noticeably above, for example, the rate for a partner who was handling Relationship Advice.

On occasions, I found individual partners trying to impose two different rates upon clients: one rate for Relationship Advice and a higher rate for Rocket Science to reflect the fact that sometimes they were dealing with day-to-day matters, and on other occasions they were dealing with Rocket Science. This was not a successful strategy. Clients judged individual partners and categorised them based upon their experiences with them, and they were not happy for one person to claim two different rates when charging. A Relationship Work partner needs to refer the client to a different partner if Rocket Science work and prices are appropriate. It also seemed that the cost of being a Rocket Scientist was the need to truly specialise and therefore cope with occasional work famines, rather than filling up with lower grade work at lower prices during quiet periods and risk undermining their position.

One fact that leapt out from my research was that there were originally quite a number of cases where my firm had not been successful in a proposal for Rocket Science work, even though we actually had the relevant expertise. To an extent that is inevitable. There will not be only one expert and it is not uncommon for a client to want to talk to two or three potential advisers and then choose the one that is the best fit. If we didn't have the best fit and another firm (in fact, a specific partner) did, then it was appropriate that we lost. However, what came out of the research project was the realisation that our proposals were quite unfocussed. They would often talk about the expertise of the whole firm, which was actually irrelevant. What is needed is to focus directly upon the issue that the client is facing and then produce quite a simple document which demonstrates the specific expertise of the relevant partner and show how it matches the needs of the client.

What I learnt from this was simple – the need to ask more questions. When asked to propose for Rocket Science work, I needed to understand the problem in considerable detail. This meant sitting down with the client to gain a deeper understanding of the outcome they needed, the challenges they anticipated and how they wanted the project to work. In some cases there was simply a lack of the required expertise, and my firm gained credibility for acknowledging that. In other cases our proposal won because it demonstrated the exact expertise of the relevant partner or partners and showed how their track record matched the client's needs. The adviser who does the best job of matching track record to needs in this way is the one that is chosen, and quite often at no point has price been discussed at all.

PRICING RELATIONSHIP ADVICE

It is here that my research starts to show clients talking about price as one of the factors in their decision making about which firm to use. Interestingly, *it was very rarely the deciding factor*. Clients were very clear in saying that the two most important factors were a belief that the firm could handle the work, which is based on their track record on similar work and for similar clients, and personal chemistry with the team that was going to be carrying out the work. Contrast this with partners who often tried to work out what competitors are charging and then go in under that, on the assumption that this would win the work. In fact the client is choosing based upon other factors.

Price was one factor, but not the most important. Track record and a good cultural fit with the team were considered much more important.	**Key point**

This helped me to understand all of those situations where clients had told us that price was not the most important issue, but then chosen a firm that was lower in price than us. The client's decision had been focussed very strongly on picking the firm that they thought would be best at doing the work, and would form the best cultural fit with them. If that firm happened to be cheaper than my firm, then so be it. But price was not the decider. As one client put it: *If you are not the right firm for us, then you are not the right firm – even at half price.*

I was both surprised and greatly encouraged by this finding. All of the partners that I had talked to about this worked upon the assumption that 'all other things being equal, the lowest price wins', and this led to a vast amount of time being taken up by partners retelling anecdotal stories of how cheaply direct competitors were selling their services, and how we needed to cut our own prices by more if we were to be successful. This was a deeply ingrained belief. However, the key fallacy was this: in services it is rarely the case that all other things are equal! The clients were directly telling us that they *first* judged which team of advisers they preferred, and only then did they turn to the issue of price. If it turned out that their preferred team was the lowest price, then (unless it was very low, in which case the client started to doubt that team's abilities) that was that. If, however, their chosen firm was the highest price (again assuming that they were not off-the-scale expensive), then the client would simply negotiate fee rates with their chosen team. I deal with this scenario in detail in Chapter 3; for now it is just crucial to understand that for Relationship Advice, going in low does not, of itself, increase the chances of success. What it does create is an inability to price yourselves at a higher, more reasonable rate at a future point – why, when they were offered Rate C for you, should they then pay Rate A for the same partners a short while later? Pricing low positions you and it is very difficult to reposition at a higher rate later on.

Firms need to change their approach to winning Relationship Advice to match this finding. You can massively increase your chances of success if you meet several people from the client side, so that you gain a much better understanding both of what the client is looking for in terms of the work (which would help you to demonstrate the best, most relevant track record), and also give you a feel for your culture. Rather than obsess over price, simply adjust your proposed team to reflect the client's culture and demonstrate your deeper understanding of their needs and the challenges they face. If you are the best fit for the client, then it doesn't matter that your price is higher than the competition (it couldn't be ridiculously high, but there is no problem if it is the highest of the group). In addition, having meetings with the client gives you the chance to start creating chemistry between you, to show how you are similar to them and why you are the best (cultural) fit.

Key point	You do not need to obsess over your price. Being the highest priced offer wasn't a problem (if anything it confirms your superior quality). Clients expect to negotiate price *after* they had chosen their preferred firm.

Clients often expect to negotiate on price *after* they have chosen their preferred firm. With that in mind, being higher than your competitors is not fatal to your success as the client will probably try to negotiate you down (how to handle this pressure to cut your pitch price is discussed later). There is an exception to this rule in relation to government, public sector or highly procured contracts where the client will seek first to prequalify who could do the work, and then after that will ask for a single bid and reserve the right to take the lowest bid (although not be bound to do so).

However, it is also in this area of Relationship Advice that clients are looking for alternative methods of charging by their service firms. My research revealed that there was real dissatisfaction with simply charging for the time taken. Clients were not simply looking for this to be addressed by negotiating discounts off hourly or daily rates, but were also looking for a different approach to pricing. Given that price was going to be a factor, if the client saw two firms that were very similar, then an offer by one of those firms to charge on a *different basis* (not just lower) could be decisive.

In fact, this was not just a matter of principle. Clients displayed a visceral dislike of charging based upon time spent for Relationship Advice, unless it was tied into a tight overall cost. It actually felt unprofessional and reminded clients of similar situations, such as where they called a plumber to their home to resolve a blocked drain and instinctively 'knew' that the plumber was not going to work quickly, and would be quite likely to find further problems, because the longer the plumber was on their premises the more money they would have to pay. Interestingly, there is ample research that shows that *everyone* displays this aversion to being charged 'by the hour'. This is often called the 'taxi meter effect' and is a function of the fear of uncertainty that charging on a time-based system causes, so that a fixed fee is preferred even in circumstances where that leads to a higher overall cost[2].

From a client's' perspective, these are the problems with the old way of unlimited time-based billing:

- There is no incentive for the service firm to be efficient or to develop any processes that would speed up the work. In fact the opposite is true, not just for the firm as a whole, but for all the individuals working on that client's matters who would be under pressure to hit budgets and to record and charge for more time, and so have no incentive to work faster or more efficiently.

---

[2] See Itai Ater and Vardit Landsman, 'Do customers learn from experience? Evidence from retail banking'. *Management Science* (2013) Vol. 59(9), 2019–35.

- The longer the matter took, the higher the bill. The more problems that were discovered, the more hours would be needed, and the more staff that became involved, the better for the firm.

- Clients are typically tied into annual budgets for spend. These cannot be exceeded; indeed, for a client to tell their manager that they had blown through an allocated budget could end their career. So how do they then cope with service providers who cannot agree budgets in advance?

- There is little link to value. It might take a long time to produce quite a poor result. Charging by the time taken simply passes on all of the costs and inefficiencies in the system to the client.

There is no alignment between the interests of the client and the interests of the firm; they are pretty much in direct opposition. This is hardly the ideal position for partners who are seeking to become trusted advisers to their clients, and yet Relationship Advice is the area where achieving that status is the most important.

Key point   One client complained: 'Would you take your car to be repaired at a garage if you knew that every mechanic could earn bonuses based upon how many faults they found in your car?'

The level of dissatisfaction with time-based charging led clients in some areas of work to demand a change to fixed fees. Even where a project could not be specified in detail at an early stage, the client took the view that they were dealing with firms with considerable experience who should be able to draw on past data showing typical costs in order to create a realistic fixed fee proposal. In this way the client could compare the proposals from several possible firms before making a choice, safe in the knowledge that they were not going to go over budget. Even if a firm was reluctant to offer a fixed fee on an uncertain project, the firm will be told that all their competitors have agreed to do so and that if they fail to join in, then they will simply be excluded from the work. The more streetwise clients were still going to choose their advisers based upon track record and chemistry, but introduced a fixed fee competition to drive down the prices of their preferred firm.

Although a fixed fee sounds like a simple answer to all the problems, in practice it actually had as many shortcomings as charging for time taken:

- There is a real incentive for firms to bid low in order to win the work. Typically, firms do not have easily accessible data in order to create a realistic estimate of the work involved, the actual path of the work, and the time cost, could vary dramatically. This led to the typical fixed fee transaction running well over cost, made worse by the lack of fixed fee project management skills inside the firm.

- While the client may be unconcerned by the matter running well over its fixed fee, inside the firm the partner running the matter will find increasing reluctance of good people to work on it, given that all of their time is simply going to be written off.

- There is no incentive for the client to be efficient. The client could change their mind, substantially alter the terms of the project and argue over every issue. It doesn't matter to them because they have a fixed fee no matter what.

Switching to fixed fees is not a sustainable solution for Relationship Advice. By definition this advice involves important and somewhat complex projects which cannot always be sufficiently specified in advance to create a realistic fixed fee. While firms may be prepared to take risks in order to keep the flow of work, it is very unlikely to be a sustainable, long-term business model.

Eventually, at my firm, I started to explain to clients who demanded a fixed fee on an uncertain project that their approach was a little like going for an operation but telling the surgeon that they only wanted to pay for two hours of their time, so that, at the expiry of the time they just wanted to be sewn back up, no matter at what stage the operation was. Because that was what was going to happen on a fixed fee deal – of course we would complete the job, but there would be real pressure to cut corners and reduce losses.

> Switching to fixed fees wasn't the simple answer that clients had hoped for. Transactions typically overran the somewhat optimistic fixed fee, and good people became very scarce. **Key point**

It became increasingly obvious that it was this area of Relationship Advice that required the most focus on pricing skills. This is where service firms needed to up their game and behave just as more advanced businesses had for the last 50 years: devising clear pricing strategies, developing a better understanding of the market and, as a result, being able to produce prices and a method of charging that would be both profitable for the firm and realistic for the client. The aim is to build long-standing, mutually sustainable relationships with your clients. This is the primary area of focus for this text.

PRICING ROUTINE WORK

Fixed fee. It is almost as simple as that. When it comes to Routine Work, clients are expecting a fixed fee and even if it is accepted that some pieces of work will take substantially longer than others, the firm will be expected to average these out so that a single fixed fee can be charged. This is the case whether a single client is providing sufficient volume to average out the cost, or the volume comes from a group of clients.

Procurement could be expected to be involved in producing a tight specification and running bidding processes (quite frequently online). This is definitely not an area for relationships. Clients would move the work for a relatively small difference in price. Partners who excel in this work are good at process, data and creating and managing junior teams. The best excel at continuous improvement and designing their service to closely match the client's needs. Despite its downmarket image, many highly reputable firms are able to produce substantial profit from highly leveraged teams, leading to a high profit per partner. Just as budget airlines often carry more passengers than the national 'flag carrier' airlines and earn more profit in a typical year, so it is with Routine Work.

Provided that a relatively low-quality hurdle could be met, lowest price, combined with evidence of an ability to cope with the planned volumes of work, was pretty much the deciding factor. However, clients did show a willingness to pay higher prices for differential services. In other words, the best of the firms actually take time to understand what might make the service being provided on Routine Work more valuable to the client. Given that Routine Work typically arrives in substantial volumes, small changes in price can have a very substantial effect on profitability. Not untypically, a 1% improvement in the price being charged increases the actual profit on this work by 10% or more.

| Key point | Even in this most commoditised area of work, there are opportunities to differentiate your firm and to earn higher fees as a result. |

This means that there are opportunities for value-based pricing. For example, you could say that Price 1, the lowest price, is to be charged per matter provided that certain performance criteria were met, but Price 2 and Price 3 will be charged if specified better results are achieved. This appeals to clients because it met a need for continuous improvement and extra payments are only triggered if the better performance is actually delivered. It allows a firm, even in this most routine and commoditised area of work, to create a differentiated service. The firm could say that its aim is not to be the cheapest firm delivering the most basic level of service, but to be better than competitors and to earn more fees as a direct result of delivering better outcomes.

Understanding the client's drivers of value, as discussed in Chapter 8, is particularly relevant to this type of price variation, which depends upon facts and data. This is not an area for grand and fuzzy claims to be better than competitors.

With these fundamental pricing principles in place we can now examine how we can put this into practice to improve firm profitability. Unfortunately, this is not simply a matter of increasing prices. If it were that simple, then no books would have been written on the subject. It is about using the inherent flexibility of services delivery to your advantage. With services, a unique feature is that the terms are agreed before the services are delivered; they are intangible and you can agree with the client the actual type of delivery as part of your negotiations. Contrast this with the typical situation for physical goods, where a supplier may have a warehouse full of the completed product that they need now to sell, with little chance of alteration.

As a next step, it is important to understand the most basic principles behind how the price of services is calculated, what options are available, and which will have the best chance of improving profitability while maintaining client satisfaction. It is to this topic that we will now turn our attention.

Cost-plus pricing and beyond

If you are to develop a successful pricing strategy for services then there are effectively two pillars: first, the method you use to calculate the price of your services and, second, how you competitively position your services.

The first pillar involves deciding how you will calculate the prices that you are going to charge your clients. There are three widely used techniques:

- cost-plus pricing;
- client-based pricing;
- competitor-based pricing.

They each have different drivers and each can help you to understand what price you should be charging your clients, but they also have real drawbacks that you need to understand, or they will cause you problems when you come to execute your strategy. You are very likely to be able to recognise some of these problems in your current situation. My aim is for you to create a strategy which moves towards 'value billing', where the fee you charge most accurately reflects the value derived by your client.

The second pillar to a successful pricing strategy is to understand your basic competitive strategy – why should clients choose your firm rather than your closest competitors? Harvard Professor Michael Porter set out three generic strategies in his seminal work on competitive strategy.[1] He called these strategies cost leadership (your claim is that you are as good as your competitors but cheaper than them); differentiated (more expensive than your competitors but providing benefits that clients value more than those provided by those competitors); or niche (focusing on a specific sector or skill and offering benefits from that greater knowledge).

A very basic understanding of these two pillars will transform your approach to how you price your firm's services. Let's start by looking at the first pillar, the underlying approach you use to calculate your prices.

COST-PLUS PRICING

The traditional method of pricing for service firms is called 'cost-plus'. In relatively stable times, with steady demand for work, the

---

[1] Porter, M. E. (1979). 'How competitive forces shape strategy.' *Harvard Business Review*, March.

cost-plus formula delivers the results the firm wants. The firm covers all overhead costs, produces the desired pre-planned margin of profit, and leads to everyone being paid what they expected to be paid.

This method is built upon the assumed costs (overheads) of the service firm for the coming year. To this is added the required level of profit. This creates the total income that is needed and that income is then spread across the hourly charging staff with rates based upon seniority, and on the assumption that a certain number of chargeable hours will be both recorded and recovered by those staff.

For example:

Total assumed overheads for coming year for the whole firm £1,100,000

Profit required for division among partners £400,000

TOTAL INCOME REQUIRED £1,500,000

We then divide that income across the service staff:

One partner @ 1500 hours × £500 an hour = £750,000

One director @ 1500 hours × £300 an hour = £450,000

One assistant @ 1500 hours × £200 an hour = £300,000

TOTAL INCOME PREDICTED £1,500,000

Of course, across the year there will be some bumps in the road: not everyone will recover exactly 1500 hours of time and unexpected costs may arise in the business. However, with practice, and after building in contingencies, this 'cost-plus' method has served service firms very well in the past.

In a stable or a rising market, the main criticism of cost-plus pricing is that it does not maximise profit. It is a somewhat lazy and inefficient approach as it does not look at what profit each area of work is capable of generating and then try to maximise that, but typically treats all areas of work the same (irrespective of market demand, expertise and so on). The end result is that it is not maximising the return that could be made by the firm. In fact, it does most damage in relation to Rocket Science work, where an obsession with counting the number of hours taken to deliver the results typically leads to undercharging. Simply counting hours does not reflect the actual value delivered to clients. In practice, individual partners may get this right by using the recorded time as only the basis for a discussion, but that will not always occur. As mentioned previously, the better approach in terms of Rocket Science work is to talk to the client about putting a safe budget in place, with discussion of the price being left to the end of the matter when the outcome can be seen – a value-based approach.

These days, relatively stable times have long gone and competition is much more intense; firms can no longer afford to use what is an entirely internally focussed pricing model, and one which suffers from the following problems:

■ It analyses the cost of delivering the service and charges the client on that basis, wholly irrespective of the actual value of the work to the client. It is like charging for works of art based upon the amount of paint the artist used (which would inevitably vary from painting to painting, but have no effect on the perceived value to the buyer) and also on the number of hours the artist takes (so that faster artists charge less for their works of art than slow artists).

■ In order to construct an hourly rate, you need to allocate all of the overhead costs of the business onto individuals. The actual method of allocation (there is no universal one, so it will vary from firm to firm) affects the price that is going to be charged for each member of the service team. Partners in a firm who have 20 years' experience and are seen as some of the leading experts in their field often would be allocated an hourly charge-out rate which would be affected by the salary of their secretary, but wholly unaffected by the number of years of expertise that they had. A newly qualified partner with no particular expertise may be charged out to a client at the same rate as a much more experienced partner. However, from a client's perspective, they would place much more value on the most experienced partner and be prepared to pay extra for that expertise.

■ Being entirely internally focused, the prices charged for individuals take no account of market demand for services. In situations where there is a huge demand for a particular area of the firm, and therefore likely to be considerable opportunity for price increases, the actual price charged would be the same as an area where demand has collapsed.

■ In order to calculate the hourly charge-out rate of each team member you have to decide, several months before the start of the year, when the budgets are being put together, that you will sell the agreed maximum number of hours for that person (e.g. 1500 hours). This information goes into the formula and then all of the relevant overhead costs of the firm are added to it so that an hourly rate can be produced. The result is that if there had been an increase in overheads, then the hourly rate that comes out at the end of the formula will be higher than the preceding year.

In practice this means that if you have increased your marketing budget in order to attract new clients, you will charge all existing clients more per hour for their work in the following year; similarly if you have taken on newer, more expensive premises. From a client's perspective it is hard for them to understand why the price per hour has increased in these situations, when the actual service that they receive is unchanged. In addition, cost-plus pricing assumes that you can predict the number of hours of each person's time you will sell in the coming year, *irrespective of the hourly charge-out rate*. In reality, increasing the hourly charge-out rate might lead to a drop in demand (some work might be lost to a competitor which the client rates as equivalent to you, but is now cheaper than you) such that only 1200 hours can be sold. However, a cost-plus pricing formula ignores this real effect. In fact, the fewer hours you predict you will sell, the more the formula increases the price!

Cost-plus pricing has been around in service firms for so long that there is no question of it being thrown out. The tracking of hours forms a key part of the management information of the firm. However, the cost-plus calculation should be seen as only the first step in putting together a price. It is, after all, important to know what your running costs are planned to be in the coming year so that you can correctly measure breakeven points and then assess profit beyond. With this in mind, it is equally important to understand that simply applying an X% mark-up to create profit should not be the end point. As well as the problems that we've seen above, it does not involve the firm in seeking to understand the value it is delivering to each client to see what the clients would be prepared to pay. If the firm delivered a different service from the one it is currently delivering, would the client value it more and therefore be willing to pay a premium for it? In other words, it takes no advantage of the potential price increases which would be available if firms delivered a service which better met the client's needs, or which reflected the expertise of its people or the demand for that type of work. This is an issue we will address in Chapter 8 when we explore value-based pricing in more detail.

> Cost-plus pricing fails completely in Rocket Science work – where **Key point**
> both the service firm and client know that the number of hours
> recorded is not the issue, but rather the end result – so what value
> did the work add?

If we look at consumer goods we can see an interesting example of how cost-plus pricing fails to maximise profit – there is even a legal case about it. The case is *Reckitt & Colman* v. *Borden Inc.* [1990] 1 All ER 873. This was the case involving the Jif plastic lemon whose manufacturers were seeking to prevent other firms producing similar plastic lemons to compete with them. In other words, the manufacturer wanted to stop others putting their lemon juice into similarly shaped yellow plastic containers. They went to a huge amount of effort to protect their rights. What was the real reason they did that? It was neatly explained in the case when it was revealed that if you are selling lemon juice to the public, then by putting it in squeezable plastic containers you are able to charge almost three times as much per fluid ounce as you can do if you put the lemon juice into bottles. Therefore, it was hugely valuable to Reckitt & Colman to be the sole provider of the squeezable plastic lemons because it would enable this price differential to be maintained. They were successful in their claim and therefore retained their ability to charge a much higher price for their lemon juice (not one just based upon the price of the juice itself).

If a typical services firm had been asked to price the lemon juice in the squeezable plastic lemon and in the bottle, then it would have used its well-established cost-plus approach and there would have been no price premium added to lemon juice in the squeezable plastic lemon, completely ignoring the consumer benefit. If you think about it, this is exactly what service firms tend to do. They do not see the issue of price from the client's point of view so as to better understand what the client would value and what the client is prepared to pay, but rather are obsessed with internal calculations and ignore the marketplace.

However, as I noted above, cost-plus pricing should *not* be abandoned. Knowing how your costs are made up is an important element in creating your pricing strategy. It can tell you what your breakeven point is, and that can help you to decide whether particular areas of business are going to be successful for you or not. The important issue is not to be driven entirely by cost-plus pricing but to see it as only part of the picture. It is an entirely internally focussed part of the picture, so it is a good time now to turn to look at other methods which are more market-facing.

CLIENT-DRIVEN PRICING

Client-driven pricing seems intuitively correct, in that you cannot make clients pay more than they are prepared to pay for your services. This type of approach is determined generally by your sales staff. Once you have fallen into the trap of client-driven pricing then the whole pricing operation ends up focussing on your ability to negotiate the best price with the client. In fact, it is not then unusual for service firms to send front-line staff on courses to learn these types of negotiating skills. The price that each client pays can then depend upon how well each client negotiated with the particular firm and how skilled the relevant partner or salesperson was at negotiating back!

For those firms where partners negotiate price, there are also some fairly complex interpersonal issues arising from the partners' role in selling the firm. First, whenever partners have to make a formal presentation to see whether they will, or will not, gain some particular work from a client or prospective client, there is a huge level of personal involvement by that partner. Partners are very keen to win the work because it will give them kudos among their peers, and, even worse, there are considerable risks from being seen to lose a potential client. There is also a level of personal rejection involved – if a client says no, then often the client is not just saying no to the firm, but to that particular partner or team that was assembled. There is a very similar situation where you have separate sales staff who are typically rewarded by reference to turnover (sales made) rather than the prices achieved.

Key point	If you put the client in charge of your prices, you may find they are rather lower than you had hoped.

Given those pressures it is not surprising to find that partners will typically drop the price as low as they possibly can in order to win the work, and will easily be persuaded to throw in all kinds of additional services at no extra cost, without any regard for how much those services actually cost. In fact, because ancillary services (free secondments, use of research services, free training and talks, etc.) do not generally detract from a chargeable hours budget, added value can often be the first port of call when someone selling the core service wants to offer sweeteners to conclude a sale (the cost of which added value could quite easily exceed the profit to be gained on the work).

This dual role of both selling and delivering the work causes pressures where a firm wants to gain a 'trophy client', or the partner otherwise fears being light on work, or failing to meet growth targets. Where, as is quite often the case, the role of selling and delivering the service is split, the risks are even greater because the sales role will be judged on the client gains that are brought in and the turnover produced, often wholly irrespective of the price at which the work is won. This is increasingly the case where key clients are assigned a relationship partner and then the firm launches initiatives to grow the work from those key clients. When a partner wants to agree a very low rate with a client often there will be talk about this being an important trophy client, or the claim that this initial low rate is simply a way into a valuable client that will subsequently offer the firm huge amounts of work (but this time at good rates). In reality, all the evidence is that going in at a low initial rate has the opposite effect – it tends to place your firm in that price bracket, as a low-cost provider. There also might be an explanation by the relevant partner that all of the competitors for the work have dropped to even lower rates than this partner did, typically without any actual supporting evidence for the claim.

It does not end there. Even after the work has been won, clients soon realise that if they contact the average service firm and say that for budgetary, strategic or whatever reasons there has been talk about a panel review and there is a need to reduce costs, most service firms will knee-jerk react by agreeing quite readily to fairly substantial percentage reductions in prices. One client even admitted that they had a game between managers to see who could achieve the biggest drops from a single phone call, and that they had been trained by their manager to do this. The manager had explained to the team that if they did this every year, they would know when they had pushed a particular firm to its lowest price when the firm actually refused a reduction, but in their experience that was often several years and very large percentage reductions down the line.

Given all of these problems, how does a firm tackle this? There are basically two issues to be addressed. First, partners who are on the front line need a general programme of awareness to improve their pricing skills. Secondly, there are issues of honesty and integrity: agreeing different rates with different clients for exactly the same work is not a fair or sensible business practice.

An example, given by a secretary who had joined a major firm from a much smaller firm, threw this issue into sharp relief. One of the reasons why she had left her previous firm was that she felt the firm was dishonest. She said that they had two completely different pricing structures for their work. There was one price for clients who rang up and, before instructing the firm, asked how much it would cost, in which case the firm came in at a very competitive figure. However, in more than half the cases, they were instructed by clients without being asked in advance to agree a clear price, in which case they charged much more. She really didn't like being part of that subterfuge and it had certainly been a powerful element in her decision to leave her previous firm.

Key point	Put simply, it felt dishonest to charge clients less if they asked the price in advance, but more if they didn't.

Most service firm partners hearing that story will empathise entirely and feel that some improper practice has gone on. However, my consulting experience shows that in most firms you end up with two groups of clients. Group A clients have asked you to go through a formal tender process (they may even have involved procurement). Group B clients haven't done that; they have either instructed directly or are a repeat client. You are doing the same work for both groups, but due to the nature of how the working relationship started, you end up charging them two different amounts.

How do you explain to the long-standing existing client (Group B) that they are paying much more for the same service than one of their competitors who put your firm through a formal tender process? This is the end result of allowing client-driven pricing.

There is also an element of abdication of responsibility if a company simply says that they cannot charge more than clients are prepared to pay. Any normal client will want the best service that they can get at the lowest price possible; they don't have the same interest as the service firm. If you have a strategy behind your pricing which you have thought through, it will stand up to examination. You can then be confident enough to stand firm, even in the face of client pressure. There is a good example of that in the next section where we look at how water softening equipment is priced. The important issue here is that while cost-plus pricing has a role in informing pricing strategy (indicating costs and breakeven points), client-driven pricing is a slippery slope and needs to be avoided.

However, client-driven pricing does have a contributory role in the creation of informed pricing decisions, in the sense that the more that you talk to clients about price, the more you will learn about what they value or do not value. Having structured conversations about this will help you to create a more valuable service that clients are prepared to offer more to receive. In both Rocket Science and Relationship Advice, where the actual final price is uncertain, partners talk very little to clients about price, but clients want to talk much, much more about it. The role of client-driven pricing is about understanding what is good and not good about your pricing in the eyes of the client, to help to shape how you will charge. That said, you cannot abdicate the actual pricing decision to clients; you have to create your strategy and be prepared to defend it, not just give in at every client resistance. As we will see in Chapter 8, one way of creating client options is to offer different levels of service at different prices – so allowing clients to choose which they actually want, per transaction.

COMPETITION-DRIVEN PRICING (MARKET-DRIVEN)

Again, this is intuitively attractive. If you are up against a competitor firm that all of your peers would see as pretty much equivalent to you, and they have dropped their price by 15% (or so your client says), then how on earth can you charge more than them? There is no question of gaining or even retaining a client if your competitor is making that type of offer to them, is there?

You immediately have all of the partner/seller issues which we saw in the previous section. I'm sure that many readers have been involved in situations where competitors have offered cut-throat prices and if we pause to think about it, there are other situations where our competitors would be saying the same things about us.

If you put yourself in the position of a client who has interviewed three different firms, all of whom – to varying degrees – could supply the service that is needed, why not choose the one that is 15%

cheaper than the others? In fact the client would be mad not to, wouldn't they? However, to the surprise of many service firms, this is not really how clients go about choosing their service firms. As we've seen, they don't do that for Rocket Science work, where the key issue is getting the right expert; here, a lower price is indicative of a person not being the right expert.

What may come as a surprise to you is that clients do not automatically choose the firm that is 15% cheaper when they are looking at Relationship Advice. When clients say they don't put price first, they actually mean it. If they have gone through any type of formal tender process or have just been interviewing a few firms to get a feel for them, then they actually will have already ranked those firms in order of preference *before* they look at the prices. It is never as simple as just quoting the lowest price. I can probably best illustrate this by giving a real-life example: I had just bought a holiday cottage in the countryside. After moving in, when I turned on the taps I found that the water coming out of them was somewhat milky in appearance. In fact, it turns out that the cottage is in an area of very hard water. By asking around among my neighbours I discovered that my cottage was the only one that didn't have a water softener fitted. Realistically, I had to buy one and have it installed onto the mains water system.

After enquiring of my neighbours and carrying out some research online, I identified three potential companies that could do the job and contacted them to ask for quotes. At this stage I didn't have much idea of what the cost was going to be, so getting a few quotes was also a good way of trying to find out what was the going rate for a plumbed-in water softener.

From my point of view the work was hardly Rocket Science, but neither was it Routine. I was going to have it carried out once and I wanted it to be right. It fitted neatly into the category of Relationship Advice. The first tradesman to arrive was from a locally based company: after inspecting the pipes in the kitchen he explained that he might have some difficulty fitting the water softener under the sink, where it needed to go, but he was fairly confident that it would just about fit in, after the kitchen cabinets had been cut back. He also explained that because of a recent European Regulation it would be necessary to leave the cold water tap in the kitchen untreated because there has to be one source of untreated water left in the house. This was a problem to me because obviously this is the tap that was to be used for cooking and for making drinks, so it would be a shame if it was still very hard water.

The second company was the local franchise of a national organisation. This salesman spent some time running chemical tests on the water from the taps to test the actual degree of hardness, took me through the process and explained each of the results and what they meant. He confirmed that it was some of the hardest water he had personally encountered. The end result was that he was able to specify a particular model of water softener based upon the number of people living in the house, its likely usage and the hardness of the water. He measured up and said that their unit would fit comfortably under the kitchen sink. He also mentioned the recent European Regulation which means that there has to be one untreated tap in the house. However, he suggested that they fit a mini-tap (like a spout) into the kitchen sink, so that would mean that the main tap in the kitchen could be treated and I wouldn't end up with hard water in my tea. I really warmed to the salesman and felt that he was professional and competent. I instinctively knew two things from this visit. First, that I really wanted this company to carry out the work and, second, that they were going to be the most expensive.

The third tradesman also appeared to be reasonably professional. He measured up and confirmed that they could fit the water softener in the correct place, but also mentioned the European Regulation and again proposed leaving the main kitchen tap untreated. He didn't carry out any tests on the water or ask many questions. The visit was very brief.

Sure enough, within a week or so the quotes arrived and the first supplier had quoted £900, with the national organisation coming in at £1400 and the third tradesman quoting £1350. As a buyer you know what you need to do – which is to persuade the best supplier (£1400) to carry out the work for the same price as the worst supplier (£900). *How often have your clients done the same to you?*

There is an absolutely crucial piece of understanding here: if a client calls you to negotiate price *after* this type of competitive tender it is because they have (firmly) decided that they actually do want you to do the work. However, they also want to get you down to the price of the worst supplier *if they can*. This is really just human nature. It is also competition-driven pricing. You are letting your competitor, probably even the one who is doing the worst job in the industry (and therefore has to charge less or they simply won't get any work at all), set the lowest price at which your services are going to be sold.

Key point | In these situations clients try to get the very best supplier to carry out the work, but at the price quoted by the worst supplier.

So what happened with my water softener, and what deal did I get? In fact, I did end up with the best supplier (I was determined to do that) but they handled the price conversation very professionally. I called them to explain that while I liked their approach, their price was much too high. They took me through the reality of the situation, which was that they were the best in their industry and there was no question of their being able to do the job at the price of their least competent competitors. They wished that they could. However, what they could do was to reduce the price by £50 if I was prepared to confirm within the next 48 hours that I wanted to go ahead, and they would provide me with vouchers for free supplies of salt for the first three years of operation of the water softener (which I established later on as being worth about £25!). All in all I was fairly happy. I felt that I had negotiated a discount and, in fact, their resistance to dropping the price made me more confident that their price was fair.

This again is a crucial point. I have often witnessed partners quickly agree to a discount demand from a client, motivated by a desire to be seen as being flexible and helpful. In fact it just makes them look disingenuous because the client is left feeling that the partner was 'trying it on' at the higher price and would have charged that if not challenged, so thank goodness the client did make the challenge (and maybe they should have asked for a bigger discount). Certainly it teaches the client *always* to challenge that partner's quotes and to tell others to do the same.

To recap:

■ Post-tender: if the client calls you to negotiate on fee, then you are (more likely than not) their preferred vendor.

■ Once you are clear about your market position and how you rank against your competitors, then you can have a robust and confident approach because your price is right for the service that you are providing.

■ Suddenly dropping the price considerably undermines your clients' trust in you from the outset.

■ Knowledge of competitor pricing, and of how you relate to those prices (same, higher or lower), is important for two reasons:

- First, price needs to match your method of competing (as discussed in the next section). If you are competing using a differentiated strategy, then you need *to charge higher prices than the relevant competitors* to reflect the extra benefits you bring. That is what my chosen water softener company was doing. They understood their market proposition and positioning, and you need to do the same.

- Secondly, your price needs to be in the same area as competitors – if it is massively different (higher or lower) then clients are likely to dismiss your proposal. We will look at the importance of 'price grouping' in Chapter 3.

So it is now time to look at that – what exactly is your market position? How do you compare with the competition and what makes you think that you are the best firm for this client?

HOW SERVICE FIRMS COMPETE

More than 20 years ago, Professor Michael Porter at Harvard Business School set out the three main strategies that businesses can choose when they are competing with each other (see page 25). These strategies apply across different businesses and across the world. Your clients use them just as much as you can, although they probably do it more consciously. We are going to focus here on Relationship Advice, because other approaches are more relevant for Rocket Science and Relationship Work and are covered at the end of this chapter.

Despite all that has been written about the way that service firms compete, there are essentially only three ways. In terms of the offering to clients, a firm will say one of the following:

1. We are just as good (for your purposes) as the other firm, but we are cheaper than them.

2. We are better than the competition, and more expensive.

3. We focus on an area of work.

In a diagram, it looks like Figure 2.1. Deciding on a strategy for your firm is really important, because pricing follows from the chosen strategy.

Because the correct pricing is inextricably linked to which competitive strategy your firm is using, the purpose of this section is to help you to decide which *one* strategy to follow. This is an important decision. In my experience service firms often want to

Figure 2.1

Choosing a competitive strategy

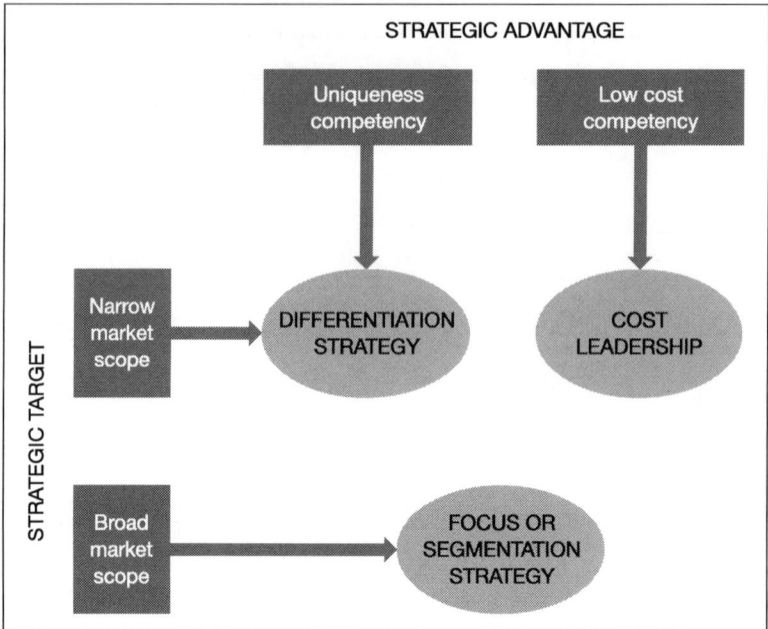

be both better and cheaper than the competition, which is illogical and an economic fallacy. Where else do you choose 'the best' (when buying a car, wine, food, clothes) and find that the best is also the cheapest? When we decide something is the best we are really focussing upon higher value to us. We are conditioned to believe that price and quality are linked; that higher price means better quality. In fact, experiments at California Institute of Technology and Stanford University (see page 66) have shown that when people were told that a wine was expensive, their brain registered higher pleasure when drinking it than when they drank exactly the same wine having been told that it was much lower priced. However, just as strongly, when we discover something is cheaper, we naturally begin to question its authenticity and/or quality. We will examine this issue in much more detail when we look at competitive tenders for work and the best approach to pricing in that situation.

Strategy 1 – We are cheaper (cost leadership)

This really says to clients that they will receive the same service/result from you as they will receive from your competitors, but at a lower price. That may not always be the reality, but this is the selling proposition. It doesn't have to be exactly the same service.

A trip on a budget airline is very different to a flight on a flag carrier airline but it achieves the same result in moving you from City A to City B (or thereabouts). The joy of service firm marketing is that no one firm is going to win the whole marketplace. Different clients look for different services, and there will always be clients who will be attracted by lower prices, whether or not that turns out to be a false economy or a genuine one. Most firms pride themselves on being 'better' than the competition and don't see themselves as cut-price, cheap or trying to win business simply on price. However, firms often enter into a tender or beauty parade by deliberately cutting prices with the intention of coming in below competitors. This immediately leads to a mixed message not just to the client, but also to the people working in the firm who start to have a confused vision about what their firm is trying to say to clients.

> In almost every area of your personal life, you will recognise that **Key point** more expensive choices are usually much better quality. However, when it comes to addressing clients, often service firms not only say that they are they better than the competition, but they also undercut them on price. Actually, if you were better, would you need to undercut them on price?

Having a 'we are cheaper' strategy is not necessarily a low-profit strategy, quite the contrary. You only have to look at the high profits of budget airlines or discount supermarkets to see that. Well-run service businesses that take this approach can be just as profitable, if not more profitable, than those that seek to take the high quality/high price position. What you need to understand is that if you have decided to compete on price then the focus of your internal efforts must be on cost reduction and efficiencies, because in order to successfully sell at a lower price than your competitors, but still make an acceptable profit, you must be able *to produce the service at a lower cost*. It's as simple as that! Don't compete on price unless you have an overheads advantage over your competitors, or have used technology, scale, different team structures or some other way of producing the service at a lower cost than competitors.

The problem for this technique in services (which is certainly not the case in manufacturing) is that the great majority of your overheads are likely to be staff costs, and therefore having an 'efficient' operation in these terms can mean paying your staff less and making them work harder than they would in a competitor's business.

That does not sound like a recipe for success in a business where the staff are the real service you are selling. Therefore, if you are going to adopt a 'cheaper' strategy it is important that you sell on being more efficient, project managing the work or using technology to make your great staff even more productive. Without a clear and understandable reason for your position as cheaper, your message to the client effectively becomes 'we are cheaper because we use less qualified and worse people'.

Without doubt, some service firms are going to be cheaper than other firms offering very similar services. Any client asking for quotes is going to find that out. This is a *big* strategic issue for your firm. When clients think of your firm, do you want them to think of you as lower cost than your competitors? Clients do 'bracket' firms by price and they are going to find it difficult to understand your market position if you are inconsistent on this: sometimes cheaper than a similar competitor, sometimes the same price and sometimes more expensive. A 'we are cheaper' strategy can be very successful but you need to carry it through and be consistent. In tough economic times, or indeed at any time when the client is under pressure to cut their costs, any firm that uses a cost leadership strategy is going to become more attractive to clients. However, clients will need reassurance about *why* you are cheaper, as they will (typically) not want to see much of a quality drop in Relationship Advice where (as we will see) the decision is not primarily about price.

There is an interesting cultural feature here. What if your client, in their business, adopts a market strategy of cost leadership? Does that change their relationships with suppliers? My experience is a resounding 'yes'. If your client is a budget airline, a discount super-market or similar, then they will negotiate hard with you over fees because the client's own market strategy demands that they con-tinually drive down the costs of their business, and that includes fees paid to their advisers. Unless the client is a trophy client and delivers on that (see Chapter 7), then it could make business sense to avoid carrying out Relationship Advice for them.

Strategy 2 – We are better and cost more (differentiation)

According to clients, almost every services firm claims that it is better than its competitors. In fact, it is similar to the Garrison Keillor quote that in his (fictional) hometown, Lake Wobegon, 'all the women are strong, all the men are good-looking and all the children are above average'.

However, it is quite interesting to find that if you ask service firm partners why a particular client should use their firm rather than a competitor firm, they are often reduced to fairly bland forms of answer:

Our advantage	Reaction of client
We are better than our competitors.	They all say that. What do you mean?
We are better lawyers/ accountants/PR agents/ actuaries/financiers, etc.	They all say that too. What do you mean by better?
We are much bigger than our competitors.	So what? As long as the other firm is big enough to do the particular task I have for them, I can't understand what benefit your being large brings, apart from extra cost.
We are innovative.	They all say that, and they all are not.
We could charge less than our competitors.	I thought you'd end up saying that.

The reality is very often that you do not know whether you are, in fact, 'better' than your competitors. For all you know, you may only be hanging on to your clients because they haven't actually experienced your competitors and found that they give a better service. If you want to know how the market perceives you against your competitors then you need to have market research under-taken (always by a third party, because clients find it difficult to speak honestly directly to you). If you commission such research you are likely to be disappointed by the answers, because clients are generally intelligent enough to work out that you are not best at everything in the world. In some areas they choose you because they genuinely believe you are giving them a good combination of performance and price, and in other areas they choose other firms for similar reasons.

The main reason you cannot say *to the world* that you are 'better' than your competitors is because each client is going to judge 'bet-ter' in a different way, and therefore it is absolutely impossible to be better in every case unless you have worked with each one of your clients to make sure that you are offering them a genuinely enhanced service. In fact that is the core theme of this book, and it is worth looking at some of the ways that clients rank one firm as better than another in ways that they value. For example:

Benefit	Explanation
The firm achieves actual completion on more transactions (i.e. fewer fail to complete).	A statistical analysis of the different firms that the client used found that one was more likely to bring deals to completion than others. Abortive deals are hugely expensive to the client in terms of management time and lost business, so the client hugely values (and will happily pay more for) a firm which completes a greater percentage of transactions.

Note: You need to gather statistical information (data) on your own work and then spend time with the client seeing how you can improve your completion rates, and how you can beat your competitors at this. No data, no real benefit.

Benefit	Explanation
The firm completes its work more quickly than its competitors.	Easily measured and do not underestimate the value of this to clients. A large matter completed faster has a real cash value to the client, and in fact there is likely to be a direct link between speed and completion rates.

Note: Again this only works with the facts to back it up. You need to measure your performance so that you can compare it with competitors. As you can see, a theme is emerging: in order to charge more than competitors for Relationship Advice you need facts and data, not merely empty claims of superiority.

If you are interested in understanding how you might be better, arrange to base yourself at your client's premises for two or three days and spend that time understanding exactly what they would value as a benefit in terms of a different services that you could provide. For more examples see Chapter 8 which shows how to explore a client's drivers of value.

Very importantly, Michael Porter warns that going head-to-head in competition with another firm where you both want to be 'the best' is likely to be a destructive strategy where both firms end up competing on price. Why? Because if you occupy the same space as another firm you can end up becoming indistinguishable to clients in terms of the service that you deliver, and then clients can just play off the firms against each other on price. Can you think of current examples for your firm? Porter says that it is crucial that each firm finds its unique space in the marketplace where it can legitimately claim that it is different from other firms. In that way it can meet the diverse needs of its target clients and compete by innovation rather than imitation. (Matching another firm head-on is a recipe for fierce and unproductive competition.) Let's look at one way of addressing market segments using niche focus.

Strategy 3 – We focus (niche)

If you look at the most profitable service firms in your sector, you might be surprised to find that there are a number of relatively small firms that get quite close to the top (or even are at the top) in terms of profit. Although the largest firms typically do extremely well, following close behind them you will often find some distinctly niche, much smaller, practices.

That is the key issue about these successful firms. They have focussed on a specific area or areas; it is not just that they are small versions of the very large firms. There are a number of advantages for a firm that specialises in this way:

- Focus brings with it all of the benefits of experience such as familiarity of the staff with their subject matter, a sector-specific bank of experience and focussed knowledge management systems. It is likely that they will spend less time on the work and are less likely to get it wrong.

- One of the most quoted reasons for clients to choose a particular firm for Relationship Advice is because it is recommended by their peers in the industry. Having focus greatly multiplies the chances of receiving such recommendations.

- Focus allows you to achieve a very high reputation in your chosen marketplace (a bigger fish in a smaller pond) and to have real empathy with the chosen sector – to actually become a part of that sector in a way that a huge firm cannot.

- The partners will be able to give great 'war stories' to potential clients which clearly demonstrate their level of expertise and empathy with the chosen market sector.

There is an interesting divergence here between service firms and their clients. Many partners in a large firm will believe that there are benefits for the client in sourcing more and more services from their firm. Sometimes this is referred to as a 'one-stop shop' approach, enabling the client to source all of their services needs from one firm. What is interesting about this viewpoint is that when you talk to clients they are often more interested in choosing firms that have specific expertise in that client's sector. The client has no great desire to feed an increasing amount of work types into any particular firm, unless it finds itself with too large a panel of advisers, in which case the client may take the initiative to reduce the number of firms.

This is probably the reason why so many cross-selling initiatives in service firms don't work. While there are obvious advantages in cross-selling for the firm, there may well be no immediate or apparent advantages for the client – quite the contrary. Is it likely that a firm that is expert in one area is also going to be expert in every other area? Clients tend to think not. Again, peer group recommendations play the major role. When searching for a firm to handle a new type of work, a client is much more likely to speak to peers and ask whom they recommend for that specific type of work than they are to speak to the (highly biased) partner who handles their other work at a particular services firm. Cross-selling can work but it must be built upon delivering greater value to the client rather than simply increasing the income for the firm.

Really successful niche firms can find themselves under pressure to diversify into other sectors because there are clearly some limits on growth if you are niche. In fact, the typical niche firm knows that there is real business risk in a focussed approach. If its chosen sector is in recession then the available business may drop precipitously, leading to pressure to diversify into other sectors to spread risk, but at a cost of perhaps diluting its current focus and strength. From a pricing perspective, the clearer and more narrow the focus, the stronger the argument for having a price premium against less focussed competitors. One strong argument for a premium is where basic charging is going to be measured on a time-spent basis, which is the normal hourly or daily based method so typical of Relationship Advice. A firm with real focus can claim that focus enables it to do the same work in less time, or to spot real issues that would be missed by those without such deep sector knowledge (even though the other firms may be cheaper by the day or hour). If niche is your positioning, you need to make sure you communicate these points to your clients in order to justify premium pricing.

Large, diversified firms can try to capture some of the benefits of focus by dividing themselves into sector-focused business lines (at least in terms of how they approach the market). This can draw them closer to the niche firm and ahead of large diversified firms that have not demonstrated such a focus. This is a strong and useful strategy. If the client is in the retail sector, it makes a real difference if they are going to be dealing with people who spend all day, every day, working with other clients in the retail sector. The empathy, language and understanding of the market will be so much stronger than a more generalist approach. That's why we talk of a niche or sector-based approach – the latter being a version of niche available for more diversified and larger firms.

WHAT NEXT?

The challenge for you now is to think about the twin pillars. First, what can you gain from reassessing how you create your prices, learning from cost-plus, client-driven and competitor-driven pricing issues. Second, think about which of Michael Porter's three competitive strategies are appropriate to your firm. Think also that in an ideal situation you would have *one* competitive strategy across the whole firm. Is that possible? If it is, then it gives you the greatest chance of creating a clear brand (reputational) message to clients. If you are going to run several strategies, then how will you separate them, and will partners really understand what they are trying to say to clients about the firm? For example, the message might be that for tax work you are better than competitors and charge more for better results, but for insurance advice you have systematised the work so you can give clients the same service but at lower cost than competitors and for business strategy advice you are niche players in retail, food and energy only. That's quite a complex message, isn't it? Can you pick one? If not then you may need to address brand in a more structured way. Do you need to have separate brands or a family of brands (with different names) so that you can communicate more than one market position? What would be the impact of that for your overall brand?

In the table below I have examined all three generic competitive strategies across the three types of services:

Work type	Cost leadership	Differentiated	Focus
Rocket Science	NO	YES – the usual strategy. I am the right expert. I cost a lot but this is no time to be saving money.	MAYBE – I am the expert AND I focus particularly on problems in your sector – no one understands your sector like me.
Relationship Advice	YES – we can do this work and what we add is a commitment to cost control and efficiency that our competitors lack. We have developed systems that make us more efficient.	YES – we understand what our clients want better than our competitors and have tailored our services to better meet those needs – we cost more but we bring you better results.	YES – no one understands your sector better than us – as a result we can deliver the same results faster and at lower cost than our competitors/give you better results at an extra cost.

Work type	Cost leadership	Differentiated	Focus
Routine Work	YES – the usual strategy – we can do this work to the quality level that you need, but at a lower cost than our competitors.	YES – our prices are still low but we deliver better results than our competitors at a small extra cost.	YES – no one understands your sector better than us – as a result we can deliver the same results faster and at lower cost than our competitors/give you better results at a small extra cost.

CLIENT MESSAGING

If you look at the grid above, it starts to affect the way that you talk to clients about different work types, and this is really important. Your language needs to be appropriate for the services that you are selling. For Rocket Science work there is no point in arguing that you are the right firm to handle the work when you are not – it's about individual track record and expertise, so the language needs to be about that person, not about the firm as a whole. For Relationship Advice you need to be clear to your clients where you stand against your competitors and what advantages there are in choosing you.

In Chapter 8 we will take our basic pricing strategy to the next level and look at how to build an approach to value pricing your services, so that you start to tailor them to make them more valuable to individual clients (rather than having more of a 'one size fits all' approach).

THE COMPETITIVE LANDSCAPE – WHAT IS YOUR MARKET POSITIONING?

Understanding your firm's market positioning is important because clients group firms into bands and their expectations in terms of the quality, breadth of service and price of the services that the firm provides are conditioned by the group in which you are. To explain this it is useful to look at how hotel groups segment their industry and position themselves within it, creating differences in service and style rather than engaging in a simple price war.

In major towns and cities you should see every type of hotel – from five-star luxury hotels through four-star, three-star, budget hotels, guesthouses and bed and breakfast accommodation. There are implications in each strata of hotel and we can learn from their behaviour. Interestingly, it's worth noting that the major hotel groups have separately branded hotels focussing on each level so that they can compete for different market segments (different groups of clients). Unlike many service providers, they don't try to use one brand across many different levels.

From the entrance foyer, the style and luxury of the building, to the number and welcoming nature of the staff, everything about a five-star hotel has to be coherent with its status. Note how different hotel groups will adopt very different styles of luxury, from ultra-traditional through business-friendly to fashionable, in order to target different parts of the five-star market. Even though they are aiming at different audiences, the quality level is going to be very similar.

There will be a price expectation that will be high and while it will vary from city to city based upon supply and demand and overall living costs, the prices of five-star hotels within any locality will be quite closely grouped. Competing on price between market segments would be somewhat foolish, given that they have targeted different types of guests. Would someone who liked a modern hotel really want to switch to a very traditional one based upon price? If one hotel successfully competed with lower prices, it is the work of a moment for the other hotels to match or undercut those prices and now the hotels are back where they started, but all at lower rates.

Similarly, four-star hotels will vary greatly in their style and the segments of the market that they are targeting. While they will offer a very high standard, their prices will be grouped together at a *lower level* than their five-star competitors. Their strategy, while clearly upmarket, is to be cheaper than a five-star hotel. If they try to charge the same as a five-star hotel then the market will 'find them out'. They do not offer the same standards or facilities as a five-star hotel so their price needs to be lower to reflect that fact, but neither do they have the same running costs. The primary competitors for four-star hotels are other four-star hotels. An individual four-star hotel can compete on any of the three possible routes – it can use a differentiated strategy to be a little more expensive than another four-star hotel because it has a swimming pool and spa, or it can use a cost leadership strategy to be a little cheaper because it has cut back on facilities that are rarely used. Or it could specialise: using a niche strategy to focus on a specific type of traveller and aim to be their number one destination, whether that is silver-haired travellers who want home comforts or über trendy media types who want to sit around the pool and do deals.

Services firms can think that they are in competition with everyone else who carries out the same services, but in fact they are grouped in bands by their clients, just like hotels are, and that band sets the pricing parameters for the firm. If you are not sure of your actual competitors and which band you are in, then the answer is to see which firms your clients invite to pitch alongside you when they are running a competitive tender. That is, who your clients think your competitors are, which will show you the broad band into which your prices may fall.

In among these layers of hotels you will find the boutique hotels – the niche players. They can compete alongside any level, but what they need is a focus. So a five-star boutique hotel might be a one-site operation built in a city as one of its oldest hotels, or it might be found inside an original town hall or castle. It offers something unique and then decides in terms of its target clients 'realistically what are their other choices' – if they don't come to us what other hotel might they choose? That sets their price band. However, they are not afraid of then being the highest priced hotel in their band, because they offer guests something unique (a differentiated strategy). This is the approach that sets the scene for the next chapter on pitching for work, because it forces you to write down in detail what exactly is your pricing offer; and therefore how you position yourself against your direct competitors in terms of your prices – higher, lower or the same. Before we turn to that, we are going to look at the issues around launching entirely new services, where there are no obvious direct competitors.

NEW SERVICE LAUNCHES – SETTING THE MARKET PRICE

How much do you charge for a service where you are the first to offer this service, and therefore you cannot simply investigate the 'going rate' among competitors against which you could then position your own service?

There are whole courses run on new product launches (and it is actually rare in services for a wholly new service to be launched as opposed to an improvement to an existing one), but there are some basic rules that can be helpful in the services sector:

1. **Price based upon the closest alternative.** If the client wasn't using your service, what service would they use? An example occurred when online training first appeared. Many clients had

compulsory training programmes in force at the time. This training might have been required by regulation (for example safety training or compliance with antitrust, money laundering or anti-bribery laws), which at the time was being carried out in classroom style, face-to-face with groups of employees. When online training appeared it actually offered the client *substantial advantages* over the traditional methods. It could guarantee the quality and uniformity of training, could incorporate auditable tracking of who had taken the training and who had passed an online test, and was available 24/7, 365 days a year, so that a new employee did not need to wait months for training but could self-serve it within hours of joining the company.

The right thing for a supplier of this training was not to work outwards from their costs of creating and delivering this training (an old cost-plus approach), but to calculate the cost to the client of delivering the training using the old method and then add to that the extra value that the online training gave. For example:

> *Your existing classroom style training ties up the time of senior managers delivering training, has weak auditability, is of variable quality and will miss new employees (putting the company at compliance risk) until the next cycle of training takes place. It costs your company £100,000 a year but for just £130,000 a year you can have all the advantages of online training, a better service, lower risk and higher (auditable) compliance.*

2. **Start high.** If you genuinely have a new service, or a new innovation on a service that competitors do not have, then it is best to start at a high price, working on the assumption that you can always reduce the price if you are not finding enough clients for the service, or in order to catch a second wave of clients. This is explained in Chapter 9, dealing with skim pricing. Setting a high price tests the extra value that clients place on your innovation (and bear in mind that you may need to take time and effort to communicate this value, given that it is a new service). This type of practice is widely used in the electronics industry, where manufacturers realise that they can maximise profit by skimming different customers at different price points. So, if you have just built a larger TV than the competition, or one with better online facilities, it would not be unusual to launch it at £3000 because the 'early adopters' – those people who have to have the latest gadget or want to install something special in their hotel or offices – will be prepared to pay a premium. After just

six months the price may drop to £2000 or less as newer models are introduced, and this attracts a different level of customer, and so on, with the price decreasing at regular intervals. If the new TV had been introduced at a lower price it would not have captured the extra income that the early adopters were prepared to pay.

It is the same for a new service. If nothing similar is available then start high. If something similar but not identical is available, then the starting point must be to examine how valuable the differences are in the eyes of the client and add the value of those services to the base cost of the competing service.

3. **See through the client's eyes.** When we develop something new we tend to be acutely aware of the cost to us of developing the service, but have little grasp of its monetary value to a client. Of course, the best starting point for new service development is to explore added-value options with the client (see Chapter 8); but in the absence of that it is an absolute minimum to discuss new developments with clients, to really understand the savings or extra profit that *they* will realise, and then factor in a proportion of that to the cost of the new service.

4. **Don't start with low prices.** This is sometimes used to gain high market share quickly. Where scale is crucial, for example where a standard (think music files, video encoding) is going to be set, market penetration can be important. You want to be the one who sets the standard so that others fail, or are seen as the minority choice. There can be a temptation to start low (or free if it's online) in order to take market share and only worry about profit much further down the line. That strategy requires very deep pockets and while there have been successes, there have been many more failures. The problem with starting low is that people have a deep-seated emotional barrier to paying more later on. Once a services pricing standard has been set, clients equate the value with the set price and it can be difficult – if not impossible – to raise it later on. In other words, the value in the mind of the client gets tied into that price point and no one wants to hear that this was a false premise and that the real price is much higher. Imagine that you find a local restaurant that doesn't just serve great food, but which has prices much lower than you were expecting. You start recommending the restaurant to your friends and connections but the feedback that you receive is that while the food is indeed great, the prices were really high too. You are surprised and revisit the restaurant

only to find that your friends are right: the prices are much higher than you paid. It turns out that you visited in the first month when prices were halved to create a great impression. If anything, you feel cheated. It may have been a quite clever idea from the restaurateur, but you recommended it without realising that you had a special and temporary price cut. Beware of doing this to your clients by 'going in low' on the first piece of work.

We will continue that thought into the next chapter, where we examine the behaviour of normally rational service firm partners who are put through a formal pitching process, and whose energies become diverted into deciding 'how low can we go' rather than what price is appropriate and sustainable for this particular client.

3

Pitching for work

My considerable experience of being on the front line in pitch situations has shown me that partners behave in a very specific way when placed into a competitive environment for the winning of work. Driven by the need to win, perhaps even more so by fear of the embarrassment or shame of having to report that they failed to win a client or a piece of work, they forensically examine every possible factor that might help them win. When it comes to price, their almost universal conclusion is that 'we must not risk losing this by going in too high'. I have sat in on numerous meetings and conference calls when the main topic was '*How low* can we bid and still make a profit?', with partners working assiduously to create unrealistic team compositions (lots of junior staff, little call upon partners) in order to show how a profit is perfectly possible even at the low price they were proposing; or making claims that they 'know' that competitors are going to bid low, so that they have to bid even lower in order to win. This approach appears to be endemic to almost all service providers and even more so after the 2008 crash, where oversupply and a loss of business confidence has added to the worries.

The only problem with this approach is that *it is almost always wrong*. Which, of course, means that in some cases it is right. So the skill is in being able to predict in advance whether the circumstances of a pitch require lowest prices or not – that is the primary purpose of this chapter. There are some other interesting factors around pitching for work that you also need to understand if you are to maximise your chances of winning in competitive situations (or price will be blamed unfairly when a loss occurs), which include:

■ how to win retenders (and how to lose them);

■ post-pitch negotiations on price;

■ the tactics of pitching.

Of course, the rules on pricing depend upon the type of work, with the main complexity being around Relationship Advice, where I have seen most mistakes being made. However, let's start at the top.

PITCHING FOR ROCKET SCIENCE

If a client needs a Rocket Scientist, then the importance, urgency or potential consequences of failure ensure that price is not uppermost in the client's mind. If anything, 'reassuringly expensive' is the order of the day. In very many cases the client is not actually spending their own money but that of their employer, so price sensitivity is further removed. For the Rocket Scientist, the important foundation is to make sure that the work truly is Rocket Science and that the client understands that as well. This means that the Rocket Scientist can often be heard talking to clients about the risks of failure and the fact that a true specialist is needed, in order to explain the value of employing them. It is also crucial that the Rocket Scientist takes time to deeply understand *the exact issue* that the client is facing and does not make assumptions – we have all seen too many failures caused by that.

When the client is choosing which person to instruct (and it is the person, not the firm, that matters), it is the *closest match* between problem and successful track record that wins. Think about a brain tumour and how you would choose the right surgeon. You want to know the track record of *this* surgeon (not of their colleagues, or of the hospital), and you want as much hard data as you can find on actual success rates.

So, does that mean price is completely irrelevant? Almost: Rocket Scientists need lengthy training and during that period they will absorb the cultural charging norms of their seniors. Those norms may undervalue true Rocket Science work. There is a tendency for these people to want to act on the most prestigious and complex matters because it feeds into their expertise and reputation, and they probably value recognition by their peers above everything else. So, to the Rocket Scientist, maximising price is not often a strong driver.

As explained in the previous chapter, the pricing solution is to use your expertise to give the client a safe range of total cost, not to exceed that, and to have a final price conversation at the end of the matter so that the value to that client of the outcome can be reflected in the final bill.

Does going in at a low price in a pitch situation help your chances of winning? Emphatically no. If anything, a low price might cause the client to doubt that you are the right expert for the job: '*If this person is so good, why are they cheaper than everyone else?*'

I have found that the main problem faced by Rocket Scientists is when they are pitching for work which the client sees as being at the top end of Relationship Advice, whereas they have seen it as Rocket Science. This mismatch can cause the Rocket Scientist to fail to focus on the right issues and as a result fail to maximise their chances of winning. We will look at what the key factors are for a win in Relationship Advice in the next section.

PITCHING FOR RELATIONSHIP ADVICE

If price is not the key driver for a win in Rocket Science, then it becomes much more of a factor in Relationship Advice, doesn't it? To the surprise of almost everyone, the answer to this is a clear *no*. When teaching this principle on Executive Education programmes I take partners through the steps involved in having a new kitchen put into their homes, because once they see how they behave when they are the client in pitch situations, they start to understand better how their clients are behaving with them.

It starts with your agreeing with your spouse or partner that you really do need to have a new kitchen installed. Once that point has been passed, you will need to set a budget – a figure that you are happy is a proper price for the type of design that you have in mind. Let's say that you have settled upon £50,000.

The next stage is to choose a number of kitchen designers and invite them in to give you a quote. For this purpose you have chosen (after some research, but quite likely referrals from your peer group) three designers called Alpha Kitchens, Beta Kitchens and Zeta Kitchens.

Within a couple of weeks, their representatives have visited you in your home, talked to you about what you have in mind and have promised to mail you quotes. In practice this is what happened:

- Alexander from Alpha Kitchens arrived spot on time, smartly dressed and appeared well prepared. As you talked to him about your own ideas he made suggestions and pointed out the benefits and downsides of some potential layouts you had in mind. He offered suggestions on space-saving options that had not occurred to you: clearly here was a man who 'lived kitchens'. You liked him and felt confident that he would deliver a good result. He offered numerous referees and ideas on how best to cope during the disruptive building period, and how he would keep that to a minimum.

- Bertie from Beta Kitchen was also prompt and smart. He didn't seem to listen as much as Arthur, but he had brought with him some pretty attractive designs. You were left with a feeling that he could deliver a competent job, but you wouldn't expect it to be as good as Alpha Kitchens. Not bad though.

- David turned up 20 minutes late from Zeta Kitchen, explaining that he was filling in for Zachary who had been called off to another job. He was a bit rushed and hadn't had time to create any bespoke options. In fairness, the standard designs that he brought with him looked pretty attractive, but he was relying more on his brochures than actually tailoring a solution just for you. You had some doubts about how good a job Zeta Kitchens would deliver.

Sure enough, after a few days the written quotes arrive. Alpha Kitchens have come up with a quote of £64,000; Beta Kitchens quoted £54,000 and Zeta Kitchens came in at £47,000.

So here is the crucial question. You are going to phone one of these suppliers. *Who do you call?*

Let's look back at our research findings on Relationship Advice (and this type of kitchen project fits in well because it is not life-threatening but it is important: you only want it done once). My research said that the purchasing criteria would be:

1. track record;

2. chemistry;

3. price.

It really is in that order, with price last. Track record is a kind of precondition. If the client isn't convinced that you have the right level of experience of the work, then you don't cross the first hurdle, so don't need to be considered any further. In many cases the clients are sophisticated enough only to choose firms to pitch for the work which have the necessary track record, so it is actually removed from the equation – all of the firms satisfy the criterion. But next was chemistry, which I have found is really shorthand for 'liking'.

To many professional people it seems counterintuitive that clients looking for Relationship Advice are choosing their advisers on something as subjective and unscientific as 'liking', rather than on the technical expertise of which they are so proud – but this was very clearly what my research project showed. As humans we are hard-wired to 'like people who are like us'. We seek similarities, even to the level where I have seen clients who have a casual dress code prefer to work with lawyers or accountants who (sensitive to the issue) arrived at a tender presentation casually dressed. I think the key issue here is that there is a technical ability hurdle. Once a number of potential advisers have jumped that hurdle, then other factors come into play. That is the point about Relationship Advice. It is not so specialist that there are only very few possible advisers. There will be many who *could* provide the advice and my research showed that chemistry came in as the key decision factor, once technical ability had been satisfied.

In our designer kitchen example, the natural response to the three quotes is to telephone Arthur at Alpha Kitchens to see if you can buy one of their kitchens (£64,000) at the price of Zeta Kitchens (£47,000). This is *exactly* how clients behave every day of the week in every country of the world with their service firm suppliers! They garner competitive quotes then *they telephone the firm that they actually want* in order to try to negotiate price.

There are some important implications from this:

■ If you are following a differentiated strategy (as are most professionals in this Relationship Advice space) then you are claiming that you are better than your competitors. If this is the case, then you should not have partners in a pitch situation sat around trying to calculate the lowest price that they can submit. For your price to be congruent with your strategy, it should be *the highest of the prices* sent to the client. It should be in the same range, but it undoubtedly should be the highest because the client is going to call you if you are the favoured firm and seek to negotiate price. Look at the (confident) behaviour of Arthur from Alpha Kitchens in terms of the price put forward.

■ There is a good way of working out if you really did lose the pitch on price. Did you get the call? In the kitchen example, it is Arthur at Alpha Kitchens who is going to be called and it is just about conceivable that if Arthur refuses to move by even one penny, you might decide to use Beta Kitchens. So when a partner tells me that they 'lost on price' I respond by asking if they got the call (and messed it up)? In almost every case I have ever dealt with the partner says no. In which case I tell them: you didn't lose it on price, you lost it because they didn't like you! We are going to examine this in greater detail later on in this chapter. Of course, it is conceivable that the loss was on track record, but in my experience this is quite rare because clients tend to be fairly expert themselves and so only invite competent firms to bid.

■ Assuming that you did everything right, then you will receive the call to negotiate price. How do you respond? In my experience most professional people drop their price to that of Zeta Kitchens or close to it! They didn't need to. Let's look at how Arthur the kitchen designer handles the call. First, once he receives the call he knows that he has 'won', that he is the supplier you want. He also knows that he doesn't need to drop to the price of Zeta Kitchens for you to stick with him. Typically

Arthur would say that he wouldn't have stayed in business if he had sold his kitchens at unrealistic prices, and that all the referees that he gave you paid his price and thought that the kitchen he installed was worth it. However, for face saving Arthur knows that he should move. So, he will typically have some option built into his specification that can be downgraded or removed so that he can lower the total cost. He might say that he could change the inbuilt oven to a very similar one that happens to be on offer at the moment which would save you £500 without materially altering what you receive; and also change the internal finish, saving £750, and that if he is able to schedule the work for next month (when he has a gap) he could give another £1000 off the total so that you will get him down to £61,750 – and that's a deal. Remember that the next time a client telephones you to negotiate the price of a quote. Price and scope (the work that you are actually going to do) have to be linked. Notice also that Arthur derived confidence because there was real substance behind the quote that he gave. It was carefully constructed and detailed and created after discussion with the client. We will return to this issue when we address the issue of alternative fees in Chapter 6, when I will describe an alternative to hourly/daily based pricing that better serves both service firm *and* client.

Example   ## A useful example from the motor industry

Some years ago I needed to buy a new car and settled upon a Mini made by BMW. I had done my research, read the reviews and spoken to happy owners. I duly turned up at the dealers to agree the exact specification for a new car. As a cash buyer I expected to be able to get some money off and as I had not specified the most basic model, I felt that I had some leverage.

When I asked what was the best price they could give me on the specified model, I was told that there was a waiting list for the car, they could sell more than they could get from the factory, it would take six weeks for delivery and so they couldn't offer any money off! However, they did have a scheme under which, if I prepaid just £120, I would have the first two years of servicing included, which was not just a substantial discount but gave certainty that everything would be covered during those two years.

So at the end of my skilful negotiation, I agreed to pay the car dealer £120 more than when I had started my skilful negotiation, so truly demonstrating my skill!

In fact, I was rather reassured by the refusal to move on the core price. I was told that no one was getting a discount, and their confidence actually reassured me that this was a fair price for the car because this was what everyone else was paying. I wasn't going to find out, while drinking with friends in the pub, that everyone else had been given 15% off and I was the only idiot who had paid full price – but the dealer did have a face saver for me of discounted servicing.

Some great lessons for us – first, don't have oversupply. Of course BMW could have made more cars but with these cars piling up everywhere it would have become increasingly hard not to discount them just to move stock. Oversupply is price corrosive. If you have too many people chasing too little work then the solution is to reduce supply. That may mean losing people but it can also mean moving them to other work or seconding them to clients at a discount. Get them out of the supply chain.

Secondly, have confidence in your prices and don't feel the need to drop them as soon as you are challenged. Clients don't appreciate your immediately agreeing to discounts – rather, they feel that your first quote was something of a try-on and they wish that they had asked for a bigger discount in the first place.

Third, it can be useful to have some variable items which you can remove or reduce in return for a negotiated small reduction in price (or even better if you have a discounted add-on, as did the Mini dealer).

■ Only if your market positioning is to be low priced (the Porter strategy of cost leadership that we explored in Chapter 2) should you be aiming, in a pitch situation, to be the lowest priced offer that the client receives. Your message to the market is essentially this: 'We can provide pretty much the same service as our more expensive competitors, but we are lower cost so we save you money.' No matter what are the macroeconomic conditions, there will always be some clients who are attracted by the idea of saving money. This is essentially a segment you *should* lose if you are running a differentiated strategy. You could only win this segment by matching prices with lower priced competitors (who in any case would most likely react by dropping further). The best comparison is between traditional flag-carrying airlines and their budget airline competitors. The flag carrier cannot win by price matching, because its overheads will not allow that without incurring continuing losses. This is an area (cost leadership) where cost-plus pricing, with its indication of breakeven prices, can help you to understand the competitive situation. You should only embark on a cost leadership strategy if you have a cost base advantage over your competitors (think budget airline), or you will lose.

■ No one will win 100% of their pitches. You should arrange for a debrief telephone call after each pitch (win or lose) so that you can learn and refine your techniques. Very often, if you lose a pitch, the client will say that you lost it on price. There are a number of reasons why clients will say this even if it is not true. It is less embarrassing for everyone than the client having to say that the team who presented were ill prepared, bad presenters or disagreed in front of the client. It stops any argument, whereas if the client says that they weren't convinced about your experience you may argue back. You cannot argue back about losing on price. In addition it unsettles you so that, if anything, you are going to lower your prices next time (which is hardly bad news for the client). In practice, debriefs should be carried out by an independent person (not involved in that pitch) but even then, clients can use 'losing on price' as a quick way of disposing of the call.

What is crucial for your pricing policy to be aligned with your market strategy is that you understand you should not be trying to work out 'what is the lowest price that I can offer on this pitch?', *unless* your market strategy is to be the lowest cost provider in your band of firms.

THE LINK BETWEEN CHEMISTRY, LIKEABILITY AND PRICE

When I first carried out my research on pricing and discovered that there were three different categories of services with different rules on pricing, I then needed to name them. 'Rocket Science' and 'Routine' were obvious, and in the middle I initially called this category 'Mainstream', because that identified it to me as the bulk of work in the middle.

However, the more that I read the detailed feedback from clients and even more so in face-to-face interviews, what came across were expressions like this:

- We could see ourselves working with your team, spending long days with them.
- We felt that there was a good cultural fit.
- We liked your team.
- We felt important to your team, that they took the relationship seriously.
- We liked that your team seemed really keen to work with us and made an effort to get to know us.

What became increasingly clear was that for this mid-range type of work the client was looking for a professional *relationship* with the chosen firm (or more accurately, with the team of people that they met from the firm). This was the realm of the long-term 'Trusted Adviser' where the client expected to spend real time with the firm over many years, was looking for people who would really understand the client's business and become an integrated, but external, 'part of the team'. Contrast this with Rocket Science (where typically experts were brought in to solve one urgent issue and might not be seen again) or Routine Work (where loyalty could not be maintained if a good competitor offered the same service for 10% less). That is when this area of work came to be renamed Relationship Advice, with an understanding that both parties needed to want and to put real effort into creating a deep relationship if the true benefits for both parties were to be realised. The reward for the external professional is this: clients *will pay more* to outside advisers that they like and with whom they can develop a true professional relationship. Be wary of any clients who are buying Relationship Advice but who do not want any kind of relationship (as they are extremely likely to be very difficult over price). This has been described as: 'Your lowest priced client is your highest maintenance client.'

In my consulting work, the problem that I most often see in Relationship Advice is that either or both parties have been too busy to create a relationship, with the end result that the client complains that they are not receiving the service they wanted and the professional advisers complain of low fees. This problem was thrown into sharp relief for me by the director of a FTSE 100 company who told me that they had a panel of eight firms which provided Relationship Advice to them, but that only one of these firms had made any attempt to actually have a relationship with them. When I enquired what he meant by this he replied: 'Only one firm has ever sent people to our offices to sit down with our people, have coffee with them, and try to understand our business!'

So the important takeaway is this: you must want to have a true relationship with the client and be prepared to invest your time in it if you are to reap the rewards available – loyalty, referrals and higher fees. As we shall see when we come to the issue of dealing with procurement, your main defence to a procurement director is real client loyalty. That means having people in the client firm who insist on retaining you. If you have failed in creating a true relationship then can you be surprised when procurement are unleashed upon you to beat you down to the lowest price?

Example	**Lessons from the real world: the power of 'liking'**

A famous insurance company recruited a new chief financial officer. At his first board meeting the new CFO announced that he wanted to spend two months travelling around the business to get a feel for the finance issues that they faced and what improvements could be made. It was agreed that he would then give a formal presentation.

The day arrived and the CFO stood up to present. He explained that he only had one slide. On that slide there were two columns. On the left the column was headed 'Clients we like' and on the right was 'Clients that we don't like'. The CFO explained that on his voyage around the business one of the questions he had asked front-line staff was to give the names of clients that they liked and those they didn't like, taken from a list of the major clients of the company. He had narrowed this down to the largest 20 clients of the company and had then created his two lists. There were 13 liked clients and 7 that were not liked.

The CFO announced his conclusion. 'In the future', he said, 'we should only do business with clients that we like'. As he did so, he clicked on the slide to reveal that the company was losing money on all the clients they didn't like.

Try this in your business. It is quite possible that there is a virtuous circle of your liking a client, the client liking and valuing you and a successful business relationship developing. My contention is that this is important in terms of the prices that you can achieve. Given that chemistry is a very personal attribute, if you have a problem client, the first point of action could be to change the relationship partner (even better by letting the client choose from a selection) because that change can herald a new dawn in the relationship as a whole.

While explaining this theory to a class of postgraduate law students at the University of Miami I thought that one of my students 'nailed it'. She said that she wanted to deal with people who were happy in their work. Whether this was an airline steward, a shop assistant, a doctor or a receptionist, she said that if someone enjoyed their work then she felt that they would do a better job for her. If they were enjoying their job it would shine through in a pleasant and happy attitude and make the person likeable. (Contrast your reaction to someone who is unhappy in their job and shows it.) In the zone of Relationship Advice this makes sense. Clients look for a relationship and are naturally attracted to, and prefer working with, those who are happy to advise them. My own experience has been that the same rule does not apply in the other areas – for Rocket Science I am pretty much expecting a serious expert, and if they are going to solve the problem then I won't worry about their manner. For a supplier of Routine Work, no matter how much I like them, if another supplier can give me the same service and results for less money then I really have to switch.

However, for Relationship Advice, liking really matters. How much time do you spend on that with your clients? Would you like to have a plan that, over five years, moved your business towards clients you liked and away from those you did not like? What do you think that would mean for your prices?

The aim for Relationship Advice

There are two rules at work here. First you need coherent pricing. For the typical professional who seeks to compete by offering a differentiated service, your aim is to present stage 1 prices that are moderately higher than your competitors. So, for example, at the first round of a pitch your ideal positioning is as follows:

Your price	£515 per hour
Competitor 1	£495 per hour
Competitor 2	£500 per hour
Competitor 3	£505 per hour
Competitor 4	£420 an hour

This establishes that your price is in line with the market, but that it enjoys a premium and most clients will assume that more expensive is better. Competitor 4 will most likely be discarded as being suspiciously cheap. Similarly, if you had started at £600 an hour you might be discarded if the client views the other competitors as very similar to you.

Example	**The price placebo effect**

Do you gain more pleasure from a glass of wine when you know that it comes from a £90 bottle of wine rather than a £45 bottle, or a £5 bottle? The evidence says yes. In an experiment run by researchers at California Institute of Technology and Stanford University, volunteers were told the price of the bottle of wine before being asked to taste it and rate it while inside an fMRI machine which detected brain activity. Consistently the subjects said the more expensive wine tasted better (even though in each case the participants had been given the same wine but were told it was two different wines). Using fMRI allowed the researchers, by subtracting the common areas of activity, to see what the difference was when the 'more expensive' wine was tasted. They saw more activity in an area of the brain associated with pleasure – so the subjects actually experienced more pleasure simply because of the association with higher price.

The lesson for us is explained by Baba Shiv, co-author of the study, who says: 'We have these general beliefs about the world – for example, that cheaper products are of lower quality – and they translate into specific expectations about specific products.'

That is why it is so important that your price is congruent with your positioning. Clients will assume that a higher price indicates better quality. Why claim that you are 'better' than your competitors but then price yourself lower than them?[1]

As mentioned previously, part of being able to position your pricing in this way is to use debriefs after each win or loss so that you start to gather data on competitors' prices. Simply asking an innocuous question such as 'How did our pricing compare with the others?' can enable you to build up a picture of the competitive landscape and indicate where your premium might appear. Another way of gathering this information is by talking to recent recruits from competitors. I am always surprised that firms do not do this in a structured way. Most firms recruit from competitors on a regular basis and, while not seeking to obtain any confidential information, it is easy to achieve an understanding of whether your typical prices are higher or lower than those of your competitors.

---

[1] Plassman, H. et al. (2008) 'Marketing actions can modulate neural representations of experienced pleasantness.' Proceedings of the National Academy of Sciences of the United States of America, January 22, vol. 105, no. 3, 1050–1054, 10.1073/pnas.0706929105

Alternatively, if your competitive positioning is to be cost leadership then you need to use similar techniques to make sure that you are priced at the bottom (or close to the bottom) of the pack – but without looking so cheap that you are dismissed. Having staked your place as the lowest (or lowest realistic) price, your task to win the (price-sensitive) client will be to establish that you can deliver materially 'the same' service as your more expensive competitors.

Now we come to the second rule that is important for a win in Relationship Advice: chemistry. In a pitch situation it is really important that you obtain face time with as many people as possible in order to build this *before* any formal presentation. Spending time on this before you reach any presentation stage will make a dramatic difference to both your chances of being chosen, and the resilience of your prices. So much so that whether or not you actually proceed with a pitch can depend upon whether you are able to achieve face time pre-pitch. (I will address this in more detail in the tactics section at the end of this chapter.) .

PITCHING FOR ROUTINE WORK

For Routine Work we depart the land of chemistry and enter the world of data. Here, price is typically the leading factor, and decisions on the choice of professional adviser are often delegated to a low level or taken over almost entirely by procurement professionals. The most difficult problem faced by providers of Routine Work is that the discussion can become rather one-dimensional. It can focus upon a fixed fee per matter and buyers use competition to drive down prices year-on-year (or usually every two years, so as not to cause too much effort or disruption for the client).

Once the client is satisfied that a particular contender has the technical skills and track record (usually by requiring evidence of similar clients for the same work type), then the client can be remarkably promiscuous – although more typically they will use the threat of competitors taking a share, or all, of the work in order to remain with the incumbent suppliers but at ever lower prices.

The ideal endgame for the client is actually as follows:

- Maintain a broadly stable panel of advisers.
- Make sure that they all receive enough work (and the possibility of even more work) to keep prices low.

- Every so often, lose the worst performing adviser and introduce a new and hungry competitor to the panel.
- Drive better performance and lower prices on a continuing basis.

The end result is that the client acquires keen advisers who are making *just enough* profit to keep going. In fact, from the supply side, this can be something of a dangerous game. A typical route for the professional adviser who is delivering a great service at low prices is to be 'rewarded' with more and more volume (often with little extra profit), so that they end up in a position where they cannot 'afford to lose the client'. The loss of such a major client would cause redundancies and unused accommodation and equipment, such that suppliers even put up with losses rather than face the disruption that losing the client would cause.

The solution is to stop being one-dimensional. Once you accept the proposition that every professional is delivering exactly the same service with no differentiation, then it is inevitable that the focus moves to price and price alone. Imagine that you were put in charge of organising the tea and coffee supplies for your office, and that one of your duties (in addition to buying a very specific brand of tea and coffee) was to source 50 pints a day of 2% semi-skimmed milk. You might like shopping in a particular supermarket, but could you really justify paying a premium to them for *their* 2% semi-skimmed milk rather than that from another supermarket. Isn't 2% milk just 2% milk? Despite it being in a differently branded container, it might actually have come from the same farm.

This is the prevalent attitude taken by those buying or procuring Routine Work from firms. Aren't all the firms invited to pitch pre-qualified as being able and willing to deliver the required service? If not, why are they invited?

In fact this is fallacious. When it comes to services provided by different service firms, they are *never the same*. There are just too many human and institutional variables for two firms to actually provide the same service. The key issue for you is to use data to differentiate your service and introduce more dimensions into the equation. When I was leading a team providing Routine Work to a group of financial institutions, I regularly came up against a particular lower-priced competitor. Apart from my describing them as 'one of the finest firms *in their price range*' in order to shake the clients' claims that all firms were the same, I had developed a considerable bank of data on the performance that my firm delivered. My contention was that while that competitor's price was fine for the service that they were delivering, I was providing something different and that difference was reflected in a higher price.

There are a number of ways that a higher price can be justified: speed, accuracy, less administrative work for the client, measurably better results and so on. An easy way to start the process to differentiation is to spend time with clients running 'process improvement workshops', where teams from both sides spend time looking at ways of reducing the work involved and creating better end results. This positions you for future price drops (if they are needed because finding shortcuts saves time and money) and also enables you to understand what performance measures are important to a client, so that you can start measuring and improving your performance on those in order to secure your position. After a few years of running process improvement workshops your own service is so tailored to and inextricably linked with the client's systems that it becomes almost impossible for a new competitor to match the service which you are providing.

Another important defence for the supplier of Routine Work is to look at ways of tying the client in to you so that their biannual threat to dump you and move to another supplier becomes less credible. In other words, to raise switching costs for the client. Examples are to create technology links (bridging between your systems and the client's) and embedding staff in the client's premises to handle the initial part of the work. Overall, though, these work best when linked into the process improvement workshops so that, objectively measured, you are actually providing a superior service that makes it hard for a competitor to offer the same.

If you are in the position of being the 'new kid on the block', invited to pitch for a share of a routine client's work, then you are often put into a no-win position. You are facing established incumbent firms that will fight (on price) to retain the work and you are untested in terms of service. That means you can only really fight your way onto the panel by offering much lower prices than the incumbents (it is not worth the disruption to the client of changing supplier if there is only a small saving on offer). The procurement team know this and that's why they invited you to pitch for the work. They might even helpfully tell you the *inside information that they probably shouldn't be sharing with you, but they will because they like you, that you need to come in under £1000 per case to have any chance of getting on the panel.*

It's actually very likely that you are simply being used as a stalking horse to come in at a ridiculously low price in order to unsettle the incumbents and to force them to reduce their prices further, so that even bidding at a very low price can be a completely wasted effort. Procurement really cannot lose once they have the advisers in this position. They don't care if you win any work; you will perform a role in driving down prices and if you do bid low enough, there is no harm in (sometimes) trying you out. I have seen this happen so often that I caution against pitching for Routine Work with a new client at all. It is often a waste of time and money, because the team involved in the pitch become invested in winning (due to all of the time and effort that they have put in), and drop prices lower and lower in order to gain some return on their effort. Typically they will comfort themselves with the fallacy that if only they can gain a foothold with the client (at any price) this will in due course lead to more, and more profitable, work. However, this is very rarely the case, as once you have established yourself in the client's mind as a low-price provider it is incredibly hard to shift their perception of you and build up your prices to more respectable levels. You can work around this by making clear that you will bear a discount of a specified amount for a short period of time, but even then it is a risky strategy.

A better approach is this: work out (realistically) what it costs you to take part in this type of pitch for Routine Work (taking into account the time of all of the people involved). Once you have that figure (say £50,000), you should proactively approach the type of new client you wish to gain *before any pitch* and offer to expend that sum in carrying out free work for them to the same value, on condition that if you are better than their existing firms they will start to send you work; and if you are not then, hey, at least they just saved that sum from their spend on advisers that year. The client should be in a no-lose situation. If they say yes, then it gives you a chance to work with the client and build a new service from the ground up that hits all their key values and so makes you a valuable part of their team – not just another supplier to be played off against all the others at the biannual contest.

Alternatively, you would need to develop a cost base advantage over your competitors using technology, process skills and team composition that is way ahead of your competitors, such that you can continuously compete with them on price and win.

RETENDERS

There is a very specific rule on a retender, by which I mean that you are an existing provider for a specific type of work and the client has decided to go through a formal process under which it may retain all existing firms, reduce their number or add others. You are faced with the possible loss of the client but you also have the opportunity to win a greater share of the work.

I am going to focus upon Relationship Advice first.

Here is the crucial point about a retender. *It is won or lost in the 12 months preceding it!* In practice I found that once the retender documents are circulated, partners swing into action, meetings are called, time is set aside and ideas are brainstormed – but that is one year too late. It is actually during the 12 months preceding the release of the tender document that the client has decided whether they want to keep a particular firm as their adviser, or as one of their panel of advisers. To a very great extent, the die is cast well before you prepare your document in response or attend the formal presentation. If you have not performed well in the last 12 months then all of the wonderful promises that you make in your glossy document will be taken with a large pinch of salt, and you may be given a very hard time at the presentation stage. I have seen a situation like this being recovered, but only once. This was where the entire proposal document focussed around the problems that had been encountered with the firm in the recent past and how the responsible partner was going to make certain that the service was completely different in the future. With an otherwise good track record the firm stayed on the panel, but it was a close-run thing. To win retenders you really need to diarise them one year in advance to make sure that you perform extremely well in the period running up to the retender.

Generally, the aim for this 12-month period should be to make sure that you really do have a relationship and that you can demonstrate the benefits of that. There should have been a series of 'off the clock' sessions where you and your team meet with the client's team to look at ways of improving your service. There should be some satisfaction surveys from the client's team showing how much they value you (or that there were issues in some areas, but this is how you have fixed them). You need to go into the retender confident that you have been doing a great job and while there will always be lower-cost competitors, overall you bring greater value than them. When you have prepared in this way, you will present in a confident manner and may well be able to increase prices (based upon inflation, improvements in the service you are delivering or other factors) because you have evidence of your strong performance.

Unfortunately it is much more typical for the retender date to arrive with everyone rushing to create a great response document. I have then witnessed nervousness about even mentioning price rises. That sets a dangerous precedent. If you skip a price rise at one retender, why wouldn't you do so at the next one? Over time the inevitable impact of inflation on your cost base (which may well be above standard retail inflation measures) can quickly erode any profit on the client. Being unprepared not only puts the relationship with the client at risk, it actually impacts on the prices that you can charge.

For Routine Work, the 12-month period before the retender is crucial in demonstrating the performance that you are delivering for the fees that you are charging. *Data* is the order of the day and across the period there should have been regular meetings and workshops aimed at improving performance in ways that the client really values (as well as looking for ways of tying the client in and raising their switching costs). In this way you can actually demonstrate with facts and figures the value (performance) that you are delivering, using soft measures such as satisfaction surveys as well as hard data on outcomes, and can justify maintaining or increasing prices.

If you were to take satisfaction surveys of a client in the 12 months before a retender and average out the scores as a percentage (with 100% being fully satisfied) the graph for retenders looks something like Figure 3.1.

| Figure 3.1 | **The impact of loyalty on prices** |

In Zone A, you have lost the client. They are really going through the motions in asking you to retender. All of your wonderful efforts on a document and presentation are wasted and could have been much better spent if they had kicked off 12 months in advance.

Zone B is the typical resting place of most service firms. The client rates your performance as fine (because all the firms are fine) but it's not special. In Zone B the client can make firms compete on price because the service they provide is pretty typical and can be provided by others (remember the 2% semi-skimmed milk example?), so the client should head for the cheapest offer. My experience is that about two-thirds of the time, firms are in Zone B (so will end up competing on price and therefore lose margin).

In Zone C the client is receiving a measurably better service. They want to keep you because of your strong relationship and knowledge of their business which is allowing you to deliver a superior service (Relationship Advice), or your commitment to continuous improvement and measurably better service makes you the best supplier that they have (Routine Work).

Finally, I have seen the creation of panels (conducted on a competitive basis) for Rocket Science where a client wants to put in place a group of top-end advisers to cope with either a steady stream of Rocket Science advice, or to have a panel of experts in place in case a crucial situation should arise in the future. In my view, when an unexpected event occurs, the best adviser is the one with the closest match of track record to the actual issue in hand, so I am not convinced that a panel is the right approach to take. However, in such cases I do not advocate that Rocket Scientists become involved in competitive pricing because it really cuts across their status as a truly expert adviser.

The best practice that I have seen in this area is for the Rocket Scientist to hold firm on their prices but to offer 'added value' to recognise the value of the client to them. For example, an offer to run a valuable workshop without charge or for junior colleagues to carry out follow-on work at discounted rates after the Rocket Scientist has been involved are appropriate, but bazaar-type haggling over hourly or daily rates is not.

POST-PITCH NEGOTIATION ON PRICE

It has become standard practice in Relationship Advice and Routine Work for the advisers to be asked to 'sharpen their pencils' or 'give your best and final offer' after the pitch documents have been submitted, and quite often for there to be second and third attempts at this post-presentation: for example to be told that 'you have not made it to the final cut because of your rates, but if you were to lower them by 10% that would get you through', or 'our target rate was £350 for a partner and you did not achieve that, so we are giving you a final chance to revise your rates down to that – aren't we kind?'.

You really need to say no. It is as simple as that. I have been involved in many hundreds of conference calls following such a request to revisit prices, where the topic for discussion is not whether to reduce prices or not but is around 'do we drop just by 2.5% or do we need to drop by 5% or 10% to show that we are serious?'

First, you honestly cannot win every pitch that you take part in, even if you are the lowest priced advisers in your country, because price is not the key decider (and even for Routine Work it is not the only criterion). You need to decide on your market position, pick prices in line with that and make sure that you provide differentiated value to your segments of the market. No one has 100% of the market!

Secondly, it is just good negotiating practice never to simply give a reduction in price but to seek to swap something in return, or to tie changes in price to changes in what is going to be delivered. So while politely declining to drop prices it is perfectly acceptable to say: 'We haven't agreed actual volumes of work yet, so I cannot look at price until you can guarantee a specific volume of work.'

Thirdly, and perhaps most importantly, it makes you look dishonest! If you drop your prices when you are challenged then it looks like you were 'just trying it on' at the original price. The client feels cheated rather than pleased that you dropped the price and may then try to ask for more discount. How do you respond to that?

For Relationship Work, it is important to maintain the attitude that the role of a tender or a retender is for the client to find the right firm (remember the example of Arthur from Alpha Kitchens), and that there is no point arguing about price until the client has chosen their adviser. An expression that I have used when I felt a client was going about things in the wrong order (arguing about price too early) is:

The task is to choose the right adviser for you. I hope that we are chosen. But if we are not the right adviser for you, then we are not the right adviser even at half the price. If we are the right adviser, then we will surely be able to reach an appropriate accommodation over price and the service that we deliver for that.

I recommend a polite refusal when asked to submit lower prices, to sharpen your pencil or to submit your best and final offer. For example, say: 'Let's wait and see if we are the chosen firm. Then we can look at price against the actual service we are going to deliver, the volume of it and all the other terms.'

THE TACTICS OF PITCHING

Over the years I have discovered some tactical approaches that have helped in pitch situations and either saved us the trouble of competing for a piece of work or place on a panel that we were doomed to lose, or improved our chances on the day. These are no substitute for a clear price strategy, but they can be useful.

Stop/go

You need to have a formal process in place to help you to decide whether or not to proceed with a request to pitch, as you should not be in a position where you simply go ahead with every request that you receive. So you need some rules. These rules will then largely be ignored by partners, but this enables you to keep records to show that where the balance of evidence was that you should stop, and this was ignored by partners, you have a 100% lose rate (or close to it). If you don't find that outcome then it shows a need to revisit your stop/go procedures and change the criteria. In other words, it might be impossible to stop partners chasing every pitch, but over a year or so you should be able to collect data that shows how much money is wasted if you respond to *every* pitch, and use that data to create a proper set of rules for the future.

What are the criteria that will help you decide on a stop/go? These are very specific to industry/work type, so you will need to create your own list based upon an analysis of your own experiences of when you have won and lost and from debrief calls (which can be massively useful in this area). However, examples of factors that can be used for a yes or no score (or a numeric score from 1 to 10) would be as follows:

1. Are they an existing client for this work or another work type?

2. Do we have a pre-existing personal relationship with the client or with someone who has just moved to this client?

3. Is this opportunity in a sector where we are strong?

4. Will this client reflect well upon us, will they enhance our brand/reputation?

5. Does this potential client look *very similar* to our existing clients?

6. Rocket Science – honestly, if we were face-to-face, could we rightly claim a great track record for exactly their issue?

7. Will we be able to get face time with the decision makers before we complete the pitch document?

Note: There is one rule that I instituted that undoubtedly saved millions of pounds of wasted efforts on pointless pitches, and this was in the areas of Relationship Advice and Routine Work. We used this when we suspected (because we had no pre-existing relationship with the client or any obvious connection that wanted us to act for them) that we had only been invited to pitch in order to 'make up the numbers' or to unsettle the incumbents but with no real intention of using us. The rule was to request face time with some of the decision makers. We explained that (as we were not an incumbent) we needed to talk to key people in order to understand exactly what they wanted so that we could tailor our offer around that. If the client agreed then we would use that meeting or meetings to gauge their 'motivation to change'. For example, we might say: 'What do the best of your current advisers do that you really like and that we need to make sure we provide as well?' and 'What bad things have advisers done in the past that have caused problems and which we must avoid?' If the client had many more answers for question 1 than question 2 then it sounded like they were happy with their existing firms, but if they had more problems to discuss than benefits then that made it a more promising opportunity.

However, the clever thing was this. Very often we were refused any face time. We then said (but politely), well if you cannot get us even one hour of face time, then we will not spend (say) £50,000 of our time and effort in preparing a pitch for you.

I am certain that this approach saved us a huge amount of time and allowed us to do a better job on the 'winnable' pitches.

The start of chemistry

For Relationship Advice, our liking the client and the client liking us was an important element in winning. Having face time with as many people as possible *before* you start to create your pitch document, let alone attend a formal presentation, is crucial. Well done: this is the start of the process of creating great chemistry by showing real interest in the client's business and concerns and actually listening to their answers. This is much more easily done if pre-meetings with the client are attended by two people, so that one is making notes when the other is asking questions. I also found that broad questions about the client's business and their concerns landed much more effectively than hugely detailed questions about the work in question. For example, questions such as 'It's one year on, your pitch process has been a great success, tell me what has changed, what is different?' really went to the heart of the issues.

In fact, in an ideal situation these pre-meetings served two purposes. First, we started to get to know each other and I could start to show commonalities ('we like people who are like us') and start to create a great relationship (particularly if we had good ideas to share from similar clients or situations – remember how Arthur from Alpha Kitchens behaved?). Secondly, we would use this face time to ask questions that were in the order of the pitch document that we had to complete, so that by the time we returned to the office we effectively had the correct answers to the questions in the pitch document. We had a real understanding about what was important to the client in each of the headings and we could then reflect that back in our response. That would include asking about their attitude to price so that we could discern whether they placed price above everything else. If they did, it gave us the opportunity to discuss other dimensions of service with them so that we could start the process of positioning the service and price that we would be proposing.

As far as possible, we wanted to walk into a formal presentation and see friendly faces from those pre-meetings. We felt like we were already halfway to a win.

The unclear brief

There can be times when, despite your best efforts, you end up trying to put together a proposal for Relationship Advice when the actual scope of work and therefore your price is very uncertain. The temptation then is to quote a range of prices to the client to indicate that the likely cost will fall somewhere in that band. For example, you might say that there are factors which will affect the actual work and price (you might even spell those out), and that as a consequence the likely cost will be between £40,000 and £70,000. Don't do that. Experience has proved conclusively that when you give a range, the client 'hears' the lowest figure (so is expecting to spend £40,000) whereas you were actually trying to 'take the edge off' what is very likely to cost £70,000 or more. For the same reasons do not quote £40,000 and then add a list of unrealistic assumptions which need to be met if the work is to cost only £40,000, because again the client ends up with a mental budget figure of £40,000 and not a penny more.

The best approach is to offer several separate, and separately costed, options; for example:

Option 1 [Full description of work involved] £39,800

Option 2 [Full description of work involved] £71,500

Option 3 [Full description of work involved] £96,450

(Note that these should be accurate figures, as there is evidence that clients trust these much more than rounded-up approximations like £40,000 or £70,000.)

This lets the client make an informed choice, or to have further discussions with you to refine and re-price the closest option (again think of a fitted kitchen). In an uncertain situation, offering several distinct choices prevents you from having to guess what solution would work best and being at risk of delivering an unrealistically low quote (which will end in tears when the final bill is delivered), or one which is too high and over-specified against the client's needs and so leads to you losing the pitch.

The silver bullet

Is there a secret to winning pitches, a surprise that puts you ahead of the competition? The answer is 'sometimes'. I have seen this occur when the client asks for solution A, but in your response you explain that you can fully understand why they have asked for solution A, but you have analysed their situation and actually applying your expertise you can confidently say that they need solution B, and here is your detailed proposal for B including an explanation of its advantages over solution A.

A silver bullet depends upon particular circumstances but, if they arise, a brave response can win the day and leave the competition standing, their having submitted a variety of solution A answers.

Rocket Science and being impressive

Just as pre-meetings (scoping) are really valuable in Relationship Advice because they can start to build a relationship, so in Rocket Science a pre-meeting can also make a big difference to success at a later formal presentation. There are two distinct reasons for this. First, it is an opportunity for the Rocket Scientist to start to impress the client with their expertise and to start dropping details of matters that they have led upon and been successful. This has more impact face-to-face than in a dry document. Secondly, in order to win, the Rocket Scientist needs to show the best match between track record and the client's problem, and a pre-meeting is a crucial opportunity to gain a detailed understanding of the exact nature of the problem that is to be resolved.

I emphasise this point because I have seen so many cases where the right Rocket Scientist actually referred to the wrong experience in the presentation documents, and so lost out to a competitor who had taken the trouble to focus the details of their track record much more closely to the actual problem at hand.

4

Negotiating price

This is often a difficult issue for service providers. If a client, or prospective client, argues over your price it can feel like an attack on your credibility and indeed your personal worth: 'Are you saying that I am not worth £750 an hour?!' I always felt that it was the one time when partner and client were clearly on opposite sides of the table, arguing against each other, whereas the heart of a good client relationship is close collaboration towards a shared goal. It can be challenging and unpleasant for the client as well. To say: 'Your quote is much more than I was expecting' could be a negotiating tactic, but it could also be a genuine expression of surprise. Clients will very often have created a budget (and had it approved even at board level) so that if that budget is actually much too low to achieve what they have promised, it reflects badly upon their judgement as well. It can feel embarrassing for a client to ask about price at an early stage – as if they are not sure that they can afford you. Mutual reticence over talking about price creates the worst-case scenario, that price is not clarified and discussed *up front*, which creates real risks of problems that only become clear when it is too late to adjust the scope of work to meet the client's budget.

There is typically an unwelcome element of emotion tangled up in what should be a sensible and commercial conversation, not driven by hurt feeling and defensive behaviour. There are also some set-piece 'discussions' that should take place over money between the professional adviser and the client (I prefer this term 'discussion' to 'negotiation' because the latter phrase is so coloured in people's minds by the idea that the best negotiator 'wins'). I am going to examine issues around scope (what the price that is at issue includes and excludes); creating alternative offers; the idea of swapping rather than just conceding (a pretty standard negotiation practice, but often underused because partners have not created possible swaps); negotiation in the middle of a matter; having to approach a client to discuss an increase in prices; and, finally, how to deal with procurement professionals.

An initial piece of understanding is important for partners who hate losing at anything. You are supposed to lose some work just because you are too expensive. If you aren't having that (unpleasant) experience, then your prices must be too low. There is much that you can do to minimise losses on price, but you should not be eliminating them. The reason is simply one of market segmentation, which is probably best illustrated by Figure 4.1.

In this graph I have mapped the price of a one-night stay at a selection of hotels from the lowest price 'budget hotel' up to a

| Figure 4.1 | Price per night and market segments for hotel rooms |

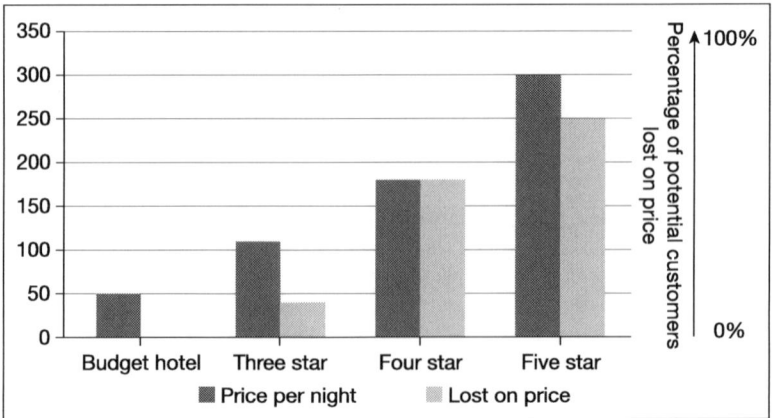

five-star hotel. The budget hotel should not lose many customers on price alone ('it's too expensive to stay here'), but for the five-star hotel the great majority of potential customers will say that there is no way that they are prepared to pay £400 and upwards per night, so those customers are truly lost on price alone. The five-star hotel doesn't believe that it has to cut its prices so as to capture a share of the four-star, three-star or budget market. It accepts that its market position means it appeals only to a particular segment of the available market of people looking for a hotel room. With very limited exceptions, the five-star hotel doesn't drop its price when challenged and neither do the four-star or three-star – nor should other service providers.

In other words, the higher your price, the more limited your potential market and therefore the greater the number of people that you will lose because they are not prepared to pay your (comparatively high) prices. Service firms often develop a hunger to take on as much work from as many clients as they can, because firms usually recognise and reward client wins (turnover) rather than profitability.

In classic economic theory it looks something like Figure 4.2, if you plot how much a client is prepared to spend (either on a per hour/day basis, or for a specific project).

In this graph we see five clients, all of whom have different price expectations or budgets. To win every client (all other things being equal) you can price at 250 which price is acceptable to all of them. For Routine Work that wins all five clients (in Relationship Advice it might raise some concerns to Clients 3, 4 and 5 as to whether you were 'the right firm'). However, pricing at 250 means that you have not maximised the return from Clients 2, 3, 4 and 5 because

Price and market share

Figure 4.2

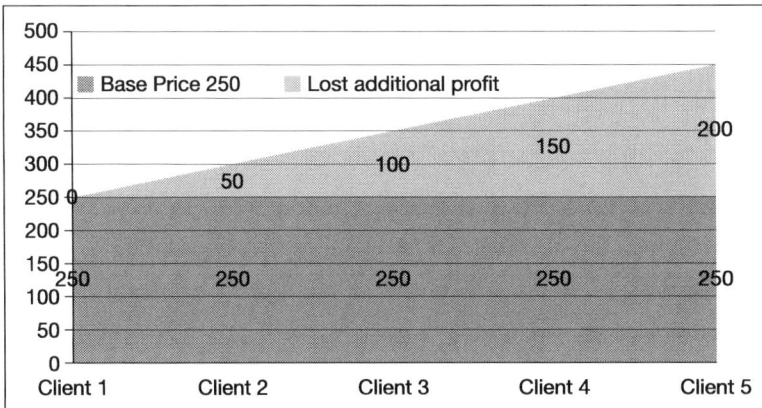

they would have been prepared to spend more. If you price at 400, then you have a price issue with all but Clients 4 and 5.

Now, you can develop different levels of service (perhaps under different brands or sub-brands) to address those different market segments – think of Intercontinental Hotels, Holiday Inn and Holiday Inn Express, which are all part of the same hotel group. Service firms often find it difficult to address different price points in a segmented market because those partners who are able to charge at the top end look down on the lower levels, which they see as diluting their brand message. I predict that in the future sub-brands will become more popular as a solution to this, but they will not be acceptable for all firms. It may come down to size aspirations. If you are and want to remain a top-end type of firm then you need to accept that you can only grow so large, due to the limited size of the available market. Note, however, that Rolls-Royce motors sits as a separate brand within the BMW Group and Bentley is within the Volkswagen Audi Group, which shows how a larger overall entity can address many different market segments.

This preliminary overview, your market positioning, is important because if you do not understand which market segments you are targeting, then you are going to have far too many difficult pricing conversations. One of my former partners summed this up wonderfully after we had endured a fruitless meeting with what we had imagined would be a valuable client, who in fact was used to using much smaller and lower cost firms and who had been genuinely shocked by our proposed prices. My partner summed it up by saying, 'The client was looking for Aldi and has stumbled into Waitrose'. (In fairness, he waited until the potential client had left.) He encapsulated a really important point. Waitrose, as a super-market positioned at the top end of the market, cannot match all the prices of Aldi, which is a successful and focussed discounter. Waitrose could spend all day and every day trying to explain to the wrong sort of customer why its prices are higher. Much better to be clear about where you are positioned and what types of clients you are looking to attract for what type of work. As we will see in Chapter 9 (Learning from industry) Waitrose did in fact very successfully create a 'sub-brand' of Waitrose Essentials in order to capture more of the available market (but not all of it). In effect, Waitrose, referring to Figure 4.2, said that it wanted to capture Clients 4 and 5 (as usual) but also some of the spend from Clients 1, 2 and 3.

| Example | **The error of emotion** |

Early on in my consulting career, I networked into a high-quality boutique firm that was starting to tackle pricing issues with its partners. The partners were failing to maximise pricing, readily agreeing discounts when challenged yet still providing a top-end service (and writing off the excess costs). As a result the firm's profits were not matching the quality it delivered to clients or allowing it to properly remunerate its people. This seemed like a good opportunity for me to provide really valuable support to an excellent firm. I met with them and then provided written details of the types of projects that would make a difference for them. Alarm bells should have rung when I was then asked to provide a very urgent price quote to deliver a series of workshops which were already scheduled to take place in the coming weeks. I provided several options at different price points just before attending a formal meeting.

It rapidly became clear that my prices were substantially above other quotes they had previously received. In error, the meeting ended up focussing on my prices and how I could possibly justify them. This felt like a challenge to my professional abilities and rather offensive, as if I had tried to trick them. My immediate reaction was to be defensive.

In fact, the correct approach would have been as follows:

■ Not to quote without a better understanding of what they wanted to achieve. In reality they had almost completed their thinking and just wanted a talking head to deliver some pre-ordained messages. That was not clear from the scant information provided.

■ Not to worry if my quote was substantially higher, but simply to ask questions about what they wanted to achieve and how much they wanted to spend on that. With that knowledge we could have cooperatively looked at possible solutions (for example, for my input to be limited to crafting the key messages and for the actual delivery to be given by a more junior colleague), rather than arguing over whether my initial quote was fair or not.

It was a valuable lesson in removing the person from the negotiation so that it could become a design discussion rather than an argument. A better response to a client who thinks you are very expensive is to wind back into a discussion around what the client wants to do and an exploration of how that might be achieved. That allows you to explore different options rather than arguing about price. If that is not done, then the discussion will be likely to fall into a defence of what the client views as very high prices.

Let's look now at some set-piece discussions that are frequently going to take place between service firms and their clients, and how they can best be addressed. We will finish with an examination of the role of, and defences to, procurement professionals, the third-party negotiators that are becoming an increasing feature of the service pricing landscape.

There is, as usual, an overlay for the three different types of services that are under discussion. The techniques are going to be largely the same for the three different types of service except that, for Rocket Science, the discussion should be limited to issues around disaggregation. There, the client still wants to have the chosen person (the actual Rocket Scientist) leading the matter and there can be very little discussion around that price. However, it can help to be sensitive to a client's pressures on spend, and therefore appropriate to examine whether more routine parts of the work could be handled by others inside the same firm (for an example, look at the near-shoring and offshoring efforts of many top service firms), or even whether routine elements can be parcelled out to specialist outsourcing operators. The Rocket Scientist must clearly remain in control because they, after all, are going to be responsible for the final outcome in the eyes of the client. So a robust rebuff should be delivered by the Rocket Scientist if they are concerned that the dictates of a client about how the work is going to be carried out could adversely affect the outcome. Otherwise, it reflects well upon the Rocket Scientist that they have facilities available which can enable cost-effective solutions to the *routine parts* of the overall task. Apart from that, there should not be much discussion about price at the beginning – assuming that the Rocket Scientist has taken the proper route of delivering realistic budget figures. I have not seen procurement involved in Rocket Science work, but if they were encountered then they must be ignored. They have nothing to bring to the party and could severely damage the outcome (see, for example, most major government procurement fiascos).

Over the past few years, Relationship Advice has seen a much greater focus upon price and much more dissatisfaction expressed by clients who are themselves facing greater pressure to control costs and to manage external advisers more robustly. Here, the market demands of the clients have met a largely unprepared group of partners who have adopted a rather amateur approach to these pricing discussions. There wasn't so much need for these negotiation skills in the past. Relationship Advice has become the main battleground on price, especially since clients discovered that pushing back on price worked and that partners were almost certain to reduce their prices when challenged. Relationship Advice is the main area where better skills are required and is the primary focus of this chapter.

For Routine Work, pricing has always been a fundamental issue and an area for much negotiation (not discussion). Partners involved in this work will be used to pretty tough negotiations about price and the relevant service specification, and so will probably be used to the various techniques outlined below. At the end of the chapter I have outlined some further thoughts that might be relevant for Routine Work.

PRICE AND SCOPE ARE LINKED

A very typical price negotiation is the one that takes place after a formal quote has been delivered to the client, in which the client seeks to reduce the price to be paid while retaining their preferred choice of adviser (just as happened in the Alpha Kitchens scenario in Chapter 3). From the point of view of the client, they typically have nothing to lose from this conversation and, much more worryingly, they are discovering that they often have a lot to gain. The more often that partners collapse when challenged on pricing, the more ingrained this client behaviour will become.

There are two issues at work here. First, most often, the partner has no real confidence in the price that was quoted as it was really a shot in the dark or a 'guesstimate'. Secondly, the quote can be somewhat vague in terms of the scope of the work that is going to be involved, so any post-quote conversations will focus upon the one obvious figure in play – the actual quoted price or hourly/daily rate – and the only thing that the client wants to hear is a lower figure.

Both of these problems are addressed if much more effort is put into creating a detailed and realistic quote. This is the ultimate 'alternative fee' that is described in detail in Chapter 6 as project-based costing which, in effect, takes services into the modern world of pricing. In pretty much every other area of commerce where somewhat uncertain projects are being commissioned, project-based costing is the answer. This could be the installation of a new kitchen, creating a new IT system for a retailer, building an office block or constructing a nuclear power station. In all these cases there is a need to fully describe what work is planned, how much that will cost and the timescales to be taken. Once real expertise and time has been put into creating this initial quote, the client can see exactly what is included and what is not and the service provider can have confidence that the fees are realistic and achievable. I call this approach 'project-based costing' (PBC) because it creates a price around a specific detailed project. This is the future for Relationship Advice (Routine Work being on fixed fees and Rocket Science using a budget followed by value-based billing).

Almost incredibly, service providers will often say that the reason why they have just quoted hourly or daily rates and given only a very broad indication of the total cost is that their work involves many variables, and it is impossible to specify the exact services in advance in order to create a realistic quote. Do they really think that they face more uncertainties and variables than a company that is building a nuclear power station, a train tunnel, a bridge or a hospital's IT system? The reality is that if you can get away with charging for your time with no limit, then you do.

The change that has hit services is that clients have decided they will no longer put up with unlimited and unspecified charging for Relationship Advice. PBC is a great solution because *it is not a fixed fee.* The actual cost can vary if something unexpected or extra comes up, provided that client has been told about the extra cost before the additional work is carried out and agrees to that extra work and associated cost. In that way the client stays in control. There is no risk of an unpleasant surprise because any changes in cost have to be pre-agreed by the client. In fact, the most important stage in PBC is the 'definition of scope' stage, which is the discussion between partner and client once the initial quote has been delivered. This enables the client to look through the detailed quotation document and ask for changes until a stage is reached where both the actual scope

The issue	Time-based charging
What a client usually receives	Details of hourly rates for each level of person who will work on the matter and sometimes an indication of a possible total fee – e.g. 'estimate is £100,000 to £140,000'. No real explanation is given of what work is included/not included in the fee estimate.
Who wins?	The service provider cannot lose. The more problems found (and fixed), the more people that can be involved and the longer it takes for the service provider to complete the work, the more income they will receive. There is no real incentive for efficiency; in fact the opposite applies because inefficiency is rewarded with higher fees. The client cannot budget and that is a real risk for the individual client, who will be expected to keep to annual spend budgets.
What happens in the 'negotiation' phase?	With just a vague estimate and hourly rates the client is likely to attack both. So there may be a demand for a cap of £100,000 or to have a 15% discount off hourly rates. The tools are blunt and large amounts are bandied back and forth, without any link to the actual scope of work. Supply and demand and negotiation skills decide who gains more in this phase.
What is the real risk for a client?	Massive overruns which only emerge at the end of the matter.
What is the real risk for a service provider?	There is a risk of an unhappy client who faces a nasty surprise on the total cost and firms often write off some of the cost when they realise how far over budget they have gone.

of work and the corresponding price for that scope have been agreed. Think of how you would behave when commissioning three quotes for a new kitchen and then refining the quote with your favoured supplier. It is worth pausing here and looking at the differences between the three most typical ways that Relationship Advice is priced by service providers as shown in the table on the two pages below.

Fixed fee	Project-based fee
A single fixed fee – e.g. £100,000. Because of the risk to the service provider of overruns, this quoted fee may well be followed by a long list of assumptions that have to be met if the actual final cost is to be £100,000. In practice the assumptions would rarely be met, so the fee would increase (i.e. it is not actually a fixed fee).	Detailed description of the work that will be carried out, typically divided into the various stages of the transaction and showing who will carry out what tasks. The cost of these tasks is added together to show a total fee for that scope of work. It will not end in a round number!
The client receives a clear budget figure which they will expect to be able to enforce against the service provider. The service firm is at real risk of overruns. The client can argue over every aspect of the matter knowing that the fee has been fixed. Gradually, based on bad experiences, the firms fight back, and start using assumptions to prevent the fixed fee actually being fixed. Supply and demand largely decide whether the client can insist on a truly fixed fee (oversupply), or if the actual fee is more open to negotiation (higher demand).	The interests of the professional and the client are largely aligned. The service provider seeks to produce a realistic scope of work in detail, the client goes through that and changes the scope/price where needed, until there is an agreed scope and price. Both win.
Clients will seek to reduce the fixed fee (usually by obtaining several competitive quotes, and sometimes by lying about how low they are). Clients may also seek to remove assumptions so that the fee becomes truly fixed.	There is discussion and agreement of the actual scope. So, rather than the client trying to reduce the quoted cost by £20,000, there is much more likely to be a detailed discussion about the scope, which then reduces the work needed and the price. For example there might be a line item of '£3800 for advice on the pensions impact of the transfer of business' and the client says, 'Remove that, I will get the advice in-house'.
Service firm agrees a low fixed price, then has to reduce the quality and time of the actual team involved in order to avoid or reduce losses.	None. Any changes from the original scope and price need to be pre-agreed (and can be declined). So the client can keep to the original scope and price.
Losses on overruns are very common as time is written off. An unreasonable client who takes every point will greatly increase losses.	None – but they need to learn how to project manage the delivery of work against the scope that was agreed with the client, and raise changes in scope in good time.

There is one final benefit of PBC. The prices created will be an exact amount and do not appear just to be guesses that have been rounded up. For example, fee quotes for hourly charges or for fixed fees tend to end in '000'. However, PBC usually results in exact amounts – e.g. £128,464. As mentioned before, there is clear research evidence that people trust these exact figures more (and seek to negotiate them less) than numbers which clearly have been rounded up.

This leads us to the key learning. It is crucial that price and scope are linked, so that if the client wants to reduce the price, then you can do that by reducing the scope. Let's look at that in the context of a typical situation where the client wants to reduce your quoted fee. There are essentially two scenarios to examine. A small reduction or a major difference of opinion on cost.

A SMALL REDUCTION

Let's say that you have submitted a PBC quote for a piece of work and that comes in at £116,430. The client calls and needs to 'talk about your prices'. In my experience there are two approaches that clients will use. One is to go through the quote with you, on an item-by-item basis, and either argue about the amount involved ('I think that £22,600 is too much for the due diligence work') or about the necessity for the item at all ('why am I being charged £1650 for pensions advice – I don't need that'). These types of challenges are exactly what PBC was designed to flush out. They enable you to change the price against changes in the scope. You can remove whole items: 'OK, let's not do any pensions work on this case. I'll let you cover that in-house'; or reduce their size: 'You are going to need due diligence, but if I limit that to high-risk issues (over £100,000) then I could cut the cost from £22,600 to £16,220'.

Alternatively, the client looks to make an overall reduction: 'I have received your quote of £116,430 but my budget is capped at £100,000 so I'm afraid you need to reduce your fee.' It is absolutely crucial that you do not drop the price (for the same scope) because the client will be highly dissatisfied. They will feel that you were just 'trying it on' at £116,430, because as soon as you were challenged you dropped your price. That just makes them doubt your probity and certainly trains them to challenge every quote that they receive from you in future. In fact, once again, a PBC quote is designed to cope with this type of challenge by a client, because

Given the frequency of clients' requests for concessions, it is really important that you create and keep to hand your own list of swaps. Areas for these would include more work, introductions to other divisions of that client, warm introductions to potential new clients, changes in payment terms ('I can only do that if you pay 50% up front'), speaking at a conference with you or giving written endorsements that you can use in your marketing materials.

The overall principle has to remain that if the client needs to reduce the price, you need to reduce the scope, but swaps are useful where the client asks for a small concession.

MAJOR REDUCTIONS

What happens if your carefully constructed PBC of £116,430 is met with the response, 'I can't do that, my budget for this job is £40,000 and you are going to have to keep within that'. This shows that there is a big gap between the client's expectations and yours. First, the very fact that you created a PBC quote means that you will have confidence in your price – it has some real thought behind it, it is logical and realistic for the scope of work described (contrast the top-of-the-head quote of 'about £100,000'). So now you have two options:

1. **Sell the quote.** This means explaining to the client why you came up with the total that you did (assuming that the client didn't realise how much work was involved in the project that they had in mind), and then going through your detailed quote to see where it could be reduced. For example, there may be elements that can be (relatively safely) removed, some that the client could carry out themselves, or that could even be passed out to a low-cost provider. The message to the client is that the cost is going to be a lot more than £40,000 ('no one could carry out this project safely for £40,000'), but that you will work with the client to reduce the cost as far as possible ('a Mini not a Mercedes').

2. **Start again with a new quote.** Tell the client that if their budget is only £40,000 then you could not carry out the type of work project that you had in mind, but you could come up with a scope for a different project and one that fits within the client's budget. You can only do this if you are happy that you can at least cover the basics at a very much lower price.

Neither of the options ends up with you doing a huge amount of work at a very low (loss-making) price.

What about negotiations that take place mid-transaction? An extremely common situation which arises (no matter how well scope and price have been discussed, specified and agreed at the outset) is that variations occur during the course of the work. This could be because new issues arise or the client asks for work that was clearly not included in the original scope. This is often called 'scope creep'. Service providers cause their own problems here, because they do not stop what they are doing and quote an additional cost. They either (begrudgingly) include the extra work because they don't want to have an argument, or they assume (wrongly) that they can sort this out at the end of the work by having a discussion about extra money at that stage. Don't do this. You need to raise and cost all extra work in writing so that the client can see the extra work and cost *before you carry it out*. We will discuss this in more detail in Chapter 6, but even if the client is *not* going to pay for the extra work, you can use its existence as a useful swap; 'OK, I'm not going to charge you for this, but I want you to get me an hour with your CFO so I can see if there are ways I could be helping her'. Alternatively, if these extras start to add up to a large amount then there comes a point where the client will start paying or at the least offer a very valuable swap. To achieve this the important rule is this: you should still send the client a 'change notice' showing the proper extra cost, but then show it being reversed out as 'agreed client concession' or something similar. This helps the client to see just how much you are forgoing.

CLIENTS ON HISTORICALLY LOW RATES

A scenario that I frequently encounter in my consulting work is where a partner has a long-term client (typically a very large one, or a trophy client) who is on very low rates, or for some other reason is producing a very poor return. This may be due to a historic negotiation when low rates were agreed by a partner eager to land a big-name client, or they may have slipped bit by bit over the years so that what were once reasonable rates have never been increased, or it may be that huge amounts of added value have been demanded by the client, or they argue over the amount of bills delivered, leading to substantial write-offs. Let's assume that this is a big client for the firm (accounting for 20% of all income) and that their rates are 40% below the full rate.

Although the iniquity of the situation is clear (the profit from other clients is effectively being used to subsidise this client's unfair deal), the partner is extremely reluctant to challenge the client over the rates that they are on. The reason is very simple. No partner ever wants to return to the firm after a client visit to have to announce to the other partners that they had a price conversation with the firm's biggest client, it went badly and the firm has been fired. The consequences would be severe. There would be job losses and even the firm's survival might be at risk. With a major and instant loss of income (even loss-making income) the firm may struggle to pay its overheads and the restructuring costs involved in staff dismissals. It's a potentially nightmare scenario.

For most partners, the issue is that they simply don't know where to start. Surprisingly, it can feel to the partner as if *they* have been disingenuous, because they have hung onto the client only by charging very low rates; and if the partner tries to increase to commercial rates, the client might leave anyway because they could employ a much better firm if those are the rates that they have to pay. For some other partners, they simply don't know where to start with a price increase conversation, as they are only used to solving clients' problems, not opposing them and creating a new one.

I had the benefit of filming numerous role plays of these conversations so that, over time, I was able to see what worked and what didn't. This enabled me to create a process for this type of situation, which is as follows:

1. **How good a service are you providing?** Before you have any conversation about fees with a client, you need to be certain that the client has no complaints with the actual service you are providing (and you need to record that fact). So the best price conversation starts with an enquiry about service levels, such as, 'So how are we performing for you at the moment?' or, much better, 'I have gathered some quick data on our performance over the last six months based on our satisfaction surveys and these show a score of 8 plus out of 10. We are really happy with this, does this sound right to you?'

   There is an important reason for this questioning. First, if there is a problem in the client's mind in terms of your service levels, then your priority is to put that right, not to increase your prices. Secondly, my experience is that, if this service issue was not cleared off the table by being addressed first, then the reaction of some clients to a request to increase prices is to immediately raise service issues, in the clear knowledge that this will put any question of price rises on ice for quite a time.

Let's assume for the moment that you have cleared this hurdle and have a positive response around your service levels.

2. **Be open, honest and specific about the price problem straight away.** When I filmed negotiations, I found that partners were so reluctant to talk about the core money issue ('we are making losses on your work', or 'your prices have not increased for seven years but our overheads have') that they tended to wait and bring these in halfway through the discussion. In that way they tended to lose impact and almost look manufactured.

    Much better to say, at the very start, 'I'm glad that we are providing the right service, because there's an issue that you can help me with'. Then get to the core straight away: 'My CFO/finance committee/managing partner is on my back over your account. I'm getting a return of just 6%, yet my firm's hurdle rate is 30%, so we need to look at how we price and deliver our work.' Other issues could be that you are writing off large amounts of time (give the exact cost of this in the last 12 months); that their required added value services are costing too much (again, state the actual cost); that every bill is being disputed and delayed; that they are on a favourable rate for large clients but they only spent £100,000 with you in the last 12 months, etc.

3. **Make a specific proposal that will help solve the problem.** I think this lands better if it contains an accommodation for the client as well as an increased cost. For example, you might say: 'I'm not expecting to make up the 24% shortfall in one year, so I'm suggesting that we phase this in by reducing the discount by 8% each year', or 'You should be paying much higher rates for a £100,000 spend, but I'm proposing to keep you on a discounted rate for six months to see if we can build up the volumes of work and if not, to only impose half the required rate increase after that'.

    Be prepared to horse-trade in this situation and see what swaps you might be prepared to accept in lieu of a full increase, but don't be prepared to walk away with nothing.

4. **Make it 'our problem'** – what are you and the client going to do in order that you can satisfy the CFO/finance committee/ managing partner and get them off your back? After all, a proper client relationship is two-way. You need to deliver a great

service and they need to pay a fair price. The fact that you are seeking to satisfy an external person or body – CFO/finance committee/managing partner – is really helpful as it depersonalises the conversation and maintains your focus upon being a great service provider.

5. **Have an exit route.** I found this to be crucial when partners were preparing for these (difficult) conversations in terms of convincing them that it could never end badly, with the client firing the firm instantly and all of the horrible repercussions of that. To create an exit route you need to think of the worst possible reaction of a client, one which absolutely rules out any increase in rates, reduction in added value or whatever. In such a case, the partner should back off. He or she should say: 'Well I hope you also appreciate the position that I am in, I'm delivering a good service to you but my CFO/finance committee/ managing partner is telling me I have to sort this out. Let's scrap the proposed increase in prices altogether, but what else might we do together so that I have something that I can take back to the office.' This should lead to a positive discussion about alternatives; for example, there might be other areas of business that could be offered to the firm (provided that these are not to be on the same, problematical, terms); there might be better ways of working together which would cut out costs; introductions to other clients that this client could make and so on. I have found that this approach plays well into the 'problem-solving' approach at which most partners excel.

6. **Let's say the worst happens** (although I have never seen a professional fired on the spot merely for raising the question of costs) and the partner has to completely back down. He or she may return from the meeting without any increase in prices or changes in terms and has, at best, just agreed a couple of small face savers which they know will not have much effect on profit. Then they need to start tailoring their service down to the price that the clients are paying, or they need to plan to replace them with better clients. This is like a three-star client staying in a five-star hotel – they are not going to change their behaviour if you continue to give them such a great deal.

If you can start to water down the service, so that the client is closer to getting what they paid for, then this should be done. Some firms are better at this than others. I think the better strategy is usually to seek out clients who are prepared to pay proper rates and once you have them, you exit the lower paying work (as opposed to the much more common strategy of winning more work and taking on more staff but *never* exiting a loss-making client). I saw this at its best when a former colleague of mine telephoned me to tell me that she would be closing down a division that I had created. She thought that, as a courtesy, she should tell me. It turned out that a few years after I had moved on, market prices for the work had declined dramatically as more and more competitors arrived and created far too much capacity. She had won a major new contract with a better client, so she told me: 'I am moving all of the staff over to the new work and ending the old.' Net result, same size building, same number of people, much higher returns. Well done Kath.

DEALING WITH PROCUREMENT

Procurement professionals should never be seen in the realm of Rocket Science (and if encountered there, must be studiously ignored), but have invaded the realm of Relationship Advice simply because it often represents such a substantial area of spend for so many clients. Apart from a very few honourable exceptions, where the procurement team have worked collaboratively with both client and professional service provider to redefine the work and create innovative solutions, my strongly held view is that they are destructive and corrosive not just to the immediate situation, but to the sustainability of the client – professional relationship itself.

I say this having joined, many years ago, the Chartered Institute of Purchasing and Supply in the United Kingdom in order that I could attend their meetings and learn how to work with them. What I found disturbed me. Here was a group of people who were tremendously well trained in the art of negotiation, who had created a real profession with high standards and training, who had then been let loose on service firm partners and it was a bloodbath. Bear in mind that it is possible to have a degree at Bachelor or Master's level in procurement and that a decent procurement director may well have attended a Harvard programme in how to negotiate. One explained to me that partners in service firms tended to be ill-prepared and assumed they could 'wing it' – a strategy that failed when met with research, data and professional negotiation skills.

In my experience, it was much worse than that. I found partners, even when faced with extremely junior members of the procurement team, discussing whether they should discount by 5% or by

10% when asked for their 'best and final offer' (whereas the correct response is 0%), and procurement professionals telling me that they had run out of extras to ask for when negotiating with partners, because 'the partners just say yes to every demand'.

While this may sound like great news for clients (and it may be so in the short term), the end result can be firms carrying out work uneconomically and unsustainably; they are then faced with a choice of whether to cut corners to save costs, or to carry a loss-leading client rather than lose the turnover. Very often, the best people in the service firm learn to avoid the client because the rates are too low, so the partner has difficulty delivering an acceptable level of service.

Even worse, flushed with their success in the first round, procurement then return every two years expecting to create similar savings, and so on. There is no end to their demand for savings, because if procurement cannot show continual savings then they cannot justify their existence and cost. The risk is that they undermine value as partners seek to provide a cheaper and cheaper service to meet unachievable promises of savings. Who is to blame for this sorry state of affairs? All of us service providers who have failed to manage our pricing and work practices so as to be able to produce the facts and figures that would allow us (and the actual client) to keep procurement at bay. We enjoyed cost-plus pricing, annual price rises where we simply passed on our increased costs, giving bonuses to our staff based upon how much they could bill clients, a culture that would punish efficiency with lower returns and celebrated ever higher incomes as a result.

The blunt instrument of competitive tenders, hard-headed negotiations, targeted reductions, online auctions and aggressive panel management were properly earned as a penalty for lazy pricing behaviour. There may have been an overdue balancing of the client – service firm power relationship. Now partners face procurement in an area where we should have been able to keep them out – Relationship Advice. Given that reality, I consider that there are two elements in a successful defence strategy. First, to build up your direct relationship with your clients, and second, to learn how to negotiate with this professional opponent. Let's look at each of these in turn.

JUST HOW STRONG IS YOUR RELATIONSHIP?

I named the middle band of work 'Relationship Advice' for good reason. It was here that I saw strong evidence of the 'Trusted Adviser' model as described by David Maister, Robert Galford and Charles W. Green in their seminal book of that name. If, and only if, you really form a relationship with your client, then your client will protect you from procurement. The client will very typically *not* have the same interests as procurement. They can be quite opposed – procurement need to show quantifiable savings (otherwise why is the company spending so much money on procurement?). The actual client user of your services has quite different drivers. They want advisers who really understand their business; they may need fast responses, ready availability, expertise, high levels of trust and so on. What are the chances that the client user will receive what they want if procurement substantially reduce the fees paid or change to cheaper advisers?

In a real relationship, the client sees part of their role as being to say, 'I don't care that they are more expensive (than the alternatives), I have to keep them as they are essential to my business'. That creates a corresponding obligation on you to truly form a relationship and to give the client the facts and figures that help to justify their defence of you. That might include satisfaction surveys, details of actual results achieved and of added value delivered. In the right circumstances you and the client will *work together* to make sure that any concessions that have to be given to procurement are minor and do not have much impact on your fees or profitability. Here are some real-life examples of creating a saving for procurement while preserving the right level of service and of fees for the client user and for the service firm. In one case we created a 'B' level of service which would be 10% cheaper than the 'A' service that we had been delivering. This B service would be made cheaper by using more junior staff, and therefore the client would choose the B service whenever a matter was not that urgent/important. Procurement were happy and went away, having booked a 10% saving. In practice, over the next two years, most of the work sent to us was marked 'A'. In another case we agreed with the client that we should aim to increase our fee rates by 12% because it had been several years since there had been any increase in rates and we had improved the service being given. This was then put on the table for procurement as part of the negotiation. In the end we agreed to reduce the increase to 7%, provided that fees remained above £1 million each year. Again this resulted in procurement booking a 'saving' of 5% (while we had an increase of 7%).

Provided that you have created a real and valuable relationship with the client then you should be able to create some 'wins' for procurement which do not damage that relationship. I have heard this called 'feeding the beast' in that it is unrealistic for procurement, given a job to do, to walk away saying they could not achieve anything (although of course you can direct them to less prepared competitors). Let's look very briefly at the actual negotiation phase with procurement.

NEGOTIATING WITH PROCUREMENT

It is usually part of the role of procurement to shake the confidence of the existing suppliers. They will use a number of techniques to do that. They will look for service delivery issues and quote these relentlessly. They may tell you that you are out of touch, market prices have been dropping fast and you need to 'sharpen your pencil' and try again. They may say that you cannot get through to round two of the procurement process unless you offer rates of under £400 an hour for partners (even when that is not true). They will find a low-cost, hopeless competitor that neither they nor the actual client have any intention of instructing, because that will give them ridiculously low rates that they can feed into their spreadsheets to tell you that your rates are '13% above the median and need to be reduced by that amount if you are to have any hope of winning the work'. The better procurement professionals will be able to achieve a massive amount without telling a direct lie.

Given the highly service-orientated, trust-built, honest, professional relationship that we are all trained to deliver, it is really easy for us to be wrong-footed by the behaviour of procurement and to believe everything that they tell us. So we need to be better prepared and better at negotiation, otherwise we will let ourselves and our clients down. Here's a plan to survive procurement:

1. **Prepare.** Procurement deal in data, and if they roll out masses of data and you have none then it puts you at a disadvantage. Have your finance team give you facts and figures and have someone from the finance team be prepared to negotiate on your behalf. You need someone who can challenge every argument that procurement use, while you stay as the service-orientated professional.

2. **Don't believe them.** If you accept everything procurement tell you then you have already lost. If I am told that I am 20% too high I would say, 'Only 20%! We should be much higher'. I ignore all statements about needing to deliver my 'best and final

offer', or that 'I need to give at least a 10% reduction' or whatever. These are all meaningless arguments. Partners tend to accept at face value what is said to them by fellow professionals. That is a mistake when dealing with procurement, who are trained to unsettle incumbent suppliers. Whenever they make a demand ask them to justify it, ask for evidence; assume it's untrue or at best partly true.

3. **Have some demands of your own.** Far too often I have seen partners go into a negotiation with procurement assuming that it is going to lead to reductions, and the only issue is how big those reductions will be. Like any negotiation you need to trade rather than concede. For example, procurement want a 10% reduction on rates. 'I can't do that, but if you spend £500,000 in the next 12 months on a new area of work for me then I could shave 2% off the partner rate.' Or I might say, 'I can't move on the partner rate, but if we reduce the number of staff seconded to you by two, then I can provide a back-end rebate of 3% of fees'. Interestingly, I have found that in any negotiation, you are entitled to 'red line' one issue, which seems to be accepted by the other side. So, if I find that on a particular account most of the profit arises from the work at senior manager level, then early on I would say that I could not do anything about the senior manager rate, but I might be able to increase the value of training, or whatever. In that way I might be able to preserve the main profit driver for me.

4. **Be clear on your value.** This advice was given by the procurement director of a major bank in a conference speech who was asked how professionals should respond when told they were (for example, £50 an hour) too high on price. It's a response that I have used numerous times since I heard it and it works. The correct response when told your rates are too high is:

> *That's rather one-dimensional isn't it. It is value that matters, not the price. There are a large number of factors in choosing the right adviser. Speed of response, knowledge of your business, geographic spread, reputation, clarity of advice, commerciality and so on. The right adviser isn't going to have all those factors and be the lowest price. If it's just about the lowest price then we don't need procurement do we? My 10-year-old daughter could do that.*

You can of course develop this response to suit your needs. I used to carry a copy of *What Car* magazine with me which (for example) showed at the time that the Dacia Sandero was the cheapest new car in Britain. So I asked if they and their clients all drove the Dacia Sandero. If they didn't then it seemed that when choosing a car for themselves they didn't want the cheapest, but when buying professional services for their company 'cheapest was best'. That simply couldn't be right.

For a period, I gave talks to procurement professionals on 'buying legal services' (in the hope I could find common ground). At the final such talk, I asked 50 of them, 'When you are having your hair cut, please put your hand up if you choose the lowest price hairdresser that you can find'. Two balding men at the back put their hands up. I challenged the 48 who were left,

So, the rest of you don't choose the cheapest hairdresser. So why do you sit opposite me month after month, and tell me that you cannot use my firm because we are more expensive than a competitor? Why is it all about price for my services, but when you are having your hair cut, it's not?

After a pause a very nice lady in the front row explained: 'That's what we are paid to say. You are supposed to ignore us, or to laugh. But no partner ever laughs. They just cut their prices further. So that's why we say it.' Fair point!

5. **Swap, don't concede.** Giving concessions to procurement doesn't stop them demanding more. Quite the opposite – the more that you show you are willing to concede, the more ambitious they become in their demands. So every concession from you has to be hard work for them, has to take time, has to involve other layers of authority and should be delivered only in return for something valuable from the client. For example, procurement are looking to cut rates by 10% (in which case I suspect they will start by demanding 20%, in order to 'anchor high' – so that if you 'only' give 10% you feel as if you have done well). The correct response could be:

Well that's interesting. It is four years since we increased our rates so inflation has given you 9.4% already across that period. This is a two-year contract, so I would be prepared to limit the increase in our rates to 10%, provided that volumes increase by at least 15% year on year.

Or you might say: 'I can't cut by 20%, that's silly. If you are able to get volumes above £1 million by year two of the contract I could give 5% off in year two.' Saying 'I can't' and 'no' are crucial tools.

6. **Drive a wedge between procurement and the client.** Sometimes the client has a common interest with the procurement

professional. For example, the client may have had instructions from their CEO to cut spend by 25%, has no idea how to do it, and is only too happy for procurement to drive the savings while they try to maintain a good relationship with the advisers affected. That would be a signal to have an in-depth meeting with the client (not procurement) to see what changes can be made in scope, team composition, timing or whatever can drive real savings (i.e. not the same people doing the same work for the client but at much lower rates). However, in the great majority of cases, the client's interests and those of procurement are very much in opposition. The client wants a great level of service, one that enables them to do their job. They don't have unlimited money but it is rare for a client to want the lowest level, cheapest service (remember the haircuts!).

On the other hand, procurement need to show demonstrable savings or they are out of a job. Can a procurement director (or external procurement company) tell the CFO that they are sorry but they simply cannot save any money from the company's services spend? External procurement companies may be on a contingent fee (a proportion of savings achieved). After the exercise, procurement want to show a saving, but the client doesn't want to see the service they were receiving being degraded. So all requests from procurement can effectively be met by asking the client which parts of the current service they want to be downgraded or removed. Remember, scope and price are linked. Imagine procurement turning up to discuss a quote for a fitted kitchen. Sure it can be reduced, we just need to agree what parts of the scope are being removed. If it is all about the hourly rate then you might talk of using more junior staff (while asking procurement if they aren't being one-dimensional).

7. **Beware post-deal demands.** A common technique is for procurement to make it look like a deal has been reached (especially if that means that you have told all your partners about it), and then to request some extras. This is quite a famous negotiating trick. It is completely dishonest and needs to be ignored. If, as the negotiations draw to a close, your side starts talking about drafting press releases, then this is petrol on the fire for this issue. A typical approach is that procurement telephone you, post-deal, to say that there has been a bit of a problem (e.g. the board or the CFO won't sanction the deal) unless you can just move a little. I was caught out by this myself with a procurement director who phoned me every three days after a major deal to

ask for 'Just one more thing'. It gradually dawned upon me I had to use the word that partners almost never use. That word is no! He was going to phone me every three days for the rest of my life until I said no.

A similar (and well-known) trick is called 'appeal to external authority'. In this device, after you have completed your meetings and agreed a deal, the procurement professional says, 'That's great, I just need to get this signed off by my CFO/finance committee/other external person not in the room'. If you agree to this, it means they get to have another round of negotiation (because the CFO or other fictional external person requires just one change before the deal can be signed off). The correct response is to say:

> *Oh, I thought you had power. If you don't, then I must also refer this deal to my CFO/finance committee/other external person not in the room. I can assure you that if your CFO wants concessions then my CFO will want twice as many; he/she is really difficult. So I suggest that we both honour the deal we have agreed today.*

8. **Use time against them.** While procurement make increasing demands upon the professional, it can often be the case that the actual client user is keen to finalise matters. When I originally came across procurement I was keen to be helpful, so dealt with all of their queries very fast. That's a mistake. Take time and explain that decisions like this have to go to your board, head of department or whatever. Make the client start pressuring procurement to stop arguing.

9. **Online auctions and other tricks.** I want you to go to your partners and suggest a new method of pricing your services. Here it is. If a client telephones you and asks the price for a partner you will charge Price A; if they use email then you will charge Price B; if they ask a partner while sitting next to them at an event then you will use Price C; if they ask at your reception desk you will use Price D, *but in every case you will deliver the exact same service* – it is only the price that has changed. That's pretty mad isn't it? So why, when presented with an online auction, do partners prepare to reduce their prices (setting a minimum level which is always reached) when the client, or more likely procurement, sets up an online auction? That's the same thing. It's saying you are going to have a lower price just because you have to type it online!

This despite the fact that the client will expressly say that they are under no obligation to accept the lowest bid and even though they will typically include one 'low-cost no-hope' bidder that will drive prices down for everyone. Here is the answer. If this is Relationship Advice, then the client (as opposed to procurement) is not going to choose their professional adviser on lowest price alone – but you have to work with your actual client to make sure that you have a service which best meets their needs so that they will insist on using you, even though you are not the lowest price. If you have done that then you should not change your price just because procurement put you through a (wholly inappropriate) online auction (whose realm should be restricted to Routine Work – see below). Enter one price and that's it, behave no differently than if there was no online auction.

10. **Understand the 'procurement grid'.** When procurement are deciding how to deal with various suppliers to their organisation they will segment the suppliers – for example measuring low vs high spend against factors such as the number of available suppliers, the cost of switching suppliers, or the complexity of the service. Score low on these factors and you will be forced to compete aggressively on price, and not just once but every two or three years. Usually, procurement will consolidate suppliers so that the few remaining ones have a lot to lose and cannot risk holding out on price. Score highly and you will find talk of long-term relationships, investments in innovation and partnering. You can only improve your position in this grid by working closely with your client (between procurements) to create a genuinely valuable and differentiated service. If you can't find the time to do that, then expect to spend vastly more time trying to make unprofitable rates work for you.

11. **Don't let procurement stop you talking to your client.** Bear in mind we are talking about Relationship Advice. Procurement don't want you talking to the user client because it undermines their power. If you are an incumbent supplier then you may have many matters on with your client, and you should feel free to work with them on any changes that you are planning to make in reaction to procurement's demands. If you are not currently a supplier then you should require face time (at least an hour) with a key user in the client firm so that you can understand their needs. If you can't get that face time then don't

proceed with a bid (why should you spend tens of thousands of pounds on a pitch to a client who will not give you one hour of face time – it's a strong indicator you have only been invited to make up the numbers or to rattle the incumbent). If you are in a controlled environment (such as the public sector), so that suppliers are formally forbidden to speak to the user client, then you should have been talking to them between bids. Bidding blind on paper is not a recipe for successful pricing – much better if you have built a great relationship before the bid (in which case if the client wants you, they will have provided great guidance before any bidding process commences).

12. **Your best and final offer has already been made.** Don't, ever, drop your price just because procurement challenge it or because they ask part-way through a bid process for your 'best and final offer'. Put in the correct bid at the outset, and only horse-trade at the very end of the process when you swap final concessions for trades in return – otherwise you simply look dishonest and the user client looks incompetent. To put forward, or to be charging, one set of prices before procurement arrive and a quite different set afterwards looks like you have been over-charging, that the client has been lazy and that procurement are wonderful. Any changes in price have to be linked to changes in scope, volume, timing or other valuable concessions.

13. **Move in small steps.** The next offer after a 10% reduction is 11% or 11.5% – it is not 15%. Don't move in blocks of 5%, that is a huge leap. Put thought into an offer and make it both conditional on a concession or benefit to be received from the buyer and only a small move upon your last position.

The foregoing might suggest that I am not a fan of procurement. I am not. That does not mean that I do not recognise the need for service firms to be efficient and for clients to save money where they can. I just believe that a more collaborative approach is needed. If anything, it has been the *failure of partners to address this issue* directly with their clients that has let in procurement. If partners had worked with clients to create data around their performance and value, they would have had a great defence to the incursion of procurement professionals. In Chapter 10 I deal with the crucial issue of saving clients money, but in ways that work for both the client and the professional. It is harking back to older times, before the procurement profession drove farmers to raise animals in intoler-able conditions, to farm vegetables chemically and intensively to create tasteless food with lower nutritional value, to award government contracts at the lowest price which then fail, costing billions, and to lead a drive for bigger and bigger, less human relationships. Apart from that procurement, are fine.

NEGOTIATIONS AND ROUTINE WORK

Just as we saw the value of swaps and clear service specification in Relationship Advice, there are additional factors involved in Routine Work where procurement may be the norm (they may be driving the purchasing project with little or no involvement from the actual users of your service). The main aim of procurement in my experience is to create a tight specification for the service, and then to ask as many firms as feasible to quote or bid online for some or all of the work.

That would be a fair enough strategy if services were like tangible goods – but they are not. For tangible goods – whether this is the proverbial 80gsm copy paper, or a pint of 2% non-organic semi-skimmed milk, or a spark plug for an engine, there is an ability to create a tight specification and then to buy against price. For the suppliers of these the battle is really over tight cost control and innovation to drive down the cost of production, because both the specification and the (low) price have been fixed. This simply doesn't work for services because of the high element of human interaction involved in delivery. To aver that a call to a call centre is the same whether it is handled by highly trained local staff or is outsourced overseas to a low-cost provider is incorrect and dangerous. It leads to poor service and (I am pleased to say) quite often to the repatriation of services back to the original country, once clients experience the big difference in actual (as opposed to specified) quality. In the United Kingdom there is in fact government support for companies who want to 'reshore' – to bring back services that were offshored to save money. If procurement is such a great idea this would not be necessary. If you use technology and innovation to drive down your own costs of delivery, you will have the flexibility to meet challenging prices while still giving a good level of service to your clients, which is quite different from using lower cost, less trained people.

If you are a supplier of Routine Work then you need to avoid it becoming a single-factor, one-dimensional discussion where the price per matter is the only one in negotiation. The crucial issue is to make sure that you both differentiate your service from competitors (see Chapter 8) and collect data on how you are different and better. Work very closely with your client between retenders in order to do this. Measures might be speed of average matter, typical results, satisfaction surveys, reduction in administrative work for the client and so on. You need to be able to talk about a number of factors (and even to tie in your price to hitting targets, such as charging 1% extra for every day shaved off the current process with a penalty of 1% reduction in fee for every day of delay).

Other tactics include charging for extra elements and variations on a strict basis so that any (even minor) changes required by the client are charged. This can often be set up post-procurement by agreeing directly with the client what types of extras they would like and at what cost. Once procurement have 'left the building' it can be possible to agree service variations that can be requested on specific matters at extra costs. This appears to keep both parties happy: procurement book the saving and then the actual user can decide if any extras are needed. Additionally, optional features are a great source of extra income – for example, agreeing to remit money by cheque but giving clients the option to have a same-day electronic payment for a fee per transaction.

It is also worth investing in creating switching costs for the client so that it is not just a matter of changing from you to a cheaper supplier. Good examples include holding substantial parts of the client's own data by digitising all of their working documents, integrating your IT with their systems, or seconding staff to the client's site to handle part of the overall process.

Perhaps the best strategy is really to collaborate with clients between bids to improve your service, rather than the much more typical flurry of activity when procurement actually arrive on the scene. This applies whether you are an incumbent or a new supplier seeking to join the panel at the next cycle. For the incumbent, you are in a favoured position to be able to integrate and improve your services so that they are delivering greater value to the client, and/or so that you have driven efficiencies and cost savings using technology or simple process improvement.

If you are a new supplier then the worst thing that you can do is to take part in the next procurement cycle. As the untested new firm, you could only realistically win a place on the panel if you offer a clear price advantage over the existing suppliers. Don't do this, as it is a dream for procurement to find a supplier like you who is going to buy your way onto the panel at rock-bottom prices.

They can use you to drive down the prices of the incumbents (unless the incumbents have read this text) whether or not you actually win any work from them. If you do join the panel, your prices will be horrible, and you will justify them by saying that you have won a new client and in any case all the existing suppliers have dropped too. What will you do in two years' time when you have another round of procurement designed to create further savings for the client?

Better that you approach the actual client (not procurement) mid-cycle and offer to carry out a set amount of work for free, 'so that you can get to know each other and because you want to create something different for them'. Most clients (provided there are not high switching costs) will be happy for you to carry out £20,000 or £50,000 or whatever of work for free so that you can test out your systems and services. You have to gauge the amount of free work that you will give based upon the size of the prize. The client then saves money, and if you can create a service which is better than their existing suppliers, why wouldn't they then want to both send you work and have you join the panel at the next retender? When the next retender comes along you are much better placed, as a known quantity that has already delivered a more valuable and more tailored service, rather than being an untried supplier just adding to the competition at the next retender date. In addition, the free work that you have provided is unlikely to have actually cost you much (assuming you are not going to take on more staff or accommodation to carry it out, but are going to handle it with your existing capacity). So you will have provided real value to the potential client at very little cost to you. It's important that the work you carry out is free. Don't offer it at low cost, or the client will bracket you at that low cost and it will be difficult for you to ever reposition yourself at a higher price.

In the next chapter we are going to look at the surprisingly high impact of relatively small reductions or increases in price, and why a pricing project at a firm can have such an exciting and positive impact upon partners and staff alike (and also explains why you should not drop the chocolate biscuits from your conference rooms).

The pricing lever

Strategy 1 – increase your prices

Strategy 2 – work harder

Strategy 3 – work smarter not harder

Strategy 4 – cut overheads, reduce the cost base

Strategy 5 – cut prices, win more work

In this chapter we are going to examine some of the options that are open to a firm that wants to increase its profits. Most service firms have a relatively simple business model which involves employing staff, housing them, selling their time (either by the hour or using fixed or project-based fees), then accounting for and billing that.

I will look at the options available to a firm that wants to increase profits, which include increasing the prices charged; working harder or increasing utilisation; the infamous 'working smarter not harder'; cutting overheads; and finally reducing prices to win more business. In each case it is going to be important to look at the effect of each different strategy both upon the people in the firm and separately upon its clients, as well as examining the financial impact that those changes would make to its bottom line.

STRATEGY 1 – INCREASE YOUR PRICES

The greatest single effect that you can have on your profit level is to increase your prices. For example, in a typical professional services firm, achieving just 10% higher prices would actually lead to profits increasing by 30% or 40% or more and an individual partner's income increasing at the same rate if the rise can be achieved without losing clients. This is based upon a firm that has an existing net profit of 25% to 33%. Other types of service firms will have an impact that is directly related to the current percentage of net profit, and this is shown in Table 5.2.

The maths on this are so surprising – yet so simple – that people often refuse to believe how powerful a lever pricing can be. If we use the example of a 'model firm' where profits start at 25%, then if you are earning £100,000 a year as a partner or shareholder at the outset, achieving a 10% uplift in your prices increases your income to £140,000 a year – and conversely, giving your clients a 10% discount would cut your income to £60,000 a year.

The reason that pricing has such a strong effect is because it all happens 'at the margin': every penny of increase or decrease in price goes directly to profits and into the individual stakeholders' pockets, be they company shareholders or a firm's profit-sharing partners. This can be easily demonstrated in Table 5.1, showing a typical firm before and after a price rise or a price cut. In all of these examples I have used a 'partnership' model to show the impact of price changes on profit-sharing partners, but the effect is the same if examining corporate profits.

| Table 5.1 | Impact of price changes upon profitability |

	Starting point	10% price increase	10% price cut
Turnover	4,000,000	4,400,000	3,600,000
Staff costs	1,500,000	1,500,000	1,500,000
Buildings costs	400,000	400,000	400,000
IT	320,000	320,000	320,000
Other costs	780,000	780,000	780,000
Total expenses	**3,000,000**	**3,000,000**	**3,000,000**
Net profit for stakeholders	1,000,000	1,400,000	600,000
10 equal stakeholders =	100,000	140,000	60,000

| Table 5.2 | Impact of price changes depends on starting profitability |

Starting profit (%)	Profit (%) after 10% price rise	Profit (%) after 10% price cut
15% (income £100,000)	25% (£166,666)	5% (£33,333)
20% (income £100,000)	30% (£150,000)	10% (£50,000)
30% (income £100,000)	40% (£133,333)	20% (£66,666)
40% (income £100,000)	50% (£125,000)	30% (£75,000)
50% (income £100,000)	60% (£120,000)	40% (£80,000)

This lever effect depends very precisely upon your starting point for profitability. Table 5.2 shows the impact of a 10% price change upon net profit for different levels of starting profit. It then shows (in brackets) the impact upon income paid to each stakeholder, if the starting point was £100,000 (and you can just multiply this to find the amount for your own income).

The higher the starting profit percentage the less impact there is. Profit-sharing stakeholders tend to think that their profit percentage is higher than it is, because they often have a dual role both as revenue generator in the business and as an owner sharing in the profits. To explain this we take again our model firm and think of a simplified situation where the firm has two profit-sharing partners and two senior members of staff (they might be called salaried or fixed share partners, directors, senior managers or whatever). Let's say that, in year one, the two profit-sharing partners earn £250,000 each and that comes from a profit of 25% on a turnover of £2 million. At the start of year two, the salaried partners (who had been earning £150,000 each) are welcomed into the firm as full profit-sharing partners but everything else stays the same (income and overheads). The only accounting change that has taken place is that the overheads have been reduced by £300,000 because the two salaried partners are no longer taking a salary, but are dependent upon taking a share in profits, as shown below.

	Year 1	Year 2
Income	£2,000,000	£2,000,000
Salary expenses	£1,000,000 (includes £300,000 for salaried partners)	£700,000 (no salaried partners)
Other overheads	£500,000	£500,000
Net profit	£500,000	£800,000
Net profit (%)	25%	40%
Each partner receives	£250,000	£200,000

Small firms in particular tend to account for themselves as per year two above and say that they have 40% profit. It should be noted that the profit-sharing partners are also working partners in the business and therefore should be assigned a 'notional salary' of, for example, £150,000 each (by comparing them with the highest paid salaried partner, for example), which means that a better analysis of profit becomes:

	Year 1	Year 2
Income	£2,000,000	£2,000,000
Salary expenses	£1,300,000 (includes £300,000 for salaried partners and £300,000 notional salary for profit-sharing partners)	£1,300,000 (includes £600,000 for notional salaries)
Other overheads	£500,000	£500,000
Net profit	£200,000	£200,000
Net profit (%)	10%	10%
Each partner receives	£250,000 (made up of £150,000 notional salary plus £100,000 of profit share)	£200,000 (made up of £150,000 notional salaries plus £50,000 of profit share)

This is a particularly important concept when firms are facing discount demands from clients. In this example, if clients achieved an average discount of 10% then income would drop to £1,800,000 and profit would drop to zero. The partners would all receive £150,000, but that is the amount that they could have earned at any similar firm just by being an employee at their level of experience and expertise – i.e. the firm has generated no surplus money for division between partners over and above the salary costs and other overheads of the staff and partners. Notional salaries are also essential if you are starting to compare team profitability or profit by client. Without a notional salary, teams with profit-sharing partners look much more profitable than teams with salaried partners, even if both teams did exactly the same amount of work at the same prices.

A project for profitability

The reason that it is crucial to understand the impact of price rises on profitability is that, for a typical services firm, no project offers such high and sustainable results as one which will achieve price rises. Developing a clear, targeted and timetabled plan for this should be very high on the agenda for every firm's management board: there is unlikely to be anything else on their desks that will promise returns like this. Take a firm with a turnover of £100 million that sets a target to improve pricing by 5%. Achieving this adds fully £5 million to the profit line and in terms of the improvement as a percentage of income for each partner or shareholder, that will make a big difference – not just in the year it is achieved, but in all subsequent years. Let's say that the project is a failure and only achieves a 2% profit improvement. That's £2 million extra profit. What other project can offer this level of reward for 'failure'?

Even more importantly, if overheads are increasing, then a failure to increase prices at an equivalent cash value will lead to profits being reduced year-on-year. That is, perhaps, the bigger driver for most partners. If overheads account for 75% of income and increase by 6% a year (at a time when income stays flat), then it takes just two years for profit to drop from 25% to about 16%, meaning that a partner who was previously earning £200,000 would see their income drop to £128,000. Most partners would react when faced with that scenario laid out in clear figures. In these examples, I have excluded growth that a firm may enjoy by winning new clients, acquiring teams or merging. These can all have a positive effect but they tend to increase overheads as well. How could you add £1 million of extra profit without also increasing the number of professionals and support staff to carry out that extra work? (Clue: A small, well-managed increase in prices.)

How to raise prices

Price rises can come from a whole host of sources; it is not about just writing to all your clients and announcing that all prices will increase by 5% starting from next month. If it were as simple as that there would be no need for any science or effort on pricing, or for a book such as this. In the following chapters we are going to examine the sources of additional income, but at this stage it is worth explaining that this can come from a number of actions:

■ reducing the amount of discount that a client is receiving – taking it from 25% to 12% is the same as increasing prices by 17% but is often more achievable. (Yes, it is 17% because if you take a standard hourly rate of £100, then a client on a 25% discount is paying £75 an hour. If the discount becomes 12% then the client pays £88 an hour. So the income from that client goes up by £13 an hour and £13 is a 17% increase on £75);

■ changing the team of people who are handling the work;

■ reducing write-offs;

■ better managing the cost and extent of added value;

■ project managing work against agreed project-based costing (PBC) quotes.

So, in looking to increase profit, there are a number of sources and in a typical firm all of them need investigation and action to contribute towards an overall growth in net profit.

Price rise – effect on staff

Generally speaking, price rises are well received internally, except that those colleagues who have to talk to clients about increases will give many reasons why it is not possible to actually impose them on *their* client. Because what client ever welcomes an increase in price?

However, all other things being equal, everyone knows that the better the firm is, the more it is going to charge its clients. There has been some interesting research which shows that at the level of brain neurone activity we believe that more expensive is 'better'. As explained in Chapter 3, there is a 'price placebo effect'. In a series of experiments at the California Institute of Technology, Antonio Rangel found that people derived more pleasure from more expensive wine than from its cheaper alternative. Time after time, the 'pleasure centres' of the brain reacted more strongly to the more expensive wine. You might find yourself agreeing with this outcome, but the issue was (and this was the reason for the experiment) that the wine the participants were tasting was always exactly the same wine; they were simply told that it cost different amounts. What is the explanation for this?

It seems that our brain is relying upon its previous learnt experiences which were that 'more expensive equals better', whether it is food, a holiday, a hotel, clothes – actually everything that you buy. Of course there may have been some disappointing exceptions, but in the main our brains assume that more expensive is better and reacts positively using that heuristic. For the staff in a services firm, there is also a status issue about working in a firm that charges more than its competitors. Logic says that it will not be able to charge more unless it is better than its competitors and its clients are of that opinion as well. In addition, a firm that charges more has more money to spend on remuneration for its staff, on training and on support – all of those things which actually enable your people to deliver a better service to your clients. If you think of the opposite situation, a firm that charges less than any of its competitors is unlikely to be paying its staff very much. As we will explore in the next chapter, underpaying staff is not a recipe for success in the services industry, where what the client is buying is the activity of your people.

It is not uncommon for your staff and your partners to worry that if you are more expensive than the local competition you will have priced yourself out of the work. I always ask them, 'Are you better than [close competitor]?', and they will usually reply 'yes'. Then, I say, 'You should charge more than them'. The client will never believe you are better if you are cheaper. Leave that competitor to be the cheap firm around here. After all, I will add, if they didn't win work on price, what work would they get? They certainly wouldn't win it on service. Clients understand that you get what you pay for and, that in pretty much every area of their life, better service costs more, just as better quality goods do. We will deal later on with those lovely clients who take pleasure in buying the cheapest ('price shoppers').

Price rise – effect on clients

A law firm has three divisions: Real Estate, Litigation and Trusts. In the current year Real Estate has been incredibly busy with staff working overtime to cope, Litigation has met its target but Trusts work has been very quiet. There is one profit-sharing partner in each of these divisions. Retail price inflation is running at 3% and overhead inflation at the firm (due mainly to staff salary increases) is running at 6%. Let's assume that profit is 25%. All other things being equal, if there is no increase in income (for example the winning of new clients, increased work from existing clients or a price rise), then profit would fall to 20.5% in the coming year (overheads having increased to 79.5%, because that is 75% plus 6% of 75%). If the average partner had been earning £100,000 then it would drop to £82,000 in the coming year, and given that retail price inflation is 3% that actually feels like £79,540. Quite a drop from £100,000.

Depending upon the level of pricing confidence among the partners, they may try to increase the firm's prices by between 3% and 6%. Or, if it's in the middle of a recession, they may not attempt a price increase but rather look for extra hours worked or overhead reductions (see pages 132–3 for the effect of these). What the firm omits to consider is the differing levels of demand for the three areas of work. Real Estate prices could very probably be increased by 10% or more and allow the partners and team there to work less hours yet earn more money, whereas increases in Trusts prices could be ineffective because the division is underutilised and may be even less busy after a price rise.

Price rises are an art, not a mathematical formula. They need to have regard to general levels of inflation and demand for each specific area of work.

At first sight, a price rise is not good news for clients. If the firm is simply going to put up its prices then that means this will directly impact on the client's own profitability pretty much pound for pound. No client is going to welcome a price increase, however much they may value you.

On the other hand, very many goods and services that the client buys (from fuel to cleaning services to accommodation to staff) do increase in price over time. So you need to be less worried about a simple straightforward price rise than you might imagine. To be successful in imposing price increases you need to take into account overall market conditions (supply and demand, competitive pressures) and also what type of work is involved. You cannot simply look to apply a percentage across the board irrespective of work type and volumes (which is why so many price rises fail to stick, being built up from a cost-plus mentality which has no connection to the value that the client is receiving). Let me give you an example which will help to draw this out.

In what I would describe as 'normal times', it is permissible to increase prices particularly if you do two things – link them to overall increases taking place in the economy, and (if possible) show that you are also taking steps that will improve efficiency or reduce the total cost. Clients want to feel that you are on their side. However, there are the usual nuances depending upon whether the client is buying Rocket Science, Relationship Advice or Routine Work as shown in the table below.

	Rocket Science	Relationship Advice	Routine Work
How much to increase	The hourly rate is not fundamental to the final cost, which should have a substantial value element. Rates should be increased every year based upon workplace inflation.	Your rates can and should be ahead of your competitors unless you are using a price leadership strategy. They should be in the same zone as your competitors, but can be the highest of them.	Will be on fixed fees. The important issue is to diarise the review dates. Use inflation as a guide. You will also be expected to have improved efficiency so as to absorb part of the increase.
. . . and how to approach the increase	Hourly rates and total budget notified to the client at outset. The rates can be higher than all of the competitor's rates.	The largest clients must be seen face-to-face. The factors that went into the increase need to be explained and it helps if you have absorbed part of the increase yourself. You can write to smaller clients but again, give an explanation.	Visit largest clients and write to others. Be prepared to negotiate and have swaps in mind (as set out in Chapter 4). Don't lose the opportunity to have the conversation annually, and have facts and figures to support your case for a rise.

In fact, if you speak to clients you will find that the strongest issue around price rises is whether or not they are happy with the service they are receiving from the firm. If they have a good firm, providing a great service and added value, then they are going to accept (albeit reluctantly) that price rises do occur. If, on the other hand, they already have real concerns about the service they are receiving, then a price rise is going to be refused by them and in fact may well lead them to look elsewhere. For that reason, it is essential to have regular checks on the service quality that you are providing. If you do not do this then you will find that requests for increased prices are met by a demand for an improved service *before* any price rise takes effect. Firms therefore need to understand that a real precondition to looking at price increases is to ensure first that clients are happy with the service being delivered.

We are dealing here with price rises that need to take place as a result of inflationary pressures on your firm. More importantly, however, for both Relationship Advice and for Routine Work, you can quite properly look for ways of increasing prices where you *change what you are delivering to the client.* In that case, although you are charging extra, the additional cost is justified if it is less than the extra value that the client sees from the change in the service you are delivering. This is called addressing the client's drivers of value and is covered in detail in Chapter 8.

Price rise – effect on bottom line

It is really in its effect on the bottom line that price rises triumph. In fact, it is not just a question of relatively small price rises having a huge effect on the business' bottom line – and the personal income of the partners or shareholders – if you do not achieve price rises then you can very rapidly see a substantial drop in profits as overheads increase. In just a few years of flat income and increasing overheads, the return can halve.

In the table below, we can see the effect of a 5% and a 10% increase in prices (or in margin if you are going to achieve the gains by improved working practices, as described in Strategy 3 below) on a typical firm. It is sensitive to the starting net margin as the table below shows, based upon a *starting income of £100,000* for a partner.

Starting percentage profit	5% price increase	10% price increase
10%	£150,000	£200,000
15%	£133,333	£166,667
20%	£125,000	£150,000
25%	£120,000	£140,000
30%	£116,667	£133,333
35%	£114,285	£128,571
40%	£112,500	£125,000
50%	£110,000	£120,000

As we can see, the higher the initial starting point for percentage profit, the lower the leverage effect. Even in the mid-range, however, small price rises (5%) cause a 20% increase in income (for a starting profit rate of 25%).

Let's also look at the other options that are available to firms that want to increase their profits and the return to partners.

STRATEGY 2 – WORK HARDER

Perhaps surprisingly, given how hard everybody tends to work in service firms, this is quite a common first approach, even if it is sometimes dressed up to look like Strategy 3 below (Work smarter, not harder).

It just means that everyone needs to record more chargeable hours next year or to produce more fixed fee services. Unfortunately, this is the right solution *only* if the problem was that people were not working enough hours in the first place (even though they had enough business to work those longer hours), or if they were working long hours but just not recording and recovering them.

However, anyone familiar with modern firms will realise that it is extremely unlikely that people are not working pretty much flat-out already. So increasing their targets, with the increased hours feeding through to an increased billing budget each month, is going to increase the pressure on people who are already very busy. Nonetheless, let us say that you currently target staff to record 1500 chargeable hours each year and you decide to increase that to 1600. What effect is that going to have on your people, your clients and your back pocket?

Working harder – effect on staff

Pretty bad really. It is simply a cracking of the whip, sometimes accompanied by explanations such as 'If you cannot bill more hours, then I cannot see how we can pay you more'. However, most staff will already be working and charging as many hours as they physically can, so it is typically demotivating to have more demanded. This strategy can work if the hours being worked (recorded/recovered) are out of line with the average in your sector. So, on a consultancy project, I came across a firm where people were targeted to achieve 1000 chargeable hours whereas their most direct competitors were achieving 1500. In that situation, unless you can show some real benefit to the client which would justify their paying 150% of a competitor's price for each hour worked, then you have an underperformance (or recording/recovery) issue that needs to be addressed first.

Generally speaking, staff will look for a connection between effort and pay, and if you expect extra hours of work each year then your staff will expect an appropriate pay rise to go with that.

Staff working in the firm will not be motivated or led by a strategy of simply working harder – they need something that will grab their attention and show them that the firm is progressing. How is the firm planning to grow? What is it planning to do next year? Increase the target to 1700 chargeable hours?

Working harder – effect on clients

Increasing the chargeable hours budget for staff is really just a hidden price rise as far as many clients are concerned. In the course of each day the relevant member of your team can only work so hard and if they are doing that anyway, then all the firm is doing is making them record more of their time as chargeable to clients (as opposed to administrative or personal time), so the client will pay more for the same amount of effort. For example, if someone is working 9am to 6pm every day with an hour for lunch then, working on the basis that there are effectively 45 working weeks after holidays, bank holidays, sickness and training, etc., that means there are 225 days, and on each of those days your people will have to record 6.2 chargeable hours. This rises to 6.66 chargeable hours per day at 1500 hours; but in percentage terms this is quite a drop in the amount of non-chargeable/personal time – in fact it has dropped by more than one-third.

Unless this strategy is linked to some brilliant new method for gaining clients (to whose work the professionals will devote the extra time each day), then the increase is simply being added to the bills of the same clients as before. So, if I am a client I would argue that if the required chargeable hours increase by 7% then my bills are likely to go up by 7% as well. There is no talk of added services or better value – just a 7% concealed increase.

In fact, if you come from the school of thought which says that pretty much all professionals can produce the same amount of genuinely chargeable hours in each day, then you might argue that firms with very high chargeable hour's targets are simply charging more per effective hour.

Let's say that you take 1500 hours as a standard, then it could be argued that a professional who is charged out at £200 per hour in fact costs the amounts per hour shown below:

Effective price of one hour		
1500 hours	1750 hours	2000 hours
£200	£233	£267

But maybe all of this is wrong! Maybe you can actually get people to work longer hours and each hour is still just as effective as the others. If this argument is correct, then you have to ask yourself – as a client – would you want to use a firm that makes its staff work 2000 chargeable hours as opposed to one that targets 1500 hours?

Perhaps it is easier if I put it another way. If you need to have a cartilage operation on your knee, which is pretty routine and could be carried out by any number of surgeons and teams, would you prefer to have the surgery performed by Team A (who are targeted to do four operations a day), or by Team B who have to get through five every day? What about if we change the operation to a triple heart bypass. Which team do you want now? Oh, and by the way, your operation is taking place at 4pm on Friday – and the hospital is understaffed, so teams regularly work all weekend as well.

Your surgeon looks grumpy and extremely tired – but hey, he is a professional. Good luck with the operation.

Working harder – effect on bottom line

Well, if it works, increasing chargeable hours by 100 hours will have a really impressive effect on your bottom-line profit. In fact, if you moved from 1500 to 1600 hours and had a starting profit of 25% then you could see actual profit increasing by more than 25% of that, which is well worth having. However, in order to achieve that growth in profit you have to assume a few things:

■ That people, on average, achieve the new targets. The problem with this assumption is that at 1500 hours you probably had a number of fee earners who were actually achieving 1600 hours or close to it, so they are not greatly affected by this new target. They will carry on working as they are and are unlikely to simply add 100 extra hours. Similarly, there will be a number of people achieving 1300 hours or thereabouts and they have a very long way to reach the new 1600-hour target. In addition, all those who are already on reduced targets (such as managers, team leaders, etc.) are unaffected and so do not contribute to the improvement.

- So, although the effective increase in hours will be 6.67%, in practice it is much more likely to be half that. This still gives a worthwhile rise in profit (around 13%).

- That all work is based on chargeable hours and therefore any increase in recorded hours will actually be recovered from the clients. However, there are a number of problems to this. Firstly, you may already have many arrangements for fixed fees and staff may be quite used to giving quotations and estimates to clients who ask. They will not take into account this new increased target in those quotes (i.e. if they were going to quote £31,400 they probably will still do so and will not increase that quote by the necessary 7%).

- That you not only record this higher number of hours but you are actually able to recover them. Recording the hours and billing them are two quite different things, and quite often people apply some art to the decision on what is billable. Again this is something which tends not to be affected by an increased target, and there are likely to be greater write-offs.

- That no one wants more money for working the extra hours (except of course for the profit-sharing partners or shareholders who receive this automatically). However, the most basic fairness to your staff will be that if they are asked to work extra hours then they will need to be paid more, particularly when compared with direct competitors with lower chargeable hour targets.

- That you do not lose any staff because of your working harder approach. Not a single one. If you do lose any staff then there is a cost of replacing and retraining, and turnover is hugely costly to firms and extremely annoying to clients. But we will ignore that for the present.

- That clients are happy to pay the same rate for your (more tired) staff and that therefore they are happy that you have just effectively hiked your rates by 7% without telling them. If you were planning to increase the actual rate per hour this year as well (let's say by 10%), then the client is now being expected to pay £235 per hour for the same person that was just costing

£200 an hour before the hike (you put the rate up to £220 and you increased the hours by 7%).

Working harder – summary

It does work and produces a short-term effect on the bottom line, but you can see all the assumptions you've had to make in order to ensure that much of the increased hours stick – and it is strictly a one-off. We need not rule it out as an option, particularly if you are currently budgeted to produce less than your most direct competitors in terms of chargeable hours per year per member of staff.

However, you will have to come up with something a bit more imaginative for the following year. The best response I ever heard to the 'let's work more hours' argument was from a partner at a board meeting who had just listened to the managing partner suggest that if we were able to turn just 100 hours of the current non-chargeable time of our fee earners into chargeable time, then we would all earn an extra £20,000 the following year. 'Yes', said the partner after listening patiently, 'and if idiots could fly, this place would be an airport.' The point is that this is an internally faced argument, which really ignores the effects on clients and on staff. It has a role if your firm is out of balance with your most direct competitors in terms of culture and hours recorded and charged. I have seen that happen and then you have a choice to make: all earn less than competitors (but have a less pressured culture), or rebalance working hours over a period of years to bring them into line.

Looking across the three different types of work, you can see the varied impact. For Rocket Science, professionals already tend to be working extreme hours, and if they are pricing correctly there is a substantive value element based upon budget predictions and (even if extra hours are worked) there should be little or no impact upon the final bill. Routine Work is typically on a fixed fee per matter, so is unaffected by increases in hourly budgets. It is in the zone of Relationship Advice that increased hourly budgets make the greatest impact, but that impact (unless there is a serendipitous and parallel increase in clients and work gained that will absorb the extra time) just means a price increase for all existing clients. The gamble is whether or not they will notice, but it hardly feels like appropriate behaviour for a client with whom you have a professional relationship. There are better ways of increasing prices, based upon increasing the value you deliver to a client, and these are explored in Chapter 8.

STRATEGY 3 – WORK SMARTER, NOT HARDER

I don't think there is anything much more annoying than being encouraged to 'work smarter, not harder', especially when the person doing the encouraging is pretty thin on the details of how you are to pull off this magic trick.

It is correct to say that you always need to pay attention to how much time groups of partners and their teams are treating as chargeable as opposed to non-chargeable, and look out for disparities. Some people are manifestly better at recording chargeable time than others, and that may mean that some clients are not being charged enough for perfectly proper work; but as an offset some others may be charged too much by those who are 'too good' at recording their time. For the firm, that should be just as much an issue.

The whole theory of 'working smarter' seems to revolve around the idea that in the same number of hours a day you can make more effective (by which is meant more chargeable) use of that time. That is correct if highly qualified people are spending time doing administrative work which could be done by others at a much lower cost to the client, and to the overall benefit of the firm as well. However, that is not always the case, and in fact where it is the case it has often come about because overhead cost reductions (see Strategy 4 below) have led to a reduction in the number of support staff, and therefore others are having to do administrative work that was formerly carried out by those more junior staff.

The closest that I have seen to this strategy working in practice is when emphasis is placed upon project managing the work being carried out either against a fixed fee or against a PBC quote and its associated scope. So, if you have an area of work where there is a reasonably repeating volume of similar transactions that are being charged upon the basis of time spent, you could average the cost and convert this to a fixed fee. (In fact, because the client has the benefit of budget certainty they would, in practice, be prepared to pay a little more, but for the moment let's ignore that to keep it simple.) So you might be carrying out a type of transaction which has cost between £40,000 and £60,000, and once you average them all out you find that the average cost was £50,000. If you agree with your clients that you will switch to a fixed fee of £50,000 then the efficiency benefit suddenly appears. Against that fixed fee, if the professional can work more efficiently – for example, the actual time taken adds up to £45,000 – then a useful extra profit can be made (using the time saved on other work) or the time released could be used for business development, training or relaxation (remember that?). The work doesn't have to be carried out all for one client; you can average the cost across a number of clients, provided that they all agree to the fixed fee.

The benefit here is that both clients and staff stand to gain from this approach, as does the profitability of the firm. Furthermore, this type of efficiency drive can play into the key skill set of service providers. Given a problem – 'How can we simplify this piece of work and so reduce the effort involved?' – many partners can switch into problem-solving mode in a way that can fundamentally improve profits (provided that a fixed fee or PBC quote has been agreed in advance).

STRATEGY 4 – CUT OVERHEADS, REDUCE THE COST BASE

When service firms decide to 'attack' overheads they almost always start by removing chocolate biscuits from meeting rooms before moving on to discuss the benefits of reducing the travel and marketing budget, making a reduction in support staff, shelving investment plans and reducing perks. I have revised my views on these activities, which I had previously considered to be rather peripheral, because the dramatic recession that impacted on many service firms in the West after 2008 showed that managing overheads can be fundamental to business health and even survival. In good times overheads become overweight and when the business environment turns cold they need to be addressed. That can make a substantial difference to a firm's prosperity and survival in hard times.

It is important to bear in mind, however, that non-staff overheads will typically only account for a small percentage of total overheads, so that even severe cuts in them cannot create huge increases in overall profit. It is not possible to cut your way to greatness in a service business. That is not to say that overheads do not need constant review, but more that they are not the only solution to falling profits. In fact, if you look at the most profitable service firms (for example the top 10 firms in a sector), then a visit to their offices will show you that they are not running their business on overhead reductions. Inevitably the largest overhead is going to be staff costs and these will come under attack in quiet times. The important issue to bear in mind is that you cannot repeat cuts year after year with the same impact. Overhead reduction projects run out of steam at some point. That is why pricing also needs to be addressed.

There is a story about a major airline that recognised it had a big problem with customer service because its staff were notoriously rude or indifferent to its passengers. This was having a real effect on passenger numbers. The airline developed a structured and apparently appropriate solution of sending all of the staff away on comprehensive customer service training programmes. After this exercise they measured what the customers said about customer service and how it had changed. Customers said it hadn't changed at all. After further investigation, the airline discovered that the problem was that it treated its own staff appallingly and then expected the staff to treat customers magnificently! There is substantive evidence, described in the Service Profit Chain as shown in Figure 5.1, that points to the foundation of a profitable service businesses being happy and well-rewarded staff. Constant overhead reductions are corrosive of staff morale.

The Service Profit Chain **Figure 5.1**

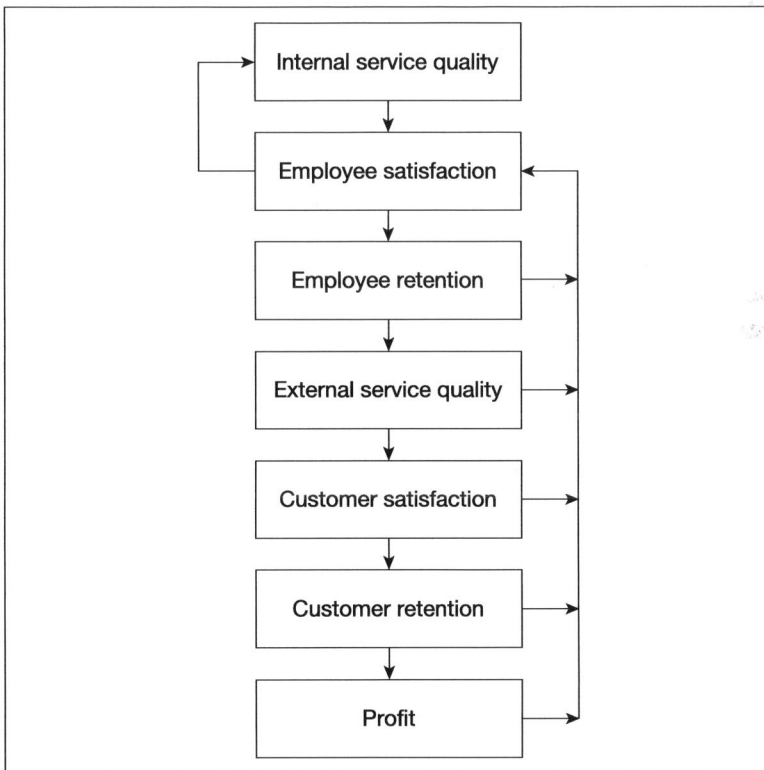

Source: Based on an exhibit from Schlesinger, L.A. and Heskett, J.L., 1991. 'Leonard A. Schlesinger and James L. Heskett, respond: Customer satisfaction is rooted in employee satisfaction', *Harvard Business Review*, November–December. Reprinted by permission of Harvard Business Review.

Overhead reductions – effect on staff

It is difficult to motivate staff through cost-cutting or penny-pinching. The problem is that most partners are much more comfortable with overhead reductions (they feel they can take control in an area where they have some expertise and something to offer), than they are when dealing with the longer-term strategic issue of changing services so that they deliver better value to clients (and so justify a higher price).

Overhead reductions also have an aura of being something of a stop-gap – presumably you cannot have overhead reductions every single year since, apart from demotivating everyone, there will be a gradual reduction in the impact that this will have. Given that the largest single overhead in a service firm is staff salary costs, most people fully understand that as soon as you talk about reducing overheads, you are talking about reducing headcount.

Overhead reductions – effect on clients

If your own staff morale drops then clients will very quickly pick up on this – you cannot expect a smiling superb service from staff who feel themselves at risk from downsizing, or who are working in an organisation that counts every penny. In addition, the most common route used – reducing the number of support staff – can directly affect the quality of service being delivered to the client. Once clients start feeling these effects they are much less likely to be agreeable to future price increases, as they will feel that they are asked 'to pay more for less'.

Overhead reductions – effect on bottom line

Whereas price increases have a lever effect, so that relatively small increases cause large effects on profits, the reverse can be true with overheads. Large percentage reductions can have a smaller effect on profit. Take the example of a service firm where overheads total 75% of income, giving a net profit of 25%. Within those overheads, IT costs might account for 10% of total overheads (so 7.5% of total income). If you cut IT costs by 20% (which is presumably quite a swingeing reduction) that would save 1.5% of actual costs, so profit increases from 25% to 26.5% (an increase of 6%). I accept that if you cut *all overheads* by a high percentage then the savings move across to the profit line, but that will not typically be possible (for example, some costs such as office accommodation will be fixed in the short to medium term).

Overhead reductions can be effective (especially if a very busy period is followed by a quiet one), but they are rarely going to be the whole answer. You will not build a great business simply by reducing overheads, because attention must also be directed externally to the clients, to your competitors and what your unique position is in the market.

STRATEGY 5 – CUT PRICES, WIN MORE WORK

The sugar rush of the pricing world, cutting your prices, may well deliver some pleasant immediate results but at horrible long-term costs. The reality is that if you win extra work *that you would not otherwise have won* through cutting your price then the immediate effect looks really good. Take, for example, a firm which was aiming for income of £2 million in the current year but is currently running behind budget and expects to bill £1.8 million, and as a result will see its profit (assuming a planned 25% return) drop from £500,000 to £300,000. A partner has been bidding on a piece of work that should have been priced at £200,000 but decides to cut the price to £100,000 and wins that work. The result in that financial year is that all of that £100,000 (even though it is at half-price) will fall into profit and increase the profit from £300,000 to £400,000! That's the upside, although you have to assume that this is work that you could not have won at £200,000. That is a big assumption because, as we have seen in both Rocket Science and Relationship Advice, price is not usually the decider.

Here's the downside. You have undermined your market position and price. Why will this client ever pay 'full price' for you again? Will they tell others that your prices are malleable? How will the competitor who lost the piece of work to you react? Won't they also start dropping their prices so that there is a real race to the bottom between all of the firms in order to fight over the available work? While this sounds like great news for the clients (as indeed it might be in the short term), this type of pricing is simply not sustainable. It doesn't generate sufficient profits to keep the firms in business.

Moreover, even relatively small drops in price have such a corrosive effect upon profit that a huge amount of extra work must be received just to stand still (make the same profit as before). Take the example of a client who is currently spending £1 million with you, who says that they will increase spend to £1.5 million next year, provided that you give a discount of 10% off current rates. For a typical firm that is a bad deal (unless they have some economies of scale on that type of work), because the £1.5 million of work at the new discounted rates will earn less profit than the £1 million at the old rates. This is illustrated in the following table, which takes as its basis a client who is giving £1 million of work to a firm and shows how much additional work is needed to achieve the same profit as before the extra discount was given:

Reduction in price	How much extra work to stand still?
5%	£0.25 million
10%	£0.67 million
15%	£1.5 million
20%	£4.0 million

Note: ASSUMPTION = Start at £1 million of work with a profit margin of 25%.

This effect can be particularly problematic in Relationship Advice, where there are low economies of scale and it is possible to build a bigger and bigger business (carrying larger risks) without any extra profit being earned for partners. Of course, bigger clients will expect a better deal from you (we will examine this when we use scattergrams in Chapter 11) but the extent of the reductions given to them is really important. Many of you will know the saying, 'Turnover is vanity, profit is sanity'.

In difficult economic times there can be huge pressure on a firm to reduce its prices. Whenever there is oversupply, prices will become soft as clients find that shopping around pays off. This is when you see a shift in market rates. Partners will tell you that whereas they used to be able to quote and charge around £100,000 for a piece of work, they are now faced with clients who refuse to pay more than £80,000. The real problem with dropping to £80,000 is that this establishes a new baseline that all firms compete against, and so it is likely to be a temporary staging post only. (Similarly with clients who attack hourly rates and drive them down and down.) In fact, we can learn from external commerce here, where they are used to feeling exactly the same pressures as us. Their answer is to maintain the usual service (as there are always some clients who are prepared to pay the 'normal' price) but to introduce a lower cost service as well. So now the client has options – if lower price is crucial you can deliver a 'no frills' service under which they still get the same team, but at a lower price (because less work will be involved), or they can have the standard service at the original price. This maintains the integrity of pricing on your standard service and (we will explore this in Chapter 8, which will cover value engineering in more detail).

In the next chapter we are going to look at ways of improving profitability, having happier clients and using that as our platform for growth. We will do this by exploring how we can use 'value-based pricing' across all of our services, as a way of aligning our interests with those of our clients.

6

Alternative fees

In this chapter I am going to describe one route which, when combined with your understanding of competitive strategy and market positioning, can fully restore confidence in your prices, both for you and for your client. It can make you look forward to discussing fees rather than dreading it, because your fees will have a solid, logical and mutually beneficial foundation. We just need to begin by talking about house painters.

Example

You have decided to have the outside of your house painted. In terms of my model I would categorise this as Relationship Advice. It's not life threatening, but on the other hand you only want it done once, so there are more issues in play than just seeking the lowest price painters that you can find. With that in mind, you decide to obtain three quotes.

The first painter says that it will cost about £25,000. He hasn't ever seen your house, but he has chatted to you on the phone. If you want, he will put the estimate in writing (if he does you will notice quite a few assumptions and conditions surrounding his 'quote'). If you have any experience in these matters at all, then you will know that the actual cost will be quite a bit more than the quote. That's because unexpected events will arise as he paints the house (rotten wood needing to be replaced, rain causing delays in completion and so on).

The second quote you receive, after this painter has visited your house and walked around it chatting to you, is that it will cost £2,000 a day for the painters to be on site and painting your house. How many days will the job take? 'I don't know', says the painter, 'because there are lots of variables, there could be some rotten boards that need replacing once we start the job, and of course the weather will have an impact as well.' But not to worry, because at the end of the job the painter will total up the number of days taken and just multiply that by £2,000 to create the final bill. You instinctively realise that the painters have a great incentive to take their time painting your house, the longer they take the better for them.

The third painter is prepared to offer you an alternative fee arrangement, because he has both 'master painters' who have at least 10 years of on-the-job painting experience, and 'apprentice painters' who have up to two years of painting experience. As a result they can offer you a blended rate of £110 an hour which you will pay for both types of painter. How many hours will it take to paint your house? 'Well', this painter responds, 'we will know that once we have finished the job, won't we? Then we will just total up the number of hours we have worked, multiply it by £110 an hour, and there's your total.' You quickly work out that this painter has both an incentive to paint as slowly as possible *and* to use as many apprentices as possible.

At this point you order some paint and scaffolding and start painting the house yourself.

Let's be clear on this. If other people behaved towards us when pricing work in the way that most service firms have typically behaved towards their clients, we simply would not put up with the cost uncertainty. The absence of any agreed and certain budget would be a deal breaker. Clients of service firms have put up with our charging by the hour because there were no realistic alternatives for most Relationship Advice. It was as if all the painters formed a cartel and agreed only to charge on the basis of time, and only to give quotes (which contain lots of conditions and assumptions which would allow an escape for the painter) if pressed to do so.

Of course, it might be different if you were an estates manager, who had to arrange for 100 houses to be painted each year. Or if there was a sudden and unexpected downturn in the demand for house painting, so that many painters were sitting around idle and were keen to get work at almost any price. In both these cases, basic economic theory tells us that the power shifts in favour of the client and the natural use of that power is to demand a move away from uncontrolled, uncapped charging by the hour.

In my view, the era of service firms being able to simply charge for time has ended in the post-recession drive for value. For Rocket Science, charging by the hour fails to reflect the value that the expert delivers, and while recording time may be a useful way for a firm to check up on how busy people are, the time taken should be merely one factor in the actual bill that is delivered to the client. For Routine Work, fixed fees have been (rightly) the norm. It is in the area of Relationship Work that time-based charging has largely remained, and it is here that it is under greatest pressure from the clients. Keeping that in mind, we will focus on Relationship Advice in this chapter and examine the alternatives and how we might align the interests of the firm and the client.

OPTION 1 – FIXED FEES

The usual demand from clients who are looking for an alternative to charging by the hour is to require a fixed fee. This is a perfectly natural reaction, although the wrong one in my view. Moving to a fixed fee for a single transaction involves risk: for the firm and for the client. The risk for the firm is obvious – that the work involved in the matter may greatly exceed the quoted fee. That risk is in fact magnified in practice by the following factors:

■ The client has asked for fixed fee quotes from several competing firms, so the actual fixed fee ends up being reduced as the client plays one firm off against another. It starts unrealistically low.

■ Firms themselves are often very poor at producing realistic quotes (having neither the historic data nor the skill to quote) – they almost always 'come in low' in any case, so the fee is never realistic for the actual work that will be involved.

■ Firms often have little experience of project managing work against a fixed fee (which would require them to monitor cumulative spend against stages of the matter and adjust their work accordingly).

■ The client can behave badly, not putting any effort into speed and efficiency, insisting on every tiny detail being covered and passing to the firm work that it would have previously carried out itself (because it has a fixed fee, so why not?).

■ No matter that the actual transaction changes beyond recognition, the client can claim that the fee was fixed and is not to vary.

At first sight this seems to neatly transfer all risk to the firm from the client and appears to be a great deal for the client concerned. However, the reality is going to be somewhat different. When I have run exercises around this, I have discovered that clients are, quite instinctively, nervous about quality once they switch to a fixed fee for a task of uncertain size and duration. Of course, at one level, clients feel that they have bagged themselves a great deal. There is no risk on the client, is there? They have agreed a clear fee; there is no small print, so that is all that the client is going to pay. However, another part of their brain is cautioning: 'But what if it goes massively over budget? Will the service provider still carry on working at a high level? Will I still be able to get hold of people, will they answer the phone and will they finish the job properly?'

These are proper concerns. When you combine a fixed fee with a partner's typical inability to build a realistic quote (so that they *always* come in low) plus a bit of competition that is used by the client to drive the fixed fee lower still, you have a recipe for under-budgeting. The almost certain end result of this is that the deal goes 'underwater', which just means that the fixed fee has already been spent (on a time basis) so that any further work cannot be billed – it must be written off. This leaves work to be done, but no money to pay for it. It is likely that those people working on the matter will try to complete it with as little time expended as possible, will try to avoid client contact and, worst of all, may have to try to persuade others in their firm to work on the project after telling them that they cannot bill any fees to it because you have already blown through the budget.

In a typical service firm, people are going to behave in a professional manner. They will not walk away and refuse to help to complete the work – but it may not be handled to the same standard as a more normal matter where they are being paid for their efforts. That is particularly the case in firms which have given their people challenging budgets for recorded chargeable time, because that means that people working on matters that are underwater are going to risk missing targets and losing out on bonuses.

When partners are forced by their clients into agreeing fixed fees and then make losses on each transaction, a typical response is for them to start using assumptions and conditions attached to their fixed fee quotes (i.e. to stop them actually being fixed fees but to give the partner some escape routes if there is more work than anticipated). I have seen that reach somewhat epic proportions with a one-page fee quote referring to four closely typed pages of assumptions and exclusions. This is not a happy solution for anyone. The partner knows that the conditions attached to the fixed fee will quite likely be breached and so a higher fee will be charged, while the client will assume that the conditions would only be breached in extreme cases and believe it is most likely that the quoted fixed fee will be charged. There has been no meeting of minds about the actual fee and both sides are likely to be unhappy at the end. It is similar to the reason that I was taught, early on in my career, never to quote a range of fees – for example, 'The fee for this work will be between £50,000 and £80,000' – because the client hears £50,000 but the professional means 'It's going to be at least £80,000, probably a bit more'. This always ends with an unhappy client and a compromised fee at the end of the matter. So these 'fudges' around a fixed fee deal are not the solution.

However, there are situations where you can have fixed fees successfully in Relationship Advice:

1. Where there is a stream of similar transactions so that you can effectively average the cost and use that as a fixed fee. Of course,

that is the default situation for Routine Work, but it is not that common in Relationship Advice. So, if a single client has, for example, 10 transactions of a particular type each year, then rather than having to calculate individual fees you look at the last 10 transactions, average the cost and charge that (typically with a mark-up to reflect the value to the client of the fixed fee). You accept that you will win on some and lose on others, but that across the course of a year it should balance out (and if it doesn't then you might adjust the fees for the next year). In theory, you can do this across several clients (so for example, Client A has one transaction a year, Client B has six and Client C has three) as the same mathematical averaging should apply. Doing this would enable firms to have a competitive edge with clients who favoured a fixed fee over an hourly charge. However, the clients would need to understand that they are in a pool and the fixed fee is fixed. If they encounter an easy transaction where the work is much less than the fixed fee then they can't require a reduction, any more than someone who has insured their car can ask for their premium back at the year-end if they haven't made a claim. So you may have some situations where 'averaging' works, but it is not likely to be the universal answer to the problem of hourly based fees.

2. Using a retainer fee. This will be explained later in this chapter; it is where you agree a one-off annual fee covering a whole area of work for a client. For example, a client may have both Routine Work and Relationship Advice needs which it is sourcing from several different firms. One firm says, 'If you give us all of this work we will agree an annual fixed fee to cover all of your needs'.

3. Where the fixed fee represents a percentage charge based upon the value of a matter. In some sectors, it has been traditional that advisers' fees are calculated as a percentage of the deal value. In such cases, the firms involved have so arranged themselves and their teams that they can (on average) carry out the required work within the percentage fee and still make a healthy profit. A cynic might point out that, when professionals have to work within a fixed fee structure, then they do. I won't do that, because I think another factor is helpful for the professionals involved: that there is, intrinsic to percentage charges, an uplift over time because the value of deals goes up (typically) year-on-year. So as time goes on, 2% of a deal value rises and rises. That's helpful.

Apart from these exceptions, I am against fixed fees for Relationship Advice. As I mentioned in Chapter 1, I used to describe a fixed fee to clients as the equivalent of their going into an operating theatre for an operation, but insisting upon only buying two hours of the surgeon's time, and after that saying they wanted to be quickly sewn up and put back on the street. Because that was what was going to happen.

Let's turn now to the best alternative, project-based costing (PBC), and how that, combined with knowledge about your competitive strategy and market positioning, can restore your pricing confidence.

OPTION 2 – PROJECT-BASED COSTING

PBC is the solution to introducing value into the client relationship for Relationship Advice and giving the client budget certainty, while protecting the service provider from unforeseen events. It's not difficult or complex, particularly given that it is the method of pricing used for almost every type of project outside of traditional service firms and has been for many years.

In the real world it works for you and me when we are having our house painted or a new kitchen installed, and it works for corporations who are installing a new or updated IT system or for a public body having a school built or commissioning a nuclear power station. Partners in some service firms have traditionally challenged PBC by claiming that their work is more complex, more demanding (and expensive) than employing a painter. I get that. I understand that, at the start of a matter, the road ahead can be unclear, that no two transactions are exactly the same and that managing a cross-disciplinary team across many continents is intellectually demanding for a project that must be completed on time – but so is building a road bridge, a tunnel or a hospital, all of which would most likely be priced using PBC.

Creating and managing a price quote using PBC takes a bit more time than coming up with a rough quote and then charging by the hour. However, it's not much harder to do and firms that cannot master this will be at a great competitive disadvantage over those that can. I became fully converted to PBC when a global client introduced a new set of rules for all of its professional advisers, which were beautiful in their simplicity and power. To paraphrase them, this is all that they said:

- When we instruct you on a piece of work, you need to send us a fee quote and we will then issue you with a purchase order number (a 'PON').

- When you interim bill for any work relating to that matter, you need to quote the PON on your invoice or we will not pay it.

- The total of your invoices for a matter cannot exceed the value attributed to the relevant PON.

- If you would like to invoice for an amount in excess of the relevant PON, you just need to get a new PON from us and you have to request this before you carry out work in excess of the original PON. We reserve the right not to agree to such extra work.

In plain language they were simply saying, 'Give us a quote and keep to that. If something new comes up, check with us before you carry out any extra work'. I found it impossible to argue against these terms. Over time these rules were refined: for example, the client said that it wasn't necessary for one-off pieces of advice under $1000 (but of course we could not then bill over $1000), and the client accepted that there were times when it was better for us to carry out some urgent work before we were given a new PON, provided we told them about it as soon as possible afterwards and there was a good reason not to ask in advance of the work.

I cannot see why any client should not impose these terms upon their service firm providers. At the service firm it radically alters how they behave when working on a matter. In practice I have seen clients who said that their bills dropped by 15–20% once they implemented PBC. As advisers we were expected to give a detailed quote and then to take notice of it as we delivered the work. However, it also meant that we did not reduce our hourly fee rates by even one penny (so we could make as much profit as we did before, or more because we had massively fewer write-offs).

Successful PBC requires the following.

Proper scoping

Here is a fundamental change in behaviour. In order to properly instruct a service firm the client needs to be clear about what the client wants them to do. Let's go back to the example of the new fitted kitchen. The client really cannot do a good job of obtaining quotes if all he or she does is telephone three kitchen installers and have a brief conversation outlining the job. The kitchen installer needs to know the exact size and shape of the kitchen, the standard of fittings and equipment, the flooring and plumbing arrangements and whether they are doing all the work or not. They need to scope the job. The client may or may not have strong views on the kitchen and/or previous experience, but the installer needs to talk it through and explore the options so that they can produce a realistic plan and budget.

For proper scoping to take place, there needs to be an agreed process at the service firm end as well. For example, all those partners and others involved in a work type need to agree how work is to be carried out and what forms and procedures will be used at each stage. There is a real need for a standardised approach to the work or no two teams will scope, quote or deliver it in the same way. So you need to agree the list of questions that you will ask a client when they instruct you or request a quote, so that you know pretty much what they have in mind.

Creating a realistic quote

The construction of a detailed quote, with enough granularity for you to have confidence in the numbers, and for the client to be able to see what work is included and what is not, is the second stage of the process. A key element in being able to create realistic quotes is that you need to gather data on past transactions, create a database of these and have them available so that partners can use them when creating fresh quotes. This doesn't need to become a huge, IT-heavy exercise. Even using junior staff over a couple of weekends to examine completed matters can start to create some useful data.

Stage 2 means creating a work plan and associated cost that covers all of the work from the start of the matter until its conclusion. Let's anchor this in the new kitchen example. In stage 1 you talked about what was wanted where and about the various options available. If the client was new to this, you took time to explain what was involved, how long it would take and what the cost implications were of some of the choices being made. In stage 2 you produce a detailed written quote against that scope, which shows costs against each stage and might detail different options with different costs if it is relevant to do so (which will enable you to deal with any areas of uncertainty). How do you do this?

The answer is that you can only construct this quote if you examine previous work of a similar nature that you have completed, and use that previous experience to map the work involved and its associated costs. You don't have to be very granular here unless you have easy access to the data. A first step might be to divide the scope of work into sections and cost each section by comparing it with previous transactions that you have carried out. You will start to see ranges of costs. So you might see:

Transaction stage	Cost	Proposed quote
1	£17,200 to £24,100	£20,500
2	£2600 to £22,800	£4100 or £20,700*
3	£4600 to £5800	£4800
4	£5700 to £8600	£8600
5	£11,400 to £13,300	£12,200
TOTAL		£50,200 or £66,800*

In this example I have shown in stages 1, 3, 4 and 5 a typical range of costs incurred on previous transactions, and then you use your skill and judgement to see how the proposed transaction compares to the previous ones in order to come up with a reasonable estimate to put in your quote. In stage 2, you find from previous transactions there is a very wide range of costs. On further investigation you see that the ones at the lower end are all matters where there are no issues of a particular type – for example, there is an acquisition of another business but no tax issues. So here you give two quotes and say that the larger quote applies if the client wants tax advice (or the proposed transaction has issues that arise that require tax advice). This is how you deal with genuine uncertainties that cannot be clearly defined at the scoping stage. You show the client the cost without and with them. You do not quote a band of prices but you give two specific separate costs that apply in the two different circumstances.

This requires practice to get right and you are going to have to pay to learn. If you say that a particular stage of the transaction is going to cost £4860, but in actual fact you incur £6300 worth of time carrying it out, then you can only bill the client for £4860. It's exactly how you would expect to be treated by a tradesperson who gave you a quote for a fitted kitchen. You don't expect to pay £1440 more than the quote because the installer found it a more difficult job to carry out than expected.

One of the new skills that emerge once you start to use PBC is that you need to assemble a quote, which quite typically involves obtaining both a scope of work and an associated budget from colleagues or fellow partners in your firm. Gone are the days when, once the job has been won, colleagues from other disciplines in your firm pile in and perform their parts of the overall task with a focus on delivering the transaction on time, irrespective of cost. The lead partner suddenly becomes a buyer of professional services *on behalf of the client*! You will suddenly find lead partners negotiating with fellow partners over the size of their quotes compared to the size of the overall project. You might hear, 'Our total fee for this job is going to be £112,000; we are not going to spend £35,000 of that on the tax aspects, think again!' I believe it is this discipline that led to clients claiming that they were saving 15–20% of their spend. There was a discipline in creating a reliable and realistic quote and the lead partner was actually working on the client's behalf in making sure that it was fair and reasonable. Imagine having your whole house decorated and never discussing the cost in advance with the decorator. Wouldn't that mean that the final cost was much higher than if there is a rigorous scoping and costing stage in advance of work commencing? In practice you will find your clients awarding work to you on a much higher PBC quote than to a lower 'guesstimate' from a competitor. So a rough quote from a competitor of £100,000 would be (intuitively) rejected in favour of a PBC quote of £127,300 because the client understood that the 'quote' of £100,000 would be exceeded without any angst on the part of the competitor firm, but your quote of £127,300 was serious, deliverable and you are committed to delivering on it.

Agreeing the quote

What happens next moves us into value-based billing for Relationship Advice. The client receives the quote from you and one option is that they are happy with the scope of the work described and the accompanying fee, which means that the client considers that the value delivered equals the fee being charged. This should often be the case as you improve your skills in scoping and then quoting for pieces of work – but, of course, that is not always going to be the case. The client might consider that the fee quoted is too high. Either they will contact you about the quote, or you need to follow up with the client and check that they are happy. At this point a vast gulf in pricing expectations might emerge. This is a good thing, because it avoids the much more typical situation where there has not been a meeting of minds over the scope of work or the fee, but this is only discovered towards the end of the matter when fees are greatly in excess of the client's expectations and both you and the client then have a real problem. Once you have a conversation with a client who was surprised by the size of your proposed fee, there are only three options:

1. After carefully examining the work you are planning to do for the fee and discussing this with you, the client comes to the conclusion that the planned work and scope actually are necessary and agrees to the higher fee. Once again, this means that you have ended up with value-based billing.

2. You find that the client expected a fee much lower than your quote. You explain that while you cannot do the amount of work that you had planned within the client's budget, you could do a different job and effectively tell the client what parts of the existing scope you could deliver for the budget they have in mind. In other words, you cut the work to match the fee that the client wants to pay. Again, you have now reached a value-billing situation.

3. You are able to convince the client that nobody could carry out a safe piece of work for their planned budget figure, and while you may be able to cut back from your initial quote you are not going to be able to do a reasonably satisfactory piece of work within the client's budget. As a result, you propose cutting back the work to what you consider to be the absolute minimum, for a fee which is a compromise amount between your original quote and the client's planned budget. If the client accepts your arguments, then again you have reached a value-billing situation where you agree to carry out work which the client values for the amount of the compromise fee.

What is perhaps most interesting about this negotiation stage is that clients become accepting of the need to vary the scope of work if there is to be a change in the fee quote. Previously, when round-figure guesstimates are provided to clients, they respond by negotiating in round figures as well. For example, after a guesstimate of £100,000 the client is quite likely to respond by saying they couldn't spend more than £80,000, and then there might be a compromise somewhere between £80,000 and £100,000 – but all without there being any variation in the scope of work (which is wholly unclear anyway). Contrast this with the negotiation that occurred when a detailed PBC was delivered and the client said they didn't want to pay £14,300 for the discovery element of a transaction, in which case you can reduce the amount of discovery work involved and reduce the fee to perhaps £12,200. Not only are negotiations being carried out with much more granularity, but they are clearly linked to changes in the scope – and that is the absolute mantra for negotiation of price. Any change in the price requires a change in the scope of work.

This third phase, when you seek to agree the scope of the work and your fee with the client at a very early stage (either before work has started, or in the first few days), is the real benefit of PBC. It means that you have agreed both your fee and the planned scope of work (or the revised plan scope of work agreed with the client), so there is no possibility of there being any argument about your fee at the end of the matter. Your fee has been agreed and this means you have the opportunity to avoid write-offs or delays when an unexpectedly high fee is received by the client. Perhaps most importantly, my experience has been that PBC was the highest driver of client satisfaction ever discovered. Partners, who devote such time, energy and expertise towards delivering a fantastic service for their clients, seldom realise that their efforts have counted for nought if they go over budget. It reflects very badly upon their expertise and professionalism.

The key issue with PBC is that once you have an agreed scope and fee, any changes have to be agreed in advance of additional work being carried out, and have to be in return for a clear and specified additional fee. That takes us to the fourth stage of PBC.

Delivery

In the delivery phase, the partner needs to project manage the work against the scope and the fee. This requires skills that many partners lack. While they may be adroit at managing a team in order to deliver the required solution for the client, they may well not have been trained in how to do that in an efficient way and having regard to the cost of delivery. It is much more common for the focus to be on achieving the desired end result, rather than checking on whether the project is running to a pre-agreed budget. There was a time when clients accepted that this was the priority, but those times have passed. In one case, a firm was planning to announce its new project management skills to its clients, only to find out that several existing clients expressed their horror at this, saying: 'We had assumed that you were using project management already, and are surprised to hear you say that this is a new skill that you are introducing!'

There are a number of important elements for successful project management of both the work and its associated budget:

- You must have in place clear processes for delivery of the work with precedents, checklists and agreed procedures for every stage. You cannot have a system where every partner has their own methodology, or you will be unable to create accurate quotes and then deliver against them. Clients assume that firms already have all this in place so that there can be quality controls, so if you do not already have this, then this is the opportunity to capture best practice and document it.

- You need to be able to correlate work carried out against the relevant part of the budget, which is (surprisingly) not that common in standard time recording systems. There is little point in assigning time to 'meetings' or 'drafting' if it is not clear what part of the overall task is being handled. At its simplest, if you can envision the overall piece of work as having six stages, then you will have scoped and costed the work attached to each stage separately, and you now need to track the actual work carried out to those stages. You need to keep records of actual performance against budget because if, for example, you typically price stage one of a piece of work at £13,250 but it regularly costs £16,800 of time, then you need either to raise the price or find ways of being more efficient in carrying out stage one. This iterative process, where you continually learn and so refine your price estimates, is important and in fact is extremely widespread outside of the service sector.

- The lead partner on a matter may be great at their professional skill, but may well not be adept at keeping the whole team to budget. They may not even want to become involved in this management task. Firms essentially have two choices here: either to upskill the existing team with project management skills, or to recruit into the team 'outsiders' whose primary skill is project management. Certainly I have witnessed real failures where firms attempted to retrain experienced partners so as to add project management to their skill set. Attempt number two was then to train more junior members of each team because those people were still trying to 'make their way' in the firm and seemed much more amenable to learning something new. The alternative is to recruit 'real' project managers into the team (I slightly incline to this as a preference): the challenge then is for the rest of the team to be prepared to 'be project managed' and also to persuade clients to pay for the project manager (when they would, by default, have paid for a junior existing team member to do that work). I have heard that, over a relatively short timescale, clients will become prepared to pay for these separate project managers once they have seen at first-hand how much value they bring. The cost of these project managers may then be openly built into quotes to clients.

- Where delivery involves cross-functional teams, then the lead partner on the matter needs to keep all of the teams to their original quote and refuse to pay them a penny more (no matter how much time they have put onto the file) unless they have followed the correct procedures to obtain agreement from the client to an increase. So the lead partner performs a really crucial role in maintaining price discipline.

- PBC is not a fixed fee. It is a fee for the particular scope of work that has been agreed with the client. New issues (outside of the existing scope) may well arise during the course of the matter. In the past, partners typically carried out the extra work (maybe motivated by the desire to do a thorough job or to complete by a deadline) and then would seek to add on the extra cost at the end of the job. That felt fine for the partner, but surprised and annoyed the client. The promise of PBC is that, when additional issues arise, the client will be notified of the *proposed* extra work and of its cost *before any extra fees are incurred.* This means that the client stays in control of the scope and of the budget. When I first rolled out PBC at my own firm I had assumed that it was this forewarning that was important – that we would advise the client of the additional problem and its solution cost and, albeit after some internal discussions to allocate a higher budget, we would then be told to go ahead. I was wrong. In half the cases that I experienced, the client said, 'No, don't do the extra work and just keep to the original budget'. There were a variety of reasons for this. Some said that they would do the extra work themselves; some said that the relevant business unit knew about the issue and it had been factored into the price; others said that after thinking about it they had decided just to take a risk on it, and could we just write to them confirming that we had raised the issue but they had told us not to address it (so that we could not be accused afterwards of missing the point or of being negligent). How interesting, because in all these cases my previous practice would have been to carry out the extra work and discuss the extra cost at the end, and here were half the clients saying they didn't want that. The other half were properly forewarned and agreed to a higher fee.

■ To make PBC work, the professional has to be alert to 'scope creep', where the amount of work involved grows bit by bit so that there is more time recorded than can be charged to the client. This is really about keeping an eye on the original scope and comparing that with the work being carried out. Sometimes the client will ask you to add in something that was not in the original scope, or in response to you serving a notice of variation the client will acknowledge the extra work but ask you to do it for free as a favour. If this happens and you are prepared to agree to the client's request, then I believe that there are two important steps to take. The first is still to prepare a proper notice of variation and associated extra fee and send it to the client together with a credit note for the same amount. This emphasises to the client that it is a real financial concession that is being given (and so that the actual write-off against the client can be recorded in your books, which becomes important when you are trying to compare the profitability of different clients). The second is to ask for a favour in return. This is the usual trading that we examined in Chapter 4. You will soon learn which clients ask more than others and be able to refuse: 'I honestly can't as I have already written off £12,800 of unplanned extras on this matter'; or you will look for truly valuable swaps: 'I can only write off another £2400 if you can get me some work from your French subsidiary, so that I have something to show to my managing partner.'

■ As you gain in experience your quotes will become more accurate, and (based upon your actual experiences) you might start to build in an amount on each matter for 'contingencies' and be able to explain to the client that it will be valuable for both of you. It means that you don't have to request additional fees for relatively small changes and the client doesn't have to keep getting authority to amend the budget (you need to be clear that if the contingency is not actually used, then it will not be billed).

■ A quote prepared using PBC should not be an optimistically low figure. It should be a realistic fee that you expect to be sufficient in the vast majority of cases. You can keep yourself honest on this by keeping records and circulating them around the teams in the firm, showing in what percentage of cases you completed work within the original PBC fee. If it's less than 80% of the time then you need to work harder on your quotes. If clients see that you continually have to increase your PBC quotes because 'unexpected' extra work arises, then they can properly call this a sham.

When facing real uncertainty

Even for firms that adopt PBC fully, there might be areas of work where the partners claim there is so much uncertainty about how it will turn out that it is impossible for a PBC quote to be prepared. Examples might be helping a client to address a sudden crisis, handle a piece of litigation or escape from an existing contractual obligation. You cannot know how this will play out, how any other parties involved will react and therefore whether this matter is going to last for a few days or over several years. So, how can you give an accurate quote for the cost? Again we are assuming that we are in the realm of Relationship Advice.

Here I found that clients do not expect you to have a crystal ball and be able to predict how the future will unfold. They are probably as aware as you are of the amount of uncertainty. However, that doesn't mean that they see you as completely off the hook on cost so that you can now just revert to hourly based charging and work out the total cost by adding up all the interim bills at the end. What you can do is to use your skill and judgement to create a plan for the matter right from now until its end (be that final resolution, a mediated agreement or whatever). You can show the activity and cost on a month-by-month basis from now until that end. This enables you and the client to discuss the ideal solution. It acts like a decision tree and enables your client to make decisions about the potential future options available. Importantly, it shows the client the monthly cost all the way to completion (even if that is several years away), so the client can see the maximum likely cost.

Of course, as the matter progresses, new information will arise and there may be unexpected events. All that is required is for you to recast the plan, incorporating that new information or event, and show the new monthly cost up until completion. This may or may not mean that the client has to revisit the original decision. What it does mean is that the client has as much information as possible about cost and outcomes. It also means that the partner is under an obligation to keep matters on target against the plan agreed with the client and, just as with the other examples of PBC, it means the partner will have to put real effort into managing the matter against the planned scope of work and cost for each month. Yet again, the client will feel that they are in control and the partner will be putting serious effort into managing the cost. Contrast that with the more typical situation where, because the outcome is uncertain, the partner lapses into unfettered monthly billing, only being accountable for the actual work undertaken during that month, rather than the final total cost.

The payoff

If you adopt a PBC approach to your quotations, and then deliver against them, you will have much happier clients. They will also have spent less money per transaction because the scope will have been refined to suit exactly what they wanted (which can often be less than the partner would have planned), and then the partner will need to manage the work involved so that it matches the fee, rather than overrunning and hoping to collect extra at the end. All other things being equal, clients will be spending less money, and so you might wonder whether PBC is such a good idea for the firm. In my experience it is, not just because it avoids the huge number of write-offs that take place when the firm overruns the original quote and then is unable to recover the excess from the client. One of the biggest benefits was the winning of much more work from clients either because we had an amazing story to tell (backed up by facts and figures) when we were involved in a beauty parade, or simply because existing clients were more than happy to send us more work because we kept to budget (and none of their other advisers had ever done that!).

Of course this was not just earning a great reputation with existing clients, but they told others, who were equally impressed with this new approach. We regained our confidence and this was of huge value. When clients asked us to match offers from our competitors we refused to do so. We pointed out that those offers were unclear in scope and there was almost no chance that the competitor would bring in the work within the guesstimate they had given. The clients knew that we were right, and we saw many examples where we beat a lower-priced competitor with our much higher PBC quote simply because the client felt safe in our hands. In addition, our partners started to take pride in delivering within (even slightly under) the agreed budget. I well remember one of our best partners saying how pleased she was that she had brought in three extremely complex global pieces of work for a client within 1.5% of the original quotes. For partners to be taking real pride in delivering to budget, and not just being concerned about the quality of delivery, was pretty amazing.

OPTION 3 – BLENDED RATES

For some reason, procurement people seem pretty keen on blended rates, as do some partners. The idea behind a blended rate is relatively straightforward. In the simplest form, you take an average of the hourly rates of the various levels of staff involved in a piece of work. For example, if you have a partner on £400 an hour, a senior associate on £300 an hour and an associate on £200 an hour, then you could create a blended rate of £300 an hour and would say that all of these professionals will be charged at that amount, irrespective of whether the work is carried out by a partner or an associate. Alternatively, you may say that you anticipate a piece of work having 10% of partner time, 60% of senior associate time and 30% of associate time, which would lead to an average rate of £280 an hour. I think partners find this attractive because it involves offering the client what appears to be a lower hourly rate than the partner's rate; and procurement like it because it enables them to compare one firm with another and then try to negotiate everybody down to the lowest figure that they are offered.

However, the end result is that the interests of the firm and the client are diametrically opposed. After agreeing a blended rate it is in the interests of the firm to use as many junior staff as they can (because they will be over-remunerated) and for the client to try to deal only with partners.

For repetitive areas of advice, I have seen blended rates operate relatively successfully (for example, where a client asked for small pieces of advice regularly). In such a case a PBC approach may be overly complex, simply because of the small size of each individual piece of advice that is needed. However, I think it a rather confusing solution.

OPTION 4 – CAPPED FEES

Capped fees are very similar to fixed fees, except they have the ability to be more amusing. In theory a capped fee sets a maximum that can be charged for a particular piece of work which is then billed (monthly) upon the basis of the actual time involved. If the total of the actual hourly charges is *less* than the agreed capped fee then the total of the hourly charges is billed to the client, but if there is an excess of total time over the agreed capped fee then the excess has to be written off. In that sense it is a one-way bet, which only the client might win if the actual work involved in the matter is less than anticipated. Just as with fixed fees, clients who are seeking capped fees will often obtain several quotes and then use the quotes to hammer the price down, so the final capped fee is often set at an unrealistically low level in any case.

These fees are amusing because if you ask partners who have carried out work on a capped fee deal if they have *ever* come in under the cap, then they laugh because they realise they never have (or almost never have). In other words, it is simply another way of dressing up a fixed fee deal, and in practice the firms almost always overrun and write off the excess.

So I would say no to a client who requests a capped fee because it has the same problems as a fixed fee in terms of getting matters completed to a satisfactory level once the deal is underwater. You might have an exception if the cap was set at a generous level and you then agreed to share savings under the cap 50:50. For example, if you expect a matter to cost £100,000, you might set a cap of £110,000 and then work hard with the client to bring in the matter under that figure. If you are actually able to complete the matter with a time charge of £90,000 then you would bill £100,000 to the client, thus sharing equally the saving of £20,000. Other than that, it is a matter of saying no to clients who ask for capped fees, but offering them instead a PBC approach which keeps them in control without unduly punishing the firm.

OPTION 5 – ANNUAL RETAINERS

An annual retainer is where a service firm agrees to undertake an area of a client's work (or even all of the work that the client is putting out to external advisers) for a single annual fee which is typically divided into 12 parts and paid monthly. The client has the benefit of certainty and a fixed fee and may well receive a discount in return for passing all work to a single adviser. Imagine a client who has a panel of three firms and has an annual spend of £1 million across them: one firm might offer to carry out all of the work for a fixed annual fee of £900,000.

I have personal experience of setting up this type of arrangement, having negotiated and then managed a deal that provided services to a client for a single fee across more than 30 countries. I might say, 'Don't try this at home' due to the difficulty of implementation in its first year, but in fact the arrangement became hugely successful for both parties and saved costs year-on-year for the client while being properly profitable for the firm. There are a number of factors that are preconditions to making retainer fees work:

- There needs to be a real atmosphere of collaboration between firm and client, so that both parties want to make it work and neither party is seeking to take unfair advantage of the other. This is important. I received some great advice from another client with whom we entered into a retainer fee, which was: 'Don't ever do this unless you know and like the client.' With a retainer fee you have created an 'all-you-can-eat buffet' and you either need stop-loss provisions in the contract (so that the retainer is only fixed if certain conditions are met and total spend does not exceed a set amount), or you need a reasonable client.
- You need to use PBC internally to make sure that you control overall cost against the monthly retainer budget.
- After the fee is agreed you should launch a series of cost-saving initiatives which are now effectively in both of your interests. By continuing to cut the costs of actual delivery it will enable you to reduce the annual retainer fee year-on-year, whereas if you were making losses (the work carried out was greatly in excess of the annual fee) then of course you would cease to act at some point. That is why it is also in the interests of the client to make these schemes work. If the chosen firm makes losses it will bow out, and the client has to start again with new advisers.

Retainer fees reward first-mover advantage. If you are on a panel of three firms then it can be very much in your interest to talk to the client about an annual retainer fee if it excludes the other two firms. In my experience, only one person gets to have this conversation.

OPTION 6 – CONTINGENT FEES

A contingent fee is one which may or may not be charged. It is often requested by clients who are embarking on a risky venture which may or may not take place. For example, a client might be bidding on a project and will need substantial amounts of advice from all of its professional advisers in making that bid. However, other people may be bidding and there is no guarantee that the client will be successful. If they are not successful, they may want their advisers to waive all or part of their fees so as to reduce the cost of failure for them.

There are important factors that you need to consider if you are asked to provide work on a contingent fee basis. More importantly, what are the chances of failure? The more speculative the matter is for the client, the higher risk the professional adviser is taking by offering a contingent fee, and where there is high risk it is much more reasonable for the professional to require an uplift in fees if the matter proceeds. A useful way of structuring this, which shows that the adviser has 'skin in the game', is to have a staged contingency which will limit exposure. For example, you might divide a transaction into four stages in the knowledge that it could fail at any of those stages. You could then offer to have your fees on stage 1 as being 100% contingent, but if stage 1 is passed then fees for stage 1 are invoiced to the client. Stage 2 is 70% contingent, stage 3 is 50% contingent and stage 4 is 25% contingent. Alternatively, you might just say that 40% of your fees are contingent on a transaction, having worked out that the 60% this leaves will more or less cover your costs.

Whatever route you take, there should be a reward to reflect the contingency that you are taking. For example, you might say that in return for having part of your fees contingent, should the matter proceed to completion then your fee will be the budgeted amount (calculated using PBC) plus 30%. You need to calculate the uplift based upon your assessment of the risk that you are taking. The greater the risk, the higher the uplift. For example, if you believe that there is a 33% chance that the matter will abort (so that you will receive no fee at all) then the fee charged for success should be increased by 50%. You can see this by looking at an example of a matter where the fees are going to be £100,000 but you are asked to make them contingent (and your best guess is that there is a one-third chance that the matter will fail). In normal circumstances, if you had three of these in a row, then you would have earned £300,000. If one is going to fail then you need to earn £150,000 on each of the others to get back to where you started – which means a 50% uplift.

If the contingent element is 50% (i.e. if the matter aborts you will charge half the accrued time) then the required uplift is 25%. In all cases I have assumed that the matter becomes abortive after all of the work has been carried out. If that is not the case, then that too reduces the required uplift. As you can see, you may need help in calculating the variables in order to offer a contingency and an uplift which is fair to the client and commercially realistic for you.

There are areas of work where contingent fees have become the norm, but they can be dangerous for the firm if too much of its income is put at risk. In addition, there should be an assessment year-on-year of the impact of contingent fees and their associated uplifts – in other words, was it worth it? If not, they need to be adjusted to make sure that it is. I understand that in times of famine, clients become less prepared to offer an uplift in fees for success, working on the basis that many firms will be prepared to offer contingency. However, I do believe that this is a line the partner has to draw because without an uplift, and given that some of these transactions are going to fail, it means that on average a potentially large percentage reduction has been given. That reduction could mean that one abortive matter cancels out all of the profit on the work that is successful and completes.

OPTION 7 – SUCCESS-BASED FEES

Again, some clients seem to like to link the final fee charged to the outcome of the particular transaction being advised upon. As we have seen, that link is best practice when it comes to Rocket Science, and can be a mechanical variation for Routine Work (for example, the fixed fee is increased by 1% for every day saved in the timetable of the matter). For Relationship Advice, one good approach is to create a 'poor, good and great' table which documents what different outcomes look like, and offers an uplift or discount of 20% (or whatever percentage is agreed in advance) tied into descriptions of particular outcomes. A simplified example is shown below for an acquisition, where time has been taken to identify (in words) what the different results look like:

Factor	Poor result	Good result	Great result
1. Completion date	After 30 April	In April	Before 1 April
2. Warranty period	Under 2 years	2 years	Over 2 years
3. Cap on warranty	Under £3 million	£3 million to £4 million	Over £4 million
4. Key personnel	<4 retained	4 retained	>4 retained
5. Actual discount obtained from due diligence exercise	Under £200,00	£200,000 to £300,000	Over £300,000

In practice this means that the client and the partner must spend some time at the start of the matter so that they can document the most important factors for the client and describe the different levels of outcome. This is really valuable for the partner because they might guess what those factors are and may well not get them right. Having them documented and circulated to the whole team working on the matter makes a real difference to their understanding of what a great result is, so that they can really direct their efforts to achieving that. Once the matter is finished, the client and partner meet again and the client decides how the actually achieved outcomes measure against the table, on the basis that if they are all 'poor' then the PBC fee is reduced by 20%, if they are 'good' the full PBC fee is paid, and if they are 'great' then the fee will be the PBC fee plus 20%. Typically, the outcomes will not all be in one column so the fee might be increased by, say, 7% for partial achievement of 'great'. This is a great way for advisers to learn much more about the client's objectives and become better and better over time at delivering against them.

Due to the overhead in time of putting these types of success fees together, I consider they are appropriate only where the client is keen on them and the transaction is large enough to merit the time. If those two conditions are met then they offer a real opportunity for the firm to dramatically increase its profitability and to have value-based billed for Relationship Advice.

I have seen some firms enthusiastically embrace combinations of contingent and success fees and make them part of the skill set that they offer to their clients. Doing this successfully requires real pricing sophistication, the ability to understand the risk in the contingency and the value of success to each individual client, but armed with that skill the firm has something very differentiating to offer its clients. We will address this in more detail when we examine the issue of pricing capabilities in Chapter 11.

OPTION 8 – DISCOUNTED HOURLY RATES

You might find it surprising that I am writing about discounted hourly rates in a chapter about alternative fees. It's because, in response to requests from clients for 'alternative fee structures', I have quite regularly seen responses offering a discount off the planned hourly rates. So, for the sake of clarity, it's worth explaining: 10% off hourly rates is not an alternative fee proposal; nor is 15% off.

However, what about clients' demands for immediate discounts off hourly rates? Clients are going to demand them, in particular if they are large clients (or, in my experience, if they are US clients). For example, I have heard: 'We would not deal with any adviser who does not offer us at least 10%/15% off their standard rates.' The primary solution is to have a standard rate card which allows for discounts without causing undue damage to profitability (again a topic addressed in Chapter 11). Effectively your headline rates have to start high enough so that you can cope with clients who insist on 10% or 15% as a starter discount. You should also tie the discount given to a particular level of spend, so you have a right to end the discount if fees do not reach a pre-agreed level. My response to such demands has been to say that this level of discount is reserved for clients who spend at least, say, £500,000 per year and that the rates will be revised if the client does not reach that level within a set period of time.

THE CONFIDENT PARTNER

By this stage I want you to start having some real confidence in your pricing. This comes from:

- Using cost-plus pricing so that you understand your breakeven point or the floor under which you should not drop.
- Positioning your firm against its most direct competitors, understanding why you are going to charge more than certain firms and having good reasons that justify the premium (or adopting a lowest price strategy and understanding the implications of that for your cost base).
- Segmenting your offer of services (more about this in Chapter 8) so that you don't simply have one level of service, but you have varied services and prices that appeal to different segments of the overall marketplace.
- Being proud to use PBC as the main method of calculating your prices for Relationship Advice, creating budgets in which you have real confidence of achieving; using value billing for Rocket Science and reserving fixed fees for Routine Work.

With this new level of confidence, you will be ready to look at how you can better understand how clients value your services and use this as a way of creating more value and higher prices, which is covered in Chapter 8. Before that, I want to examine some common pricing tactics and how you might use these in your business.

Pricing tactics

Show the discount

Lower rate does not equal less spend

Act for clients that you like (not the bullies)

From tactics to strategy

When I teach pricing on Executive Education courses, I have noticed that the most feverish note-taking occurs once I start talking about the tactical issues surrounding price. People who are having day-to-day conversations with their clients about pricing and money are keen to have instant solutions that they can put into practice immediately the course finishes.

The reality is that, for most partners, conversations about pricing are mainly at the tactical level during their everyday contact with their clients, and this is when speed and good ideas are at a real premium. Tactical solutions certainly have a place, although they are no substitute for a clear business and pricing strategy. I always warn that overreliance on short-term tactics can deflect effort which is better put into strategy formulation and execution. However, subject to that overall warning, I have set out in this chapter a number of useful tactics which I have found to be valuable in the areas of Relationship Advice or Routine Work.

FREE, NOT CHEAP

It can be very tempting to price low on the first deal with a new client, or for a new area of work with an existing client, with the view that this will lead to a long and profitable relationship. While great in theory, in practice this is a bad tactical move. Entering into a new relationship with a heavily discounted price can position you as a low-cost provider and is a recipe for an unpleasant surprise when you try to charge your normal rates later. For example, let's say that you are approached by client and you assess after scoping that the particular piece of work will cost £25,740. It is a mistake simply to offer to do it for £15,000. The next time that they have a similar job they will be anticipating a fee of only £15,000, and it would be a shock if you then proceed to charge the normal rate of £25,740. You won the work under false pretences. The same applies when quoting hourly rates – *don't start low* under the illusion that you can increase rates later. This almost never happens; if anything, subsequent negotiations bring the rates lower still.

It is much better to find a piece of work you are prepared to do for free. Call it a gift; and the size of the gift will depend upon the size of the potential prize that is available from this client, because then the client is under no illusion that the next job will not be at the same price. The aim of this approach is to have the client understand that this gift is your initial investment in the relationship.

There are alternatives around this 'impressing a new client' scenario:

- Say that the price is £25,740, but as this is the first time that you have worked on this job you will reduce this to £15,000 as a one-off to show investment in the relationship. That achieves the same effect of making clear that the true price is £25,740.

- If your pricing is a substantial premium above others, then you could put part of it at risk, for example by saying that your fee is £25,740 but that you intend billing £15,000 until they confirm that they are wholly satisfied with what you delivered, in which case you will then, and only then, bill the balance of £10,740.

Whenever possible, I favour the free approach, because it shows a readiness to invest in a future relationship, create goodwill and create an offer that the client finds difficult to turn down (which is important in the very early stages of the relationship).

However, some service firms only have very large projects – for example, they may organise conferences and it would simply cost too much to 'give one free'. If this is the case, it will be essential to develop taster products such as workshops or training sessions which can be given for free as a way for the client to try them out. It is then important to put a cash value on the free service. For example, state that the normal cost for a workshop would be £5000, but it is being provided free of charge so the client has an opportunity to see you and your service firm in action.

While free services represent real value to the client, they may well cost the service provider absolutely nothing. With an existing business it may be just a matter of the existing team 'fitting in' this extra (free) work in the same way that they might spend time on marketing activities or on administration. I have seen major offers being made which were effectively using the time that would otherwise have been spent in marketing to a potential client, so creating a win-win position.

In some cases, during the final stages of negotiation to acquire a new client, discounts are required to complete a deal. I've seen partners give away vast percentages of the total profit in order to get the matter across the line. If some form of sweetener is needed then it is important that anything offered is *limited in time*. For example, it is better to discount all fees in the first three months by 25% while the client settles into your systems (the equivalent of investing in the relationship), rather than reducing the rates of charge by 5%, because that 5% will be lost forever.

SHOW THE PRICE OF ADDED VALUE

We love listing all of the added value services that we provide for free, don't we? We can become very generous when listing the added value that we will provide to clients because in some sense it doesn't appear to be real money. However, as we will see when we start analysing client profitability in Chapter 11, the total cost of value-added services can mean the difference between profit and loss.

A useful technique is to put a clear price on added value – for example, to offer to give £10,000 worth of free training rather than to say that there will be three days of free training. Once you start doing this you can see how it starts to add up. An alternative to fairly unlimited and unstructured added value is to create a 'value-added account'. This is held in your custody, into which a percentage of a client's spend is deposited for use towards the added-value offerings. For example, you can tell your client that, subject to a minimum spend of £100,000, 2.5% of fees invoiced each year would be credited into a value-added account, which could be drawn down by the client to take free services for them and their team. Clients tend to value this more than a discount or a rebate and it costs less to provide. Apart from placing a clear ceiling on the cost of added value, it also brings in another factor that is useful in any negotiation: if your client is looking to reduce spend then you can in return reduce the amount of added value being given, allowing you to recover some of the lost margin.

GIVE THE CLIENT OPTIONS

There are times when you aren't able to create a clear project plan and cost, either because of the inability to have a proper scoping conversation or genuine uncertainty about the future path of the work. In those cases the fee that you quote may be rejected out of hand as way too high or too low, simply because it isn't clear what scale of work the client wants.

In these situations the solution is to make three different offers to the client:

1. the first at the top end, which is comprehensive and expensive (gold);
2. the second in the middle range (silver);
3. a third minimum offer (bronze).

This approach works well because the client will focus on one of these offers and then, after some refinement of the scoping, you can create an agreed project plan and budget.

When I originally started using this tactical solution it was very common for clients to choose the middle, silver, offer and to develop detail around that. However, I have noticed that more recently clients gravitate towards the minimum (bronze) offer, developing a detailed plan around that. This affirms the original concern that if you had produced a single option it might well have been very far away from the client's expectation, and so lead to an immediate rejection.

DEALING WITH LOWBALLING

Every professional I have ever met has their own horror stories of how they lost a piece of work to a good competitor who came in at a ridiculously low price. To take quite a typical example, if you were to create a PBC quote of £112,000, a good competitor might offer a fixed fee of £60,000. Strangely, I have never met a person who owned up to delivering lowballing quotes, so I do wonder whether some of these have been made up by clients.

However, be they 100% real or not, there is clearly an issue here. How should you respond when you are met with an offer from a good competitor which would be something like half of your quote? There are several effective responses you can use, and none of them involve you dramatically reducing your price or meeting the price of the competitor (this would simply cause a race to the bottom in your marketplace). Quite often it is the client who contacts the partner, wielding the lowball quote and asking for it to be matched. The crucial point to notice in such a case is that the client *has* called you. If the lowball quote was so obviously the right solution then why doesn't the client simply accept the quote? The reason is that the client is similarly unconvinced (or specifically wants you to carry out the work), which means that you have some options.

The way to respond to these quotes is as follows:

- **Exploit the fact that it's too good to be true.** When the client receives a lowball quote they are pleased to have this in their hands, but also nervous about accepting it. They know this is an unrealistically low quote, and the very fact that they have contacted you is a strong indicator that they would rather you did the work than the other firm and they are just trying to see how you will react to it. In a sense this is a no-lose telephone conversation for the client, who is hoping to use the low quote as leverage against you. If they really wanted to go with the other firm then they would have accepted their quote.

In response you need to explore the quote and their nervousness about it. You should start by saying that there is no way you can match that quote and indeed you doubt that the other firm can do anything like a proper piece of work for that money. The risk for the client is that they may actually get what they pay for, which would be very little senior-level involvement, every corner cut and most likely attempts by the other firm to actually increase the price after they have been instructed. If you are using a PBC quote then you can emphasise that the client can see exactly what is included in your scope of work, and you can be pretty sure that the competitor's quote is much less clear about the scope of work that will be covered for the quoted fee. After discussing these downsides with the client, you should end by saying that while you obviously cannot match the quote, you could reduce your total fee if you could work with the client on changing the scope. If the lowest fee was most important to them, you can go through the detailed quote line-by-line and see what could be cut out safely. In my experience this often works.

■ **You can argue with the client that the quote they are using against you is not for a fixed fee**. It is hazy and unspecific and either will dramatically increase or will be based upon leaving out much of the planned work. At that point the client will be quick to reassure you that the firm has promised a fully fixed fee; in which case I have, in the past, generously offered to send them over a short contract document which ties the opposing firm into the fee being absolutely (and without exception) a fixed fee. This helpful tactic means that the client will either end up with an absolutely fixed fee (and the lowballing firm will have to keep to that unrealistic fee) or, and this has happened in several cases, the other firm will start trying to put in exceptions and assumptions, in which case the client realises that the lowballing quote was not the fixed fee that they had assumed.

■ **You can't win them all**. There will be cases where the former arguments do not work with the client and they end up taking a much lower quote from a competitor. When you lose business to a lowball quote, the most important thing is that you make an appointment to see the client over a coffee at a time when you estimate the matter will have been completed. You need to know how it worked out for the client. There are essentially only three answers that the client can give you:

1. They will say that they received a fantastic piece of work, the firm kept to the quote, they're very pleased and looking forward to instructing that firm again. I have personally never witnessed this answer, but if it occurs then it's really important that you understand how and why. If a good competitor has learnt how to deliver a fantastic service at a significantly lower price then you need to know about it, and you need to learn.

2. The client will say that they received a terrible service – in effect they got what they paid for. I've heard clients say that they couldn't get hold of the key partner at all and that the team who were supposedly dealing with the work at the firm became severely distracted when another matter came in (generally at a better price). While it was lower cost, it was also low quality. In such a case, your visit reinforces the client's feeling they should not instruct that firm again, which is good news for you, your firm and your industry. You might also ask the client if they would act as 'referee' if another client receives such a lowball quote (i.e. to tell that client what the service from the lowballing competitor was really like).

3. The client could say that the price went up considerably (usually to a price similar to or in excess of your price) because the competitor firm kept adding extras or saying things that were essential were out of the original scope and needed to be added. The client feels misled and again, your visit is a good opportunity to make sure they don't forget this and don't fall for the same trick again (and may act as a referee).

Lowballing often occurs because a firm can see a gap in its workload and (for the short term at least) rationalises that work at any price is better than no work at all – and actually that is correct in profit terms in the very short term. Lowballing is bad for an industry because it is unsustainable, yet clients quickly become used to lower prices and start to expect them on a permanent basis.

SUPPORTING A CLIENT IN DISTRESS

Sometimes you will be approached by a client who is looking for some sort of special favour from you, typically leveraged off bad market conditions for them or a companywide cost-cutting initiative. It is in the nature of the professional relationship that you sometimes have to take the rough with the smooth and it will be a rare partner who is not receptive to doing something to support a client who has a real need.

However, the worst thing you can do is to lower your hourly rates (which you will use either for charging or for creating PBC quotes), or to lower your fixed fees if the work is repetitive and of a more routine nature. The problem is that once prices are lowered it is almost impossible to increase them again.

In these situations it is important to offer a special deal for a fixed period of time. That could be about rebating a specific percentage of total fees in six months' or 12 months' time, or having a temporary discount (shown as such on all invoices) which clearly expires on a particular date without having to have any further conversations. It must be seen to be temporary (because it's not sustainable without a change in scope) and with a clear end date. You might also seek a swap in return, such as an introduction to another area of work or to a potential new client.

THE ULTIMATUM

What happens if you have been carrying out work for a good client for a number of years and they say that they been approached with an offer of £40,000 and that you either need to match it, or they will have to switch the work? Let's also assume that the client is telling the truth. By comparison you have been charging them about £50,000 for that particular transaction type.

The worst possible reaction to this is just to match the £40,000. In a very real sense the trust between you and the client has broken down. If you were able to do the work for £40,000 then the client will feel somewhat cheated: you only dropped your price because they found a competitor and threatened you with losing the work. The client just regrets not having done this many years ago.

On the other hand, saying you cannot reduce your price almost forces the client to carry out their threat, otherwise they will be shown to have been bluffing. What is needed is for you to treat this as an opening to negotiation and to explain to the client that while you cannot drop your price to £40,000 for the work you are currently carrying out for them, you are more than happy to sit down with them and look at reducing the price by identifying whether there are different ways of working together that could reduce the amount of work involved. Treat this as an opportunity to see if there is some innovation that could reduce the price, or whether you can reduce the scope of work and therefore the associated price. If you do this, you don't need to drop to the level of £40,000. Bear in mind that the competitor is an untested service, whereas yours has been provided satisfactorily for many years: linking some price reduction to a reduction in the amount of work involved at your end is a healthy outcome.

PEDESTAL SELLING

It has been well researched that we attach more value to people if we are told of their expertise, even if it is by someone who has a vested interest, such as a colleague of theirs. Here's an example. I worked with a partner who was a real expert in managing multinational teams. She had been through some headline-grabbing transactions and really understood how to persuade everyone to pull in the same direction and overcome national differences. At first, when a client had an issue with an international team I would say, 'Let me get Diana to call you, she is great at this stuff'. That's a nice gift but it failed to communicate the size of benefit they were receiving.

I changed this to:

We actually have a partner who is a real expert at this. She has more experience than anyone I know in how to make international teams and international transactions work. As you can imagine, Diana is in huge demand and is pretty much tied up all the time. However, I did her a favour last month so she owes me one back. How about if I can get her to give you 30 minutes on the phone for free?

Doing this positions you in any future price negotiation for the services of the colleague that you have introduced, because it emphasises the high value they are delivering.

DISCOUNTS FOR VOLUME

We are hardwired to expect that we will receive a discount for volume purchases. However, for many service providers there are not massive economies of scale (except in relation to Routine Work), yet even so a major client will expect to be paying less per hour or per transaction, and this seems realistic and fair.

I have been caught out a number of times by agreeing discounts for clients who claim that they are going to spend £1 million per annum only to find that in fact their spend is massively less. It is crucial that where there are discounts given for volume they are triggered by the actual volumes, rather than predicted ones. You need to agree that the client can have an extra (say 2%) discount if they spend more than £1 million per year, and this is best paid in arrears once that spend has taken place. So, if the client only ever spends £600,000 then they will never see the reduction. Alternatively, if you are forced into giving the discount upfront, you need to have a specific term in your arrangements to say that the rates have been based on a spend of £1 million per year, and if that is not realised then you reserve the right to increase the rates. In practice, that gives you an opportunity to have a good conversation with the client at the half-year if they are falling short of their anticipated spend.

ANNUAL PRICE RISES

Apart from times of severe oversupply, service providers will typically find that their own overheads increase year-on-year because of inflation or increases in pay levels. A firm which agrees one set of prices with the client and does not alter them for three years will see a headline reduction of over 9% based on inflation running at 3% a year. Yet it is not unusual for clients to be on pretty historic rates, with the relationship partners being very reluctant to talk about increasing them.

To avoid this you need to track the rate that the client is paying against the full rate card over time (we will examine the importance of having rate cards in Chapter 11). Let's take an example of a client who starts with a discount of 10% from the rate card in year one: they are paying £360 an hour against a full rate of £400 an hour. If you don't increase your rate card then three years later they still have a discount of 10%. However, if you have changed your rate card at least in line with inflation every year (at 3%) then three years later the rate card would have grown from £400 an hour to £437. This means that the rate the client is actually paying of £360 an hour represents a discount of more than 17%. You should be able to have an easier conversation about increasing the client's rate by pointing out that they now enjoy 17% off the rate card.

In other words, if there is inflation in the economy, your rate card should not stand still even if you're not able to impose those increases on your clients on an annual basis. You still need to increase the rate card so as to show the actual discount that the client is enjoying is increasing every year.

HAVING LOWER COST OPTIONS

My guest author, Robert Browne of KPMG, says that the problem for many service firms is that they face a highly segmented marketplace but tend to have only one delivery model. In contrast, commercial organisations have become very adept at understanding the different market segments for their services, and then designing something different for them with different price points. We have only to look at the major hotel groups who have numerous very separate brands, and we can see how airlines have developed different services at different prices to target different groups of customers. Even the budget airlines are offering variations that appeal to the business as well as the leisure traveller.

One of the most worrying results of this segmentation failure is that all too often you will find that clients are paying very different prices, yet receiving identical services. The clients are segmented by price, but the service stays the same. For example, one client, who has negotiated particularly hard, is paying £400 an hour for a particular service, whereas a similar client offering similar volumes of work might be paying £500 an hour. What happens if they meet in the bar, or, even worse, if they meet at a conference organised by that firm?

One of the simplest, most effective ways in which an organisation has changed to deal with tough market conditions is the upmarket supermarket group Waitrose. At the start of the last recession, I would have confidently predicted that they would have quite a tough time because they were positioned very much at the luxury end of the market at a time when money was going to be very tight. Everyone could understand how the discount supermarkets could thrive in this environment, but it looked like tough times ahead for Waitrose. In fact, in 2009 they took the opportunity to introduce, alongside their own brand food, a cheaper brand called 'Waitrose Essentials'. Later that year these accounted for

13% of sales and contributed to growing their market share by 4% in an exceptionally tough market. These were not the same goods; they were lower priced goods that were sourced and designed from the outset to be at a lower price point.

Professionals can become tetchy when asked to produce a lower priced service: I recall one partner given this challenge asking me, 'Which corner would you like me to cut first?' In the next chapter we are going to look in detail at how you can create changes in a service allowing several different price points; but for now, at a tactical level, you should have in your armoury a lower specified service which you can offer to clients who are the most price sensitive. This gives them an opportunity to stay with you, even at times when they have to save money, by taking an alternative lower-quality service from you. Of course you have to maintain standards: a useful analogy is to think of a Mercedes A class car, which is considerably less expensive and addresses a different market from their S class, but is still undeniably a Mercedes.

In the next chapter, we will look at the staged approach to creating alternative services. At the tactical level it is important that you have some lower cost options, so that when you detect a client being difficult over the price you have a lower service option to discuss with them. That may be about having different people in the team, having support from another office (particularly one based in a lower cost centre) or limiting senior staff involvement to specific events. Without this, the firm will default to the more typical situation of only having one, very high-quality, service and providing that to all clients, irrespective of the actual price that each client has negotiated.

TEAM STRUCTURE

It's not just the price that determines profitability, but the composition of the team handling the work. This is self-evident for work which is on a fixed fee – the lower the level of staff that can then be used to complete the work the higher the profit. However, it can also be the case for work charged on an hourly basis. The way in which a team is structured, together with the level of people within the team and also the actual numbers, will have a significant impact on the profitability of a particular deal.

For example, do you have several different levels of people, at different prices, available for clients? I have seen some firms that are adept at systematising the work to enable the right task to be done at the right level. In one case an experienced partner had trained three junior assistants to work with him, giving him the benefit of leverage. This had enabled him to offer a lower partner rate because the work was distributed across a team, whereas a competitor handled all the work at partner level and at a higher rate. This new structure enabled the firm to earn greater profits on a piece of work, even with lower 'headline rates'. Have you put effort into having apprentices working within your teams?

BE IN THE PACK

When a client is reviewing fee quotes, whether they're hourly rates, PBC quotes or fixed fees, they inevitably order them highest to lowest. It's important that you are 'in the pack', unless you have an exceptionally good reason why you are not. Let's look at hourly rates (the rules are the same for all types of fees) and let's say that the client receives quotes on an hourly charged basis (Figure 7.1 – only partner rates shown).

Here, the client is likely to discount the firms at the top and the bottom of the scale. At the top end this looks overpriced if there are group of good firms in the middle who are all offering fees of around £130–£155 an hour less. At the bottom end the client starts to question quality and experience if you are £100–£125 an hour lower than your competitors.

The result is that the two extremes can be taken out of the running. Looking then at the pack, they are grouped closely enough together that the typical client would be content with any of them being the chosen firm. With that in mind, you want your quote to place you in the pack *but at the top of it, not the bottom.* I emphasise

| Figure 7.1 | **Grouping of price quotes** |

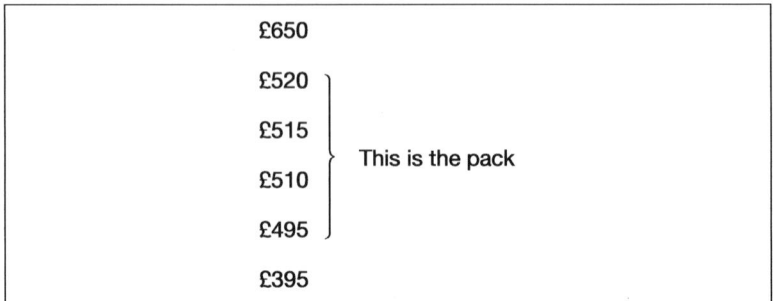

£650
£520 ⎫
£515 ⎪
£510 ⎬ This is the pack
£495 ⎭
£395

this because the normal behaviour of a typical service firm would be for the proposals team to spend quite some time discussing hourly rates in an attempt to be at the bottom of the pack ('How low can we go on this bid?'), but in fact that lowers the chance of winning rather than increasing it. That's because the client will try to choose the 'best firm' and, if anything, having the highest hourly rates (in the pack) is confirmation of their choice. The client chooses what they think is the best firm and they will not be surprised to see when they examine the hourly rates, their choice is the highest priced. Of course you can expect them to negotiate, and you will know now that you don't need to move much, but having the highest rates in the pack gives you scope to negotiate and move a little while maintaining a good level of profitability.

Unless you are using a cost leadership – low price strategy (as per Michael Porter) you must use your skill and judgement to formulate a realistic quote that would place you at the top of the pack, not the bottom. How do you find out your competitors rates? That is the topic for the next section.

MARKET INTELLIGENCE

Service firms don't generally produce public price lists so it can be difficult to know what rates competitors are charging, but having a feel for the pricing landscape of your competitors is useful in terms of your positioning. I have worked with firms where data on competitors' pricing has really helped their confidence in their own prices, for example: 'Well if Competitor X is charging £420 an hour then we should have no problem at all with our rate of £450 as we are definitely better than them.'

There are a number of sources for this data and it is worth putting real effort into gathering some of this information so that it will impact on your own pricing decisions. Where can you find this data?

■ Debriefs after tender wins and losses. You should have a practice of having a debrief meeting or phone call with a client after the result is known. One of your questions should be: 'How did our prices compare with the competition?' I tend to take more notice of the answers when it's a win, because with losses an easy brush-off (when you actually lost for other reasons) is to say that you lost on price, as this avoids the client having to tell the truth (which might be you were ill-prepared or they just didn't click with you). The response that I am looking for on a win is that 'you were more expensive than the others but in the end we thought you were the best for the job'. Anything short of that and I start thinking that we could increase our prices without damaging the win rate.

■ Interview people recruited into your firm in the last 12 months who used to work at competitors. This is a much underused resource and you should be meeting and interviewing these recruits as soon as possible after their arrival. Apart from being able to gather real information on prices actually being charged – 'How does our pricing compare with the pricing at your previous firm?' – you can also ask what your firm has to learn about its pricing policy from their previous place of work. You might be very surprised by some of the answers. One recent example was a partner who said that he had been surprised that the new firm was charging him out at £60 an hour less than his previous firm *to the same clients*, and that the budget of required time from him was 300 hours less per year! If you are short of recent recruits then look at capturing this type of information at interview stage. For example, start to ask questions that are useful generally to your business, such as 'What is your current charge-out rate?', 'Does it vary between clients?', 'How many hours do you expect to charge each year', and so on. Collecting this information in an organised way is really useful in helping to shape your own prices. Prices don't live in a vacuum, but are seen by clients in the context of your competitors' prices.

TROPHY CLIENTS

A trophy client is there to look good on the biography of the relevant partner. So far, so good. Partners do measure themselves by the quality of the clients that they advise. The problem with the trophy client is that they know that they are trophies and will very often exact very low prices or massive amounts of added value from their advisers (unless they come to you for Rocket Science, in which case you have a level playing field of Rocket Scientist versus trophy client, so the normal pricing rules apply).

Given that it is typically the partner who has very wide discretion over the actual price that the trophy client will pay, it is no surprise that the conflict over price is usually resolved in favour of the client. The partner may also talk about how well this appointment reflects on *the firm as a whole* and that while this initial deal is at a low price, there can be no doubt that it will lead in the near future to better work at higher rates and other such self-delusional nonsense.

There is nothing wrong with having trophy clients, it's just very important that you recognise them as such and make them deliver their full trophy client value. In one meeting I had been drafted in as client partner to tackle the problem of a large trophy client delivering a return of just 2%. I started by telling the client that their combination of high discounts, high added value and high partner use had led to an astonishingly low rate of return. The client acknowledged this, but their defence was that their brand was a great one to have on our client list. I agreed, but said that I needed to show some clear value from that if I was going to be able to get my finance director/managing partner/finance committee off my back. As a result I wanted the following, and you should make similar requests:

- a clear written quote about the strength of our relationship that I could use in brochures, online and in proposals;

- an agreement that the client would field three or four calls a year from prospective clients who were looking for a referee;

- an agreement to deliver a speech once a year alongside a partner of mine at a conference.

This was all agreed. After all, we were doing a good job for them and the demands that I made cost nothing, and yet were of real value to me. We also agreed to tone down some of the added value so as to add a few more points to our profit.

Don't have a trophy client unless they deliver their trophy value. Even then, don't have too many of them, or your profitability will be noticeably depressed.

NEGOTIATE WITH THE TOUGHEST CLIENTS AT THE RIGHT TIME

This is of most relevance to Routine Work, but I have also seen it have an impact on Relationship Advice. Some clients have become well organised in managing their panels of advisers and negotiate hard at each retender. They typically leverage having a strong brand and also being able to use their high volumes of work to both entice and threaten their service providers. For an incumbent who has a large volume of work, having to tell the firm that they lost the client at a retender (because they refused to reduce prices) is not an enticing thought.

To win at this game, you have to avoid fighting your battles when the client is at their strongest, which is during the tender/retender itself. At that point the client will have all the cards: new firms will be desperate to join the panel (and will be told that they have to be generous on discounts or they will not make it through the first stage), and incumbents will be told that to stay on the panel, a discount of at least, say, 10% is mandatory (ouch).

There are a number of tactics that you need to employ with these types of clients:

- Between tenders you need to work with the client to find ways of being more efficient, reducing the amount of work involved and finding savings. There is going to be great pressure to cut prices at the retender, so you need to be well prepared.

- Capture data on outcomes so that the conversation is not *one-dimensional* about price. What results are you achieving for the client, across what timescales and how do you compare with the other firms on the panel? Embed a member of your team into the client to gather data. You are going to use this data to defend a higher price at the retender (or at the least to defend no reduction). If you aren't achieving better results than your competitors on the panel then why should the client pay you more than them?

- Develop other clients and other opportunities. If you become very dependent on a single client then they will have huge power over you, because the loss of their work could have serious consequences for your team and even for the firm itself. Make certain that you spend time in between tenders nurturing new clients and new areas of work.

- Develop 'extra services', as described in the next chapter. You may have to accept relatively low prices for your standard level of service, but if you have developed add-on services that cost the client extra then they can be ignored at the retender, but provided and charged for post-tender. For example, you develop an 'express' option for when the client asks for the work in under 48 hours, which is at a higher price. The tender is about providing the standard service so you maintain the right to deliver and charge for the express service when requested post-tender.

- Lower the octane rating. If the client insists on continually reducing prices you need to find ways of delegating the work so that the client gets what they pay for. That may mean recruitment and training of more junior staff to take on more aspects of the client's work. For example, do you have doctors who are carrying out tasks that a well-trained nurse could provide?

- As explained when we looked at the issue of negotiations in relation to Routine Work, timing can be important for Relationship Advice as well. If you aspire to join a panel at the next retender (you are not one of the incumbents) then you are at very real risk of having to drop prices massively, in effect to 'buy your way onto the panel'. This tends to have the effect of reducing the value of the work for the whole panel and of setting a new pricing floor. I have seen partners who have been involved in several rounds of negotiating and feel so invested in the process (and, of course, having spent so much of their time trying to win the work) that they will offer *any* price by the end of the process, just so that all of their efforts have not been wasted. That is a really bad place to be. Much better to approach the target client *between retenders* and offer to carry out £50,000 of work for free, so that they can get to know you and you can start to understand how they like their work done. The worst case for the client is that they just saved £50,000. You use your pilot project to understand what the client wants and to create a desirable and valuable service for them, so that it is the client that 'pulls' you in at the next retender. This is a better use of £50,000 of time than fighting over price in a retender, and positions you to fight the next retender on more normal prices and complete with some evidence of what your performance is like.

DIFFERENTIAL PARTNER RATES

The biggest problem of cost-plus pricing is that its focus on internal costs (on your overheads) fails to recognise the realities of the marketplace. So a calculation is made which assigns a certain level of overheads to a partner, then adds the required margin so as to produce an hourly rate for that partner. For example, if a partner is attributed overheads of £350,000 and there is a required profit margin of £100,00 that turns into an hourly rate of £300, if the budget requires 1500 chargeable hours.

One problem is that someone who made partner last year is going to be charged out at the same hourly rate as a partner with more than 25 upwards years' experience. From the client's viewpoint the more experienced partner is worth more. Having them at the same rate as a new partner is likely to lead to the senior person being over-utilised, while the younger one struggles to build a professional relationship against what is effectively undercutting by the more senior partner. The rates need to be separated out having regard to what they are worth to clients. An easy solution is for the senior partner to add a premium of 25% and see what happens. Some clients should then switch to the cheaper, more junior partner.

Similarly, some work types allow for higher leverage than others. At the extreme, a Rocket Scientist may work with one or two people in their team, whereas those in Routine Work would expect to manage a very large team (20–50 people, or more). As a result, the actual percentage margins would typically range from 50% for Rocket Science to perhaps 5% for Routine Work, even though both of these partners are bringing in similar returns *per partner* for the firm. Firms which have this broad spread of partners often struggle to acknowledge these differences. I have seen, for example, partners given a 'hurdle rate' (don't take on work which is less profitable than this) of 20%, even though that makes life extremely easy for the Rocket Scientists (who will most likely start dropping their rates if the target is so low), while those in more mundane work have unrealistically high rates imposed upon them, leading to a loss of competitiveness and unrealistic quotes being sent to clients.

A full service firm is likely to need at least four different rates for partners or managers: one for Rocket Scientists ('expert rate'), one for seniors partners, one for more junior ones (in Relationship Advice) and one for those who lead highly leveraged teams carrying out Routine Work.

Another problem for cost-plus pricing is that it ignores the laws of supply and demand. If there is huge demand for advice on tax but a huge drop in demand for restructuring, it is a rare firm that recognises this and puts up all prices in tax while removing supply from restructuring (better to do that than to keep supply high and drop the price, because everyone else will be doing the same). There's typically an easy way to spot these opportunities: look for areas in the firm which are greatly over-utilised and try increasing prices to damp down demand. The people involved in the under-supplied work have the wonderful opportunity of working fewer hours at higher rates and earning more money for the firm.

DELIVER WHAT WAS ACTUALLY PAID FOR

Another tactic for public sector and other heavily procured clients is to make sure that you are delivering only the absolute minimum of what was paid for, and to be astute in looking for and adding on charges for extra services. This is something for which the budget airlines and the hotel sector have become famous. While I consider this to be a very bad tactic for those clients who are paying a fair price (because it will annoy them), it is acceptable for those paying the absolute minimum.

If you want to service the most price-sensitive of clients you need to be very astute in considering what could be extra. A great starting point for that is to create your absolutely basic level of service (your own, plain-labelled 'value range') so that you can minimise your costs while maximising the chance that you can sell more expensive extras. If that doesn't appeal to you, then look at the more strategic issue of whether you want to exit public sector and heavily procured work (or want to pass it to a separately branded subsidiary with a lower cost base).

Too often I see firms struggling to provide the same great service they always did, with exactly the same people, for clients who keep driving the price lower and lower. Better that you keep lowering the scope of what you provide, changing the team structure, using technology or putting the work into a low-cost offshoot.

SHOW THE DISCOUNT

If you are putting in a quote to a major client, or to a new client that you consider will become a major client, then there will be a strong desire to give them a discount from your standard rates. That will also be expected by the client. Let's say that you have set up a rate card which allows for a discount of 10% for 'major clients' (for example, those who should spend £500,000-plus per year either immediately or within a reasonable period of time).

Let's say that your rate card rates are £500 for a partner, £450 for a senior associate and £400 for an associate. I have seen partners, wanting to be helpful, simply showing that the hourly rates are £450, £405 and £360 respectively. However, the response from the new client is often to demand a 10% discount and refusing to believe you when you claim you already did that. As a result it is important that you set it out as shown in the following table:

Grade	Standard rate	Global client rate*
Partner	£500	£450
Senior associate	£450	£405
Associate	£400	£360

*Note: Global client rate is reserved for clients who anticipate an annual spend of £500,000 or more each year. If spend drops below that rate we reserve the right to remove this discount.

LOWER RATE DOES NOT EQUAL LESS SPEND

Whenever you have hourly rates as part of your pricing, even if they are being used to create a PBC quote, often clients will seek to attack the rates and lower them as much as they can. That's logical, because the lower the hourly rates, the less they will be charged, right? No, that's actually wrong. I'm indebted to one of my American clients for a story that perfectly illustrates this. He explained that, in response to an order from his CEO to cut costs immediately, he emailed his adviser panel to explain that due to severely adverse trading conditions he would have to reduce all hourly rates by 15% starting the next day, and if any adviser had a problem with that then they needed to come off the panel. All demurred. One year later he asked me, 'How much do you think I saved?' I was expecting a boast like 'One million dollars', but that's not what he said. 'Not a single cent', was the answer, 'all the firms just worked 15% slower (or anyway they recorded more hours at the lower rate)'.

This is a useful lesson. If the client's attack is on the hourly rate, then the first casualty is going to be your ability to give them the best team. It's easy for you to cave in and reduce rates, but the best professionals in the firm may see these rates and just avoid working for that client. In reality the client is going to end up with the professionals who are least busy, and therefore there is some risk that they will not be the best.

There is also no incentive for professionals to 'jump to it' if they think the agreed rates are seriously low. Why not do that work at the end of the day when you are not so fresh?

So if clients become fixated by arguing over hourly rates, it's worth taking a step back with them and asking them what they are trying to achieve by arguing over them? If it is to downgrade the type of people handling their work, then fine. If it is to reduce spend, then it is much better that you institute a spend reduction project with them and leave the rates alone. We will look at those projects in detail in Chapter 10.

ACT FOR CLIENTS THAT YOU LIKE (NOT THE BULLIES)

Every firm will have clients that they really like, who are paying comparatively high rates of charge, and aggressive, difficult clients who are paying much less but are receiving the same or a better level of service. This happens because we tend to be reactive rather than proactive, and if a client that we want to keep is difficult over money then they tend to get their way (while effectively being subsidised by the 'nicer' clients). This is a dangerous practice: how will you explain to the nice clients why they are paying more? The risk is that you lose the nice clients and spend your professional career with the more price-aggressive ones. Don't do this.

There is a simple exercise that you can carry out in your firm, as discussed previously when it was carried out by an insurance company: segment your clients into 'like' and 'don't like' (see Chapter 3). This sounds somewhat unusual, but it often produces very interesting results. It involves taking the largest clients by turnover (top 20, top 50 or whatever is appropriate for your firm) and conducting a survey with the front-line staff in your firm, asking them to rate these clients as 'like' or 'don't like'. This is a deliberately subjective question about the actual experience of the person in your firm and how they feel about dealing with the client. It is binary – they must choose 'like' or 'don't like'.

You total up these scores and create a table with just two columns so that your top clients have been divided up. The interesting addition is this: put next to the clients the profit (or loss) made on each individual client and this typically reveals an interesting pattern. If you cannot calculate profitability at a client level in your firm then you could instead list average prices paid by each individual client over the preceding year. You will almost always find that the clients that you don't like are loss-making or low profit (or low average price if using that measure)! Clients categorised as 'like' are much more often the most profitable ones. I started to explain this as 'We like this client and this client values us'.

It was just as interesting to look at the clients in the 'don't like' column. They were the ones who always had to have everything in a rush, started every conversation by emphasising that the work had to be done as cheaply as possible, argued over the bill, requested a lot of extras for free and generally treated you without respect. In some cases, they were in companies which themselves had a culture of cost-cutting and whose industry profile was to be 'lowest price', which meant that they had to keep their overheads to a minimum and so all expenditure was scrutinised and constrained. Some of these difficult clients can just feel like spoilt children who want everything but want to pay very little.

If you find the profit/loss correlation above, then it is worth spending time acquiring new clients that you like and gradually easing yourself out of the others. It may simply be a matter of passing them over to colleagues, as again it has been my experience that when one partner did not have a great relationship with the client, this did not mean that a subsequent partner would have the same experience.

FROM TACTICS TO STRATEGY

Tactics are all very well, but what is the strategic answer? It is to work closely with each client to build a service which genuinely delivers additional value to the particular client and so justifies a higher price, or to develop lower cost and lower priced services to serve clients who have less to spend. This exercise needs to be conducted on an individual basis between clients, but there are certainly common themes that emerge, and the next chapter looks at a much more strategic solution to this issue.

8

Drivers of value

This chapter is about the importance of understanding a client's drivers of value: the additional or enhanced services for which they would be prepared to pay a premium, and those parts of a service that they would be happy to forgo in return for a price reduction. This topic has become ever more important in this post-recession environment. For those firms able to understand and harness this skill, the benefits are numerous, such as:

■ Persuading clients to pay more than the market rate for your services.

■ How to present your *valuable* differentiation to your clients.

■ Creating service tie-ins for your clients, so that if they switch to another supplier it becomes costly and inconvenient for them.

■ Allowing you to vary scope along with the agreed price.

■ Rather than having one service at one price, learning to segment your clients, using their individual price sensitivity, thereby maximising profitability (and client satisfaction).

■ Avoiding pricing conversations being one-dimensional (and only focussing on how high or low a price should be) by having many factors and options in play.

In the past, service providers have tended to concentrate on polishing and refining the quality, speed and efficacy (and sometimes efficiency) of the service that they provide to their clients. The problem with this strategy is that their competitors are usually doing *exactly* the same thing at *exactly* the same time. Incremental improvements in service come in waves and very typically you will find that everyone is raising their game, standards are improving and clients are simply getting used to better service from all the providers in your sector. Using a drivers of value approach and a process to vary your service around those drivers (sometimes called 'value engineering') gives you the opportunity to tailor your service to the real needs of your individual clients, and also allows you to explore additional cost options for them which enhance your profit by costing you less than the achievable increase in price.

TYPICAL STARTING POINT

The most common problem that service firms encounter is that different clients are paying quite different prices *for exactly the same service.* This is typically because some clients negotiate much harder than others on price (or receive different quotes from partners within the same firm, offering different starting prices or discount schemes – this will be addressed in Chapter 11). It might also be the case that each client started their relationship with you at different times, and there has never been any attempt to regularise prices and the services provided for those prices.

In the real world we often encounter price discrepancies. Budget airlines sell seats cheaply at first and then at higher prices in response to demand or proximity to flight time (for exactly the same seat), and retailers will clear their shelves of last season's fashions or food close to its expiration date. The difference in such cases is that there are good business reasons for the variations, reasons built upon scarcity or perishability of goods.

For clients to be paying you different prices for the same services carries a substantive business risk. If those clients meet and compare prices, as they might, then one of them will quite properly feel cheated. That is a particular issue in the field of Relationship Advice, where there is a foundation of honesty and trust which would be shattered (irrespective of how well you are doing the work, and how satisfied that client might have been prior to finding out they were paying more than their peers). This is a real and serious issue, and in Chapter 11 we will look at how you can use analytics, including scattergrams, to identify clients who have unfair prices (high or low) and the right strategies to use in those situations.

In this chapter, I will provide you with practical exercises that you can carry out in your own organisation to help you analyse the service that you provide, and therefore think about how you could offer different versions of it.

CREATING DIFFERENT SERVICES – PART 1: BEST EVER SERVICE

The best starting point for most service providers is to imagine what the perfect, no expense spared, service would look like. This is a good group exercise: imagine that your most important client calls and says that they have a matter that is incredibly important, and so they want you to give them the best service possible. This type of thinking works even for Routine Work, because there can be cases where apparently routine matters carry high risk.

Typical factors that will be in play could include:

- the speed of response;
- the actual (named) team members who are going to be involved in carrying out the work;
- whether there is special technology that can be used to improve performance or to keep the client up to date;
- how many people will work on the task and where they will be (for example, you could embed a team member at the client's offices so that they are on call and available throughout).

Once you have gathered some ideas of your own, it is time to involve the clients. Choosing a client with whom you have a good relationship, ask them to help you to work out ways that you could improve the service they receive from people like you: if they had a magic wand, what would they wish for? Request that they focus in particular upon ways that you could make their lives easier. Can you assist in taking over some of the tasks that they currently perform in relation to matters, or can you help by streamlining delivery in a way that is consistent with their administrative system – for example, can you access their computers to update them or can you deliver the answers in a format that allows for easy upload?

It can be beneficial to think about other service businesses and how they behave when in direct competition. If a second drycleaner opens across the street from an existing one, then unless the original drycleaner enters into a price war, it is going to have to develop new value. They may collect and deliver the clothes to be cleaned (particularly if there are offices nearby which could be a good source of customers), they might use quality hangers rather than wire ones, add suit carriers where appropriate, carry out small repairs to buttons and zips. The aim of this exercise is to identify parts of your services which are valuable to the client so that you can factor them into your pricing strategy. The same process works in the reverse when trying to reduce cost by reducing delivery of the parts of your service that the clients do not value, and we will look at this in more detail below.

Resisting price pressure from a bank client | Example

It has become accepted in some sectors for there to be price reductions at every contract renegotiation. There might be two-year contracts awarded and at each retender the incumbent suppliers are told that they must offer lower prices than they are currently charging, based upon some mythical process improvements that they are expected to have achieved. This is especially prevalent where you have large companies handing out substantial volumes of work. They know that incumbents will not want to risk losing their share of the current work (because that could have staff reduction implications as well as financial ones), and that new providers will be happy to offer discounted prices to join the existing panel.

In one such situation a bank was providing a services firm with 400 transactions a year at a price of £3000 each transaction (so £1.2 million in fees each year), and was seeking to reduce the fees to £2500. After many years of continued reductions, the firm felt that this was a cut too far. It had already invested in systems, technology and training and was facing having to use more and more junior staff, which was risking the quality of service to this bank and ultimately its own market reputation. The firm wanted to achieve an increased price, not a reduced one. How could that be justified (and avoid the bank simply switching to a lower offer from another firm)?

An investigation of the drivers of value of the relevant unit in the bank discovered that their main measure of performance was their quarterly sales results. They would happily pay more to a firm that helped them improve those results. An investigation of the bank's end-to-end process found that there were effectively four stages:

1. Underwrite an application for a loan (much work for the bank).

2. If the relevant criteria were met then a loan offer would be issued and copied to external firms which would act for the bank, completing the necessary work to enable the loan to be made.

3. External firms dealt with the bank, the borrower and all other relevant parties and when satisfied that all necessary conditions were met, notified the bank to make the loan.

4. Finally the bank advanced the loan money to the borrower (and the total of loans made that quarter were the bank's sales figures, which would be compared to its targets).

An interesting issue emerged. For every 100 offers made at stage 2 above, only 84 loans were actually made in stage 4. There was a loss of 16% of the bank's business during the process. These were called 'abortives'. With an average loan value of £4.6 million, these abortives represented a loss of lending to the bank of almost £300 million on the 400 transactions passed to this firm.

The solution was to focus effort on reducing the number of abortive transactions, which fed directly into better sales results. The firm agreed a higher fee for each completed case and a zero fee on each abortive case (so aligning its interests with those of the client). Speed was found to be the crucial factor – slow transactions were much more likely not to complete. So the firm charged more, created a faster service which reduced abortives and created (substantial) extra value for the bank.

The key to drivers of value is this: you are looking for enhancements that cost less to deliver than their value to the client. This means that you can charge extra for the enhancements plus a profit element, and that total would be within the range of extra value for which the client would be prepared to pay. This can be personal to a client – something that one client values that another will not – so the more options that you can develop, within reason, the better. This exercise also helps to embed the idea that extra optional services are going to cost extra. It's not simply a matter of doing the best piece of work that you can. There will be cost implications and you need to think about whether the client will be prepared to pay more for that higher level of service. People sometimes get hung up on their inability to *promise* a particular result, because they don't want to offer something and then fail to deliver.

In one example, a firm that fitted out retail premises was stuck in a negotiation with a client. The firm wanted to charge £198,600 but the client would not move from a maximum spend of £160,000. Of course, the firm could have started to lower the specification but they felt that the difference was so large that the end result would not reflect well on them. We looked at the other variables and came up with *speed to completion*. For a retailer, each week of fit-out is a week not trading, so faster is much better. Conversations with the client revealed that they would value faster completion by £25,000 each week. If the retail space was available two weeks early then the client would happily pay £40,000 more to the company. At this point there was hesitation because a fit-out is a complex operation reliant upon many people completing their parts on time, and the project manager at the firm said that he couldn't guarantee completion two weeks early. I asked him: 'If the client said they would pay £160,000 for completion as currently scheduled, but £5 million for completion two weeks early, do you think you would achieve that?' He answered in the affirmative, to which I said, 'OK they won't pay £5 million but they will pay £198,600. Try hard and see what happens'. The deal was agreed with a variable price depending upon completion date. The value the client saw in an early completion had been successfully incorporated into the price.

Generally partners are pretty good (and inventive) when it comes to creating the top-end service. We enjoy adding extras and improving performance because it reflects well on us in the finished result. If done well and tailored to each client, this can be effective in enabling higher prices. However, there will be times, and there will be clients, where the strongest driver is about reducing costs and that leads us to the second part of the exercise, which involves creating minimum levels of service.

CREATING DIFFERENT SERVICES – PART 2: LOWEST COST

Having completed part 1 and created valuable extras to the current service, the next stage is to imagine a situation where a client contacts you to say that they are being forced to cut spend, so they want you to examine the service that you deliver and for you to tell them the absolute lowest cost service that you could deliver. You have to perform another value engineering exercise, but this time with the aim of cost reduction, therefore stripping out any aspects that you can, without compromising appropriate minimum quality standards.

Partners are generally uncomfortable during this exercise, worrying that they will deliver substandard services and will either be met with complaints or, in a worst-case scenario, professional claims against them and their firm.

This is not an attempt to hoodwink a client into believing they are getting your usual standard of service but at a much lower price. In fact, it is an attempt to create a quite different level of service at a much lower price. There are brand implications when differentiating service based on lower prices – do you want to be known for lower cost services, or would this impact on the perception of your firm in other areas of work? It is possible to have different services at different prices within one overall brand – think, for example, of First Class, Business Class, Premium Economy and Economy all on the same aircraft. With a clear and well-communicated strategy, different services at different price points can successfully hit different client segments.

As before, the variables will be around the identity of the team members (more junior and fewer senior ones), speed of delivery, location of teams, availability, use of technology, how much the client has to do for themselves and so on. In one case, I visited the managing director of a major client and was struck by the piles of reports stacked up around his office. These were our reports which we compiled with great care and at considerable cost each month. 'Do you ever read these reports?' I enquired. 'To be honest, no', he admitted, showing that these costly reports had no value to him. The reports were immediately stopped, at a saving to my firm, which then translated into a saving for the client, and the managing director was also able to clear some space in his office. Brief follow-up enquiries revealed that these reports had been requested by the *previous* managing director. Cutting out work, and the associated cost, is not a natural skill for most partners, but it is a necessary one if you are to align prices and services across a broader spectrum of clients.

Once again, after the internal team has worked to create the minimum level of service it is worth involving a price-sensitive client in the exercise in order to hear from them about how much of the existing service they would sacrifice, or carry out themselves or via another provider, in order to achieve price reductions.

CREATING DIFFERENT VERSIONS

The purpose of the previous two exercises is that if you begin with the most enhanced service that you can imagine and then work your way down to the absolute minimum, it gives you a whole series of different versions of your service. In other words, each step down from the best service to the least service gives you a possible different level of service. These versions, and their different cost bases, are crucial bargaining tools when having pricing conversations because any change in price should be met with a change in version. If you have only one level of service then the only thing in play is the price of it, and to the client there is only one direction that figure can go. As described at the beginning of this chapter, it is worth examining the following scenarios.

Persuading clients to pay more than the market rate for your services

Accepting that there is a market rate means accepting that the service you deliver is perceived as being the same as the service of all of your competitors. Much more worryingly, perhaps it is the same! When you consider that the sellers of bottled water have managed to create very different prices for what really is effectively the same product (could you really taste the difference in a blind tasting?), any service provider who allows their service to be 'the same' as their competitors is just being lazy. However, there can be markets where fees are fixed by reference to deal value – for example, at 0.5% of the value of the transaction. Here, creating a valuably different service is what will win you the work against your competitors, even if the total fee is fixed.

How to present your valuable differentiation to your clients

Inside a professional service business it can feel quite unique. From personal experience, I can say that firms can have very different cultures behind closed doors; but to the clients the firms can outwardly appear very similar.

In order to differentiate effectively, you need to focus upon delivering different results in a different way when compared to your competitors. Remember that your most direct competitors are likely to have recruited the same type of people as your firm, often from similar backgrounds.

If clients think that you are the same as your competitors then, as we have already seen, the only real differentiator becomes price. After running the exercises it is best practice to have an in-house workshop, building up a list of ideas from your team, and then to run an event with each of the chosen clients to ask them what could be changed or improved from the service that they currently receive. This aim is to create a personalised service for each of them: this justifies different clients paying different prices because the service that they are receiving is not identical.

Creating service tie-ins for your clients

The ability to tailor your service around a client's exact needs and systems is a brilliant way to gain a real edge against your competitors and serves as protection when it comes to your prices. When discussing price, perhaps relative to a low competitor quote, the discussion becomes deeper than just the numbers because your competitors, who have not spent the time that you have in making the service fit the client's needs and systems, will find it difficult to match the service that you provide. A service tie-in is a form of tailoring that differentiates your service but also raises the cost, time and difficulty of the client switching provider from you to a cheaper competitor.

For example, a client may find value in having all of their business with you digitised, with records and documents held in a secure extranet to which you and the client are given online access. This can create a service that holds extra value for the client and/or cuts time and work, leading to speed improvements or cost savings. Hosting the data yourself and having the right contractual terms can mean that your efforts in digitising belong to you and will be switched off if there is a change in service provider to a competitor. Similarly, if you carry out part of the work that was previously carried out by a client (so that they don't have the people or knowledge to carry that out in the future), or by hosting valuable performance data. We will examine the skilful use of data later in this chapter.

Allowing you to vary scope along with the agreed price

Clients have become much more interested in disaggregation of services: in seeing which parts of the overall task can be separated out and handled by the client themselves using existing resources, or by being passed to lower cost, specialised, outsourcing companies. Many firms have had to accept that while it may be somewhat easier for them to provide an end-to-end service, that approach may end up costing the client more than necessary. Having created a minimum level of service allows you to examine whether additional elements could be provided by others at a lower cost to the client, and also critically to examine even the core elements. For example, can you create a lower cost base team through near-shoring or off-shoring? Will those people be part of your organisation, or will they be contracted from a specialist provider?

Having first examined the value of the separate elements of your service, it makes these disaggregation decisions much more realistic. It enables you proactively to approach clients with solutions which maintain the most valuable parts of the work, while giving clients lower cost options for the more routine aspects.

Segment your clients

When there are pressures on price a natural reaction is to move into 'overhead saving mode'. When market conditions are tough, this can restore a sense of power because it enables the partners to focus on cutting waste and should be well within their powers and abilities to deliver tangible results. Cutting headcount, leaving vacancies unfilled, subletting spare accommodation, reducing travel and so on will have a relatively fast impact on the bottom line. Reducing costs enables the firm to give lower prices to clients while also maintaining some margin.

However, these activities are carried out at the organisational level and their impact tends to be felt equally by all clients. This is a shame because all clients are not the same in terms of price sensitivity and the level of service that they require. Worst of all, the least price-sensitive clients are those who are most likely to notice if there is a diminution of service (because they will feel that they are no longer receiving what they paid for). A more nuanced approach enables you to maintain the highest levels of service for those who are prepared to pay higher prices, in the same way that an airline will offer premium economy, business and first class seats on the same aircraft as one with economy seats. They can address the needs and preparedness to pay of four segments of clients, rather than just one.

Avoiding pricing conversations being one-dimensional

If you ask anyone who has received a beautifully prepared work proposal from a potential supplier, many of them will tell you that they will first read the executive summary and then secondly will turn to the page of prices. This is not because the decision is going to be about finding the lowest price (other than for Routine Work), but because there is a need to frame the price alongside the others that are received.

There is a timing issue: price comes most into focus when the final decision is being made. It's now that the client is going to make their buying decision and so they need to tie down the best price that they can with the chosen supplier. The conversation will be about the client seeking to reduce the quoted price and many partners will see this as a negotiation where positions need to be restated, compromises made and concessions traded. This is where having a clear understanding of the separate elements that make up your service becomes vitally important, as it allows you to offer reductions in price in return for clear and specific variations in the service to be provided. This is massively more valuable than the more typical approach of negotiating headline figures, with the partner making concessions to 'seal the deal' while reassuring himself or herself that they will sort this out during execution (which in practice very rarely occurs).

PRICE DISCRIMINATION

Beware of having higher prices which affect only a proportion of your clients and are based upon factors such as the urgency of their need or willingness to pay. This can look like value-based pricing, but if it is discriminatory it will typically cause a strongly adverse reaction. Let's look at some examples. Suppose that you are selling online and decide that people who use Apple computers are likely to be more affluent than the average, and so you set up your site to display higher prices to visitors with an Apple computer. This may not cause instant problems but could do so when the practice becomes public.

Price discrimination is often criticised by clients. For example, a store that charged double for its umbrellas when it was raining (because of higher demand) was criticised for unfair trading practices (even though it claimed it was reacting to supply and demand), and a minicab company that increased rates in line with actual demand at the time of booking, was just felt to be profiteering from people's needs (even though it said it was trying to encourage more drivers to become available). At this stage it is just important to understand that price discrimination (seen as 'taking advantage' of a client with a specific, typically urgent, need) is a very different tactic from value engineering.

CREATING DIFFERENT SERVICES – STATISTICS AND DATA

Inside most service firms there is often a huge amount of very valuable data. However, despite being in possession of such data, it is rarely gathered together, and even more rarely is it shared with the clients. This is where you can add real value and demonstrate your worth to a client. For example:

■ What is your track record in the particular work you are dealing with for this client? How many cases have you handled; what was the end result of each case; how long do they take on average; what was the overall end result; what was the client satisfaction rating of your performance?

■ Where you carry out the same type of work for many clients you can offer them anonymised statistical information showing the differences between them. For example, how long do their matters take; how much do they cost; what are the end results? Delivering this type of information to clients is of real value, showing whether they are above or below the norm and whether there are areas they can improve. If a particular client is paying much more than others per matter because they are causing additional work, then it is better to face this issue with them and look at ways you can work together to reduce this, rather than simply losing them to a competitor who is able to offer them a more cost-effective solution.

■ Performance data is not just valuable to enable better working with your existing clients, but is something of a magic bullet when seeking a new one. One of the main difficulties in winning new clients is that you are selling an intangible product. It is very difficult to demonstrate the service without providing it, but the client finds it hard to put a value on the service when they haven't experienced it – and in any case, the actual service that they receive may differ from the service that you provide to another client. Hard data is what is required in today's business environment and those who are too busy to put together this data will be at a considerable disadvantage. Imagine the contrast between these two approaches:

■ You should use us because we have this great service (just like all our competitors) and we can get some referees.

■ We have facts and figures on our actual performance. We would be happy to share that data with you and to work on a comparison with your existing service provider so that we can show you how much better off you will be if you start using us (in outcomes, costs, time, etc.).

Statistics can be the sole justification needed to increase your prices. Once you start accurately tracking your performance across a series of data points, you can agree improvement targets with your clients and link your price to achievement of them. This can make price adjustments mechanical and automatic.

USING EXISTING CLIENTS AS YOUR DIFFERENTIATOR

There are very many cases where your clients are not in direct competition with one another and that opens up the possibility that you can use your clients, as a group, as a valuable differentiator between you and your competitors. This is achieved by persuading them to share their experiences with others. For example, suppose a client tells you that they have been tasked with opening up a new production facility in China, recruiting a managing director for their Polish subsidiary, launching a new healthy eating product in Germany or organising their company's global conference in Miami.

Your existing experience in areas such as this is why they have come to you for advice, but what if you told them that you had another client who had experienced exactly the same issue as them and that client would be happy to share their experiences with them? How valuable is that to someone who is facing a substantial task for the first time?

Anyone who works in services has the opportunity to harness the real-life experiences of their clients in this way. It takes some organisation but it has the possibility of creating a hugely valuable differentiation. This works best when clients understand your approach from the outset and if you create 'client clubs' or similar so that there is real substance to this enhancement. For example, a client who is considering entering into a management buy-out (MBO) of their company will need advice from lawyers, accountants, bankers, venture capitalists and the like. What if one of these advisers said that they had created an MBO club, and the benefit to this client was that they would have the opportunity to meet and talk to other clients who had been through exactly the same experience in the last couple of years, so that they could learn what it had been like in reality, what issues to watch out for and so on? A kind of 'Everything I wish I had known about MBOs *before* I started on one'. The only condition of receiving this valuable advice and input is that the client must also agree to be available to others in the future who are seeking the same advice.

Without doubt this offers the client an enhanced version of the core service and one which provides the client with value from an unexpected source – other clients.

MOVING FROM COSTS INCURRED TO VALUE DELIVERED

Understanding and using the value to the client as the key issue in the price charged to the client is pivotal in creating a successful pricing strategy. For many service providers it is ingrained thinking that something that takes two days to deliver to the client will cost twice as much as something that takes one day to deliver. That's true so far as the costs incurred are concerned, but it fails to consider the client's' point of view. Value engineering forces you to ask the right – client-focussed – questions, which may reveal that speed is of the essence and that the client might be prepared to pay twice as much for faster delivery (in one day) rather than the other way around.

When teaching this I use the example of replacing car exhausts, and ask participants to imagine that they run such a business in a town where there are also two competitors offering a similar service. Let's assume that there is enough business for all three suppliers to be reasonably busy, and that after a period of competing on price they have worked out that service differentiation or market segmentation will enable them all to survive. There is a reasonable equilibrium in supply and demand and some price variations between the three companies.

On a trip abroad, you discover a machine which would enable you to *halve* the time it takes to replace an exhaust. Labour costs represent 60% of your overheads, and therefore even after taking into account the cost of the machinery you will be able to carry out the work for much less than your competitors. Put simply, you will be able to get through twice as many exhaust replacements per day as you could before. You secure exclusive rights to use the machinery in your country and you have it installed in your workshop. Before you installed the machines you charged customers an average of £180 and made £30 profit. After installing the machinery (and even taking into account its cost) you can now drop your price to £120 and still make £30 profit. That will really hit your competitors because if they were to drop to your price, their profits would all but disappear. What do you do next?

You have several options, but it is interesting that when this scenario is presented as a case study with many pages of information on internal costs, people tend to focus on calculations around those costs. Internal costs and the whole 'cost-plus' thinking that we examined in Chapter 2 is of interest – it gives information on breakeven points and helps you to understand the minimum price. However, it is of no help at all in assessing the highest price that can be charged, because that is a function of the value that you deliver to the client (differentiated value, if it is going to be sustainable).

In the example of the car exhaust, you are able to create a differentiated service (because of your exclusive rights to this new machine) which is quicker for the customer. It enables you to offer an 'express service' that your competitors cannot match and to offer it as a higher priced option so that customers who value saving time can pay extra and have their exhaust replaced faster. In this way you increase the margin on the standard exhaust replacement (fewer staff) and make increased profit, but it *also* opens up an enhanced service option that will earn even higher profits for the same amount of work. Charging just £15 extra for the express service would lift profit on those jobs by 50%, even before factoring in savings from the new equipment. Of course there are other options, some of them involve fighting a price war using your cost base advantage (see for example, how the deep-discounting retailers such as Aldi and Lidl have taken market share from traditional supermarkets) but your first thought should be about whether a change in service creates greater value for the client.

THE PERFECT SOLUTION – START WITH VALUE

The ideal approach to value engineering is to *start* with the value to be delivered to clients and then to build your service based around a much deeper understanding of your clients' businesses. This is truly the nirvana of the pricing world and can best be illustrated with a couple of examples.

There are several global players who can deliver complete IT solutions to hospitals. A typical project would involve running the booking, administration and billing systems of the hospital itself, holding patient records and supporting the doctors, nurses and other professionals who work there. If you are a hospital administrator or a government body looking for a supplier, you will not find it difficult to meet and obtain detailed quotes from some highly reputable companies with a proven track record in completing these types of projects. Inevitably, in the final stages of the selection, there would be considerable and detailed negotiations with each supplier about the total cost and final specifications of the system.

If you are a salesperson at one of those IT solutions providers you will be familiar with the process. You have powerful competitors who will be fighting just as hard as you to win each major contract. How do you avoid a race to the bottom on price so that you don't just win projects at the lowest price? For example, one great method of differentiation occurred when just such a supplier started to better understand the clients' point of view and to realise where one area of real value lay in hospital IT systems. This turned out not to be in the core areas of the service – that was an area where every potential supplier could demonstrate a robust system.

This supplier took time to examine the costs that were incurred when running a hospital and (probably just like its competitors) saw that there were areas where the system could save money (for example, fewer staff needed in administration, improved attendance at hospital appointments thanks to the ability to send reminders by text message and so on). However they also noticed a line labelled 'mis-prescription' which, on investigation, they found related to costs and damages paid out when patients were given the wrong medicine (or more often the wrong amount of the right medicine) at the bedside. To develop a value-based solution around this, first they worked with an existing client to understand how the hospital's IT systems could be used to help prevent a mis-prescription and to gather audit data before and after the fix was applied.

In a busy hospital mistakes are going to occur every year. Their frequency will be known and often the consequences will be very serious. The supplier's investigations revealed that each event cost the hospital $155,000 and that reductions of 75% were possible, giving a calculable cash benefit for each hospital based upon their size and current performance.

In other words, developing a robust IT-based prescription system used at the bedside which flagged up possible errors to the doctors and nurses could save a specific amount of money, and improve patient care and the hospital's reputation. This enabled the supplier to have a conversation with a hospital that was considering different suppliers for its computerisation project, along these lines:

- Of course our systems will provide all of the core solutions that you need.
- So will those of our competitors.

- But only ours has the bedside prescription built in so that it reduces mis-prescription costs by 75%.
- And although our systems cost a little more, they will create annual savings *greater than the additional cost.*
- And help enhance your hospital's reputation and the well-being of its patients.

This is a powerful answer to a negotiation on the client side which would be built upon negotiating the best cost. Of course, these types of innovation and value-based solutions can be copied, which is what drives this supplier to continue to look for a better and deeper understanding of its clients' needs so that it can maintain a price premium.

A second example involves the value of training provided to professionals by external consultants. Often brokered through the learning and development department, there will be a 'market rate' for training which sits in a band that takes into account the seniority of the professionals being trained and the qualifications of the trainer or trainers involved. That is a good example of there being a 'going rate' or 'market rate' for a service.

However, what if one training consultant created a business development workshop that used a new approach to training senior professionals? Could that be of greater value if it delivered better results? For example, a service where the focus was not upon the cost of delivering it but which tracked the achievements of those who attended the course and collated data on those results. One which said: 'It's inconceivable that the attendees will not obtain new work worth at least five times the cost of training in the six months following it.' This shifts the focus of attention to the results that are going to be achieved by the attendees, which is effectively the real value of the session – and who wouldn't think it worthwhile to invest £1 to receive a £5 return within six months?

This idea of starting to build your service for a client based upon the value that you deliver to them is likely to be the most powerful strategy that you have in justifying higher prices. It means not simply delivering the service that you currently provide, but spending time with individual clients understanding what is important and valuable to them in relation to the work you are going to provide. For one-off pieces of work this means spending time at the outset to design a more valuable service, and to explain that value to the client. You will start to use expressions like:

- So if I have this right, it would make a big difference to you if we were able to base one of our team in your offices?
- Am I right in thinking that this project must be finished inside two weeks?
- Tell me, what are the must-have outcomes from this piece of work?

This also helps the client to better understand what it is they value as they may also have given too little thought to this. You need to help them do this, because if they do not understand the value that they may obtain from the services you deliver then they are not going to want to pay for that value. It should lead to your proposal highlighting the key drivers of value that came out of that discussion: that will explain your price to them and will justify your charging a higher price than competitors who have not had value discussions with the client. Don't be too busy to have these conversations (and leap straight to standard scope and price), or you will miss out on one of your biggest opportunities to increase profits.

Let's now look at another form of value pricing, one which varies the fee after the service has been delivered and bases that fee on the actual outcome so that the service provider shares in the success or failure of each piece of work.

VALUE PRICING BY WORK TYPE

Every so often there is a news story about a restaurant or café that abolishes fixed prices but asks customers to pay what they think is fair after they have had the meal. There is an alluring logic to this formula. Why should restaurant customers pay *more* than they think a meal was worth, because that is clearly not a sustainable business model and any restaurant that fixes its prices faces just that risk?

These experiments seem to be almost entirely in the not-for-profit sector, which says a lot about their financial success, and in any event they are not a widespread phenomenon. I consider that any services business that followed this approach would be at great risk of 'selection against', by which I mean that the clients who are most attracted to the businesses are likely to be those people who are going to pay the least. If there are really successful service businesses operating on this model then they may have some interesting lessons for us all. For now I am going to assume that they are not a mainstream possibility.

Much more common is an approach that sets prices, but also has an element of variable uplift (or less commonly, discount) based upon actual outcome. Restaurant tipping is a good example of this approach. We have already outlined the approach for general services which varies by work type as set out in the table below:

Rocket Science	Budget range given with upper and lower levels. Actual fee based on outcome (and may be under the minimum stated but will not exceed the maximum).
Relationship Advice	Identify at the outset a series of desired outcomes from the work and describe in detail possible outcomes as poor, good and great. After completion, compare actual outcome, with a good result giving the agreed fee, poor being up to –20% and great being up to +20% (at client's discretion).
Routine Work	Create data points around outcomes, with the actual fee being varied in a mechanical way based upon actual performance. For example, target completion is 30 days and fee is ±3% for each day of difference.

THE BIG QUESTION: DOES VALUE PRICING MEAN THE END OF CHARGING BY TIME?

No. And yes.

Wherever you find people who charge upon the basis of time taken to complete the work you will find nervous clients who feel out of control and worried about the final bill. As we have discussed, this is a particular concern for Relationship Advice and we have seen how project-based costing (rather than fixed fees) can work both for the client and for the service provider. However, doesn't a value approach also offer an opportunity to agree a fee in advance and stick to it?

It can. You can use the techniques already discussed when creating your fee quote to understand the client's drivers of value and then design a (more valuable) service which covers those needs and has an appropriately matching, fixed price. However, I don't see a need to fix the fee (in Relationship Advice) as a project-based cost approach will work just as well. It fixes the fee for the agreed scope of work (but not for any additional work which the client agrees needs carrying out).

What is more challenging is the issue of whether those working on this matter need to record time. Once you have a fixed fee or project-based costed fee, you cannot charge the client more just because you took more time than you thought to carry out tasks within the agreed scope. So why bother recording time? I would say that recording time is often a key management tool for a firm because it enables you to see at a glance who is busy and who is not, and is often the mainstay of the management accounts. It also helps you to understand how much it has cost you (in time) to deliver a piece of work, and whether you underestimated or overestimated the time that would be needed. That is important information to help you to quote more accurately in the future.

Even where you have agreed a fixed fee or project-based costed fee with your client, continuing to record time against that matter provides you with absolutely key management information.

In the next chapter we are going to look at other lessons that we can take from commerce and industry. Can we learn from airlines with their dynamic pricing, from the makers of aero engines who sell 'power by the hour' rather than selling a physical engine, from loyalty rewards schemes, from pricing across the lifetime of a service or selling add-ons such as maintenance contracts?

Learning from industry

In this chapter I'm going to look at the wide variety of pricing strategies and tactics of very disparate businesses. They might be consumer facing, transport, technology or industrial and I want to see if there are lessons that we can learn from the approaches that they have developed in order to survive and prosper.

Some of the most interesting lessons are about how you might deliberately vary the price of a service across its lifetime (rather than just having one price); using price to match your capacity in the way that airlines do; using add-ons and maintenance contracts to dramatically increase the profit per transaction; using key client programmes to drive and reward loyalty; and how to use price matching to prevent a price war.

PRICING ACROSS THE LIFETIME OF A PRODUCT

Sometimes called 'skim pricing' because of its skill at taking extra money off early adopters, there are some valuable lessons to be learnt from a proactive approach to product cycle pricing. This is in contrast to the much more common, passive approach which occurs by way of default, where service firms drop their prices late in the service cycle when clients refuse to pay them. Let's look at this in practice.

In the technology sector it is very common to bring out the latest gadgets at a very high initial price (aimed at the segment of customers who have to have the latest technology), and then after a relatively short period (six months being typical) there is a reduction to attract the next segment of customers before finally being discounted at the same time as the next innovation is launched, and the cycle starts again.

The pricing over time would look something like Figure 9.1.

In this example, a company introduces a 40-inch television at an initial price of £700, in the knowledge that this is currently the largest size available and also that it has a 55-inch television with 3D capability in development. After the early adopters have paid £700 it drops the price of the 40-inch model to £450 at the same time as launching a 55-inch model (but holding back on the 3D) at a price of £800. Again it waits for the early adopters to pay £800 before dropping the price of the 40-inch model to £300, the 55-inch to £600 and launches a 55-inch plus 3D model for £900, and so on ad infinitum. Life-cycle pricing requires constant innovation so that new, higher specified models are continually coming along the track.

| Figure 9.1 | Pricing over time |

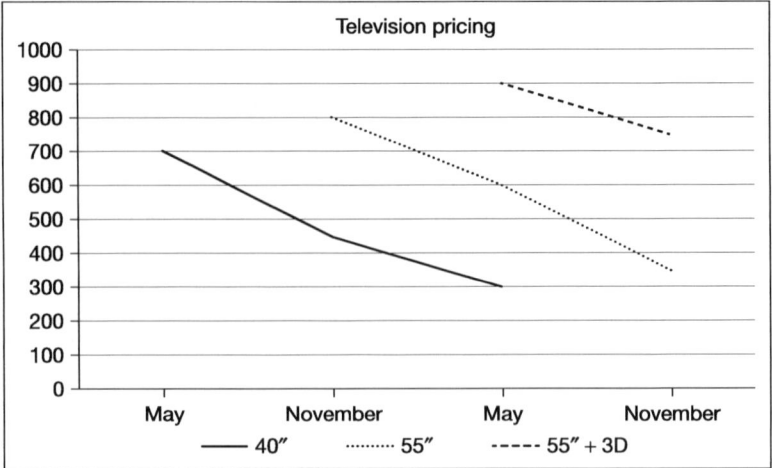

Television pricing

1000
900
800
700
600
500
400
300
200
100
0

May   November   May   November

—— 40"   .... 55"   ----- 55" + 3D

| Figure 9.2 | Skim pricing |

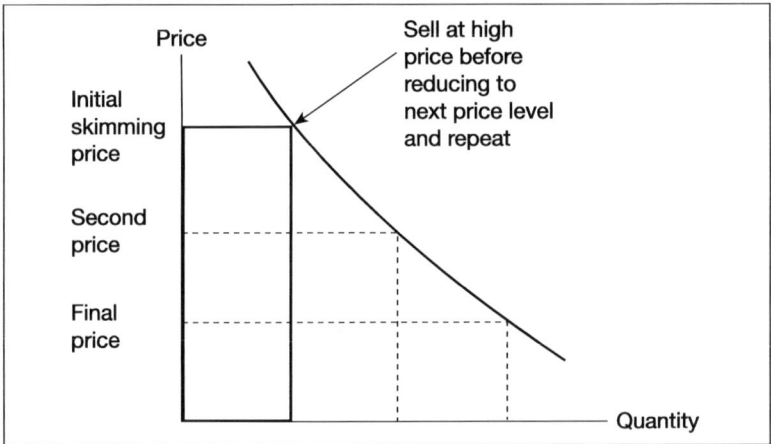

Price

Sell at high price before reducing to next price level and repeat

Initial skimming price

Second price

Final price

Quantity

For an individual product or service, skim pricing looks like Figure 9.2.

This works well in the electronics industry, which needs to keep innovating and to keep persuading us that we need to buy their latest product. The initial production run might not be huge because there could be a relatively small number of early adopters, and as scale production begins the price can be dropped against higher production runs. Notice also that this approach is very different from the more typical 'cost-plus' approach to pricing used in services. The cost-plus model tends to allocate the same price to the service *throughout its life cycle*. This means ignoring the realities of the marketplace, which could mean undercharging at the start when a service is cutting edge (and a premium is justified in market terms), but then overcharging in maturity when clients are seeking lower prices for a service that has become more commonly available. The end result is that there is a failure to realise available profits at the start and clients force the price down (switching suppliers, or threatening to) as it becomes more widely available. Cost-plus would be the equivalent of pricing at the level of the 'Second price' in the graph in Figure 9.2.

It is common for there to be a life cycle in service offerings, but it is rare for the firms involved to prepare for price drops as the market matures. That would mean planning to deliver cutting-edge services based on using Rocket Scientists to solve new problems (or to produce new answers to old problems), but in the knowledge that this workstream needs to be passed across to Relationship Advisers at some point who can then deliver well-established solutions at lower prices using teams with higher leverage. Rather, service providers tend to complain about the commoditisation of their services as their Rocket Scientists find increasing price resistance from clients. The same applies to Relationship Advice which (over time) moves to Routine Work (as some, but not all, will).

Service firms can be at a definite advantage to competitors if they introduce this change of work methodology, and therefore change pricing, over the lifetime of a service. They will end up driving the process while continuing to develop new services at the top end. What are you doing in your business to manage price across each service's lifetime to achieve that?

Try this exercise: imagine that a brand new competitor is coming into your market. They don't carry the baggage of the past. They are starting with a blank sheet of paper. What specific area of your business should they target if they are going to be most successful? Given that they are starting afresh, how should they best organise themselves in terms of location, team structures, technology and so on?

Spend some time thinking about what this competitor would look like if they got it absolutely right – targeting exactly the right segment of your market and set-up to do so efficiently and so as to maximise their profit? You could find that the design you create is very different from your existing set-up. That's interesting in itself, isn't it? Now, the good news is that this competitor doesn't exist today – but why don't you create this competing service? In fact, with your existing experience you would make a better job of it than they would. Don't wait for a new competitor to get it just right. Do it yourself!

This type of thinking is increasingly important. It will ensure that you do not complain that your (premium) services are being commoditised, but that you take the lead in seeing where you can create efficiencies due to your experience in carrying out the work. As a team handles more and more work of a similar type they will benefit from the experience curve effect: that over time the cost (time) of carrying out a task drops. This is an opportunity to revisit the team needed to carry out the work and it enables you to create different services at lower costs. That doesn't automatically mean that you need to reduce the price to clients – at least in the early stages you can simply achieve higher profitability.

Given the benefits of life-cycle pricing and using innovation to develop better services, it is a surprise that more service firms are not embedding this at their core. Innovation can create newly differentiated services justifying higher prices or it can be used to lower production costs when prices are falling. The key elements in success will include the following:

- **Creating the right internal culture for innovation.** That means having very visible support, from the top, and devoting people, time and money to innovation while recognising that these new projects carry a higher risk of failure than existing products.

- **Aligning your reward systems.** Most service firms offer greater rewards to people who *do not* innovate! Firms look for volume returns, and that may reward those who reliably deliver the equivalent of 40 televisions rather than taking time out to develop new services (some of which may fail).

- **Involving your clients.** The real dangers in internal teams being 'creative' is that they are very unlikely to produce solutions that meet current clients' expectations and needs. This is not a question of handing the project over to clients (as Henry Ford remarked: if he had done that his customers would have demanded faster horses, rather than cars), but it does mean trying out your ideas on them and asking them to help you build final services which are of maximum value to them.

- **Using external facilitators.** Teams that are wholly internal may fail to ask obvious questions because they have become institutionalised. They may accept 'the way things are done around here'. An outsider may be much more challenging.

If you do start producing new solutions and services, then reread Chapter 2 to remember the rules for pricing new service launches.

PENETRATION PRICING

The exact opposite of skim pricing, penetration pricing, is about entering a market (or creating a new one) at deliberately low prices in order to establish a foothold in a competitive market. An often-quoted example is the Lexus car, introduced by Toyota into the United States in 1989 as an entirely separate marque designed to compete with the likes of BMW and Mercedes Benz. At its launch the Lexus would have been something of an unknown quantity. It had no established track record and despite the obvious build quality, customers would have been nervous of being one of the first buyers. The Lexus strategy was to create substantial value in its product but also to price it about 40% below its intended competition. That enabled it to gain a foothold, build up its sales and then, year-on-year, increase its prices to their intended level.

Partners love penetration pricing even though they don't call it that. Typically a partner meets a potential new client and wants to be certain of winning the first job. So they deliberately go in very low on price, but as previously discussed, this tactic is more likely to position you as a low-price provider in the mind of the client and make it very difficult for you to charge realistic prices later on. However, there is one area where I believe penetration pricing can be very successful, and that is in the realm of cross-selling additional services to an existing client. In this case you have already built up a reputation and a position. You want to persuade the client to try you out in another area of work and here you could position an offer as follows:

> *I know you have not tried out our services in {new work type/new location} but I would like you to do so. To encourage you to try us out, I would like to offer you a 50% discount on the first piece of work. In that way you will have the opportunity to see what we can do and in the process will make a substantial saving.*

Positioning the cross-selling offer in this way makes it very clear to the client that subsequent pieces of work will not also be at half price, while showing them a real benefit for giving you a trial.

A second way of using reduced prices is in relation to referrals. What is it worth for you to gain another client in the same industry as an existing client? How much would you be prepared to spend in terms of marketing, hosting events and creating brochures in order to gain such clients? What is the best, most successful way of gaining a new client (and I will give you a hint, it's not the brochure)?

One of the strongest reasons for a new client coming to you is because they receive a recommendation by someone in their industry.

Putting this together means that you can actually reward your existing clients for giving referrals. If you did this directly to the introducer client, then this might look quite improper and indeed may have influenced their introduction – but there is a way of giving rewards that works for both of the clients. I first saw this approach used by an accountant. In return for the introduction he emailed both the clients, thanked the introducer for his actions and said that as a reward he would give the new client 10% off their first three months' fees. That makes the introducer client feel great as their actions have directly benefited the new client. It also gives the new client an extra incentive to test you out. Rewarding referrals through pricing is an effective and safe way of building new business.

LEARNING FROM AIRLINES

Where to start? Airlines have developed such sophisticated pricing strategies to cover a combination of yield and price management that they are generally seen as at the forefront of pricing innovation. It is worth unpacking some of their approaches to see if we can use them more broadly.

Segmentation

Addressing different parts of the flying community with very different offers is clearly at the heart of much airline competitive strategy. From the budget airlines seeking to profitably serve the most cost-conscious travellers (but then developing clever tactics to derive the maximum yield from those passengers) up to flag carriers running business-only aircraft on the most lucrative routes, and everything in between, there is clearly a high level of sophistication here. One very interesting issue that arises (and has great implications for brand) is whether a premium service provider can also provide a very low-cost service. You might think that they already do, when you step onto a large aircraft and see a small first class section, a larger business class followed by premium economy and economy. However, the budget airlines showed that a very low-cost service is actually something very different and (at least initially) is built on the basis that a clean start allows the budget airline to create low-cost services using its cost base advantage. It is not saddled with legacy costs (particularly labour costs), can buy the latest, most fuel-efficient aircraft and create lean administration and overheads (EasyJet began in a tiny cabin at Luton Airport). It can offer seats at prices that, if matched, would mean a loss on every seat for the traditional flag carrier airline. Of course, as budget airlines grow and mature there is increasing evidence that their complexity starts to erode some of their cost base advantages, but there is no doubt that their fresh start approach offers us some lessons.

No matter what type of service you are currently offering in the Relationship Advice or Routine Work space, it is likely that a new competitor could use these techniques to start afresh and create a service that looks similar to yours but at a lower price; or to create a service that is unashamedly a cut-down version of yours, but at a *much* lower price. How do you react? The risk for you is this: clients who are price sensitive may ask you to match these lower prices so that they can save money, and even very loyal clients themselves may have come under pressure to cut costs and start passing on that pressure to you. If you are in the position of the flag carrier airline then it is easy to match the lower price, but only by sacrificing all profits, which is not a sustainable strategy. If your cost base is higher than your competitors' it is not wise to start a price war.

There are three strategies that can work:

1. The first strategy is to accept that a proportion of business will be lost to the lower cost competitor and to concentrate on making a good profit from the others. For example, let's say that 25% of your customers will be lost to the 'budget' competitor. It may be better to carry on providing a better, more expensive service to the 75% than it is to fight over that 25% and have to lower prices and perhaps take your own brand downmarket in the process. In my observation of telecom companies, I have seen financial calculations that show them to be much more profitable by accepting the loss of a client segment rather than seeking to match a new competitor.

2. The second strategy is to introduce 'complex pricing'. Using this, you erect barriers to a client obtaining the lower price so that effectively the clients self-select who receives lower prices. This might include being able to order well in advance, having to accept minimum quantities, carrying out some of the work themselves (the equivalent of printing your own boarding pass) and so on. This can be really successful in beating off the lower

priced challenger by showing clients that, provided they meet some (reasonably possible) criteria, then your price is pretty similar. In fact, budget airlines realise this in reverse, because if you try to book a flight at short notice for a short trip (so that you look like a business traveller) then you might be surprised to see that their price is very similar to a flag carrier airline. I have also seen complex pricing, which is just designed to be complex and deliberately so. In these cases – and they often appear across industries in response to initial price-driven competition – each company offers a complex plethora of options so that it is difficult to know in advance which company is going to give you the best deal. Think of utilities and telecoms providers. If they all offered *exactly* the same service then customers would be left only to compare on price. If I can buy my electricity from three possible suppliers which all charge a monthly fee of £10 plus 15p per kilowatt hour, then there is no competition. If one supplier drops to 10p a kilowatt hour then I (and everyone else) may move to them, which would force the other suppliers to match it. So their defence is to create multiple, complex tariffs, some offering fixed rates, some variable, some with standing charges and some without.

For generic goods (or services) simple price competition isn't going to work because any supplier dropping prices will find that their competitors have to match them or lose the market to them. I'm not sure that any electricity supplier could convince me that they gave a valuably better service than others because I am so used to a completely reliable electricity supply (of course it would be different if the supply was somewhat erratic and one supplier was able to improve upon that). In these circumstances, the suppliers will try to segment the market. One may offer a service to low-volume users which omits the monthly fee. Another may target the highest users and pass on some economies of scale because servicing three very large homes with three large bills is easier than having to earn the same money from 20 small flats. Yet another may offer to fix the price for 18 months in advance in return for charging a small premium over the existing price. Others may target customers who buy both their gas and electricity from one supplier. That creates a veritable forest of possible costs with the result that there is no clear single route to a lowest price. It works where the buyers are small compared to the seller, but a major buyer may well demand much simpler prices.

Complex pricing can work particularly well in the area of Routine Work (although a preferable method is to adopt a drivers-of-value approach), but it can be less acceptable in Relationship Advice, where it cuts across the essence of fair dealing that is implicit in a genuine relationship.

3. The third strategy, when faced with a 'budget airline' competitor, is to take them on head-on and create a division or a subsidiary that offers a very similar (cut down) service under a different brand name. This strategy accepts that a proportion of existing customers will leave for a budget offering and that you would rather capture these (or a good share of them) by beating the budget carrier at its own game. This sounds acceptable in broad terms, but commercial history is littered with failures when this approach has been taken. The mind set of the management in a budget airline or any low-cost operator is very different from the traditional service provider. Even if you recruit such people and put them in a subsidiary, there comes a point where the parent becomes tired of its offspring poaching its customers for lower fees. At some point, the lower cost alternative is cannibalising the parent company's customers, and doing so in order to offer them lower prices. For this reason I recommend to clients that initially they adopt a semi-revolutionary approach, as explained in the discussion of skim pricing, where a team is offered the opportunity to do things in a different way within the organisation, rather than trying to imitate a low-cost competitor. This opens up the opportunity to offer different levels of service within one brand (think of the different classes of travel offered by an airline) rather than jumping into the house-of-brands approach seen in the Volkswagen Group where brands (and prices) range from Skoda to Bentley. The latter approach may be necessary in your market but requires greater resources to pull off successfully.

Loyalty schemes

Also used extensively in the hotels sector, loyalty schemes are designed to give the customer a reason to use the supplier again, other than one based upon lowest cost. This works on two levels. First, it encourages loyalty by giving better benefits to the higher levels of membership. You repeat purchase so that enough points are awarded to reach the next tier or to remain there. Secondly, it gives rewards based upon usage so that customers will see value in repeat purchases irrespective of the tiers – for example, trading in points for free flights or hotel nights. A typical airline scheme might have levels and rewards as shown in the table below:

Level	Rewards
Blue/red/ green	An ability to collect points that can be exchanged for free flights, or for discounts off flights, or for other goods and services
Silver	Above plus the ability to reserve seats for free when booking a flight, priority booking and check-in, access to business lounges, bonus additional points on each flight
Gold	Above plus access to first class lounges, first class check-in, free extra luggage, etc.

These schemes do actually create loyalty at a minimal cost to the airline or hotel. Free flights will be offered on quiet flights when there should be empty seats and similarly a hotel can fill up empty rooms during quiet periods. Business lounges and first class check-ins are already in place, so the marginal additional cost of another user is low. I would say that a key part of any successful loyalty scheme is to find benefits that are low cost to you but high value to your clients.

There is clearly a fair degree of cost and organisation associated with a full-blown loyalty scheme. If your business is one that can benefit from this then I am sure it will repay the investment. My experience of service businesses generally has been that only the largest could even contemplate a formal loyalty scheme. However, that should not mean that your loyal clients are given nothing. There are two really good reasons for this: first, loyalty schemes work because they drive loyalty and that is very valuable in profit terms to any business. They are a clear alternative to trying to attract clients with ever lower prices. Secondly, they can be a well-structured way of giving higher benefits only to your most valuable clients rather than their being handed out (often over-generously) by partners on an ad hoc basis.

A well-devised loyalty scheme on a smaller scale can be built around a Key Account Management Programme (KAM). In case you don't have one of those, KAM identifies your 'top clients', usually based upon turnover (or clients that you think have the potential to grow substantially), and puts resources into better understanding their needs so that you can look for ways of increasing your share of their spend by satisfying those needs. Here's a good question relating to the current position in your business: in terms of the quality of service, the best teams of people, the discounts and the added value, are these targeted at your KAM clients, or is it rather more haphazard? While I may not advocate handing out different coloured plastic cards to your clients, you really should be categorising them in terms of their value to your business as Group A at the top, then Group B and Group C, so that you can then carry out a comparison of prices and added value given to them (more about this in Chapter 11). Finding a Group C client who has a better deal from you than a Group A client should be considered to be a major issue (it puts the Group A client at risk because they would be rightly angry if they discovered this).

This type of categorisation also helps in two other ways. Clients may try to impose a 'most favoured nation' clause upon you. Such a clause says that as a major client of yours, you undertake not to give better terms (prices, added value or otherwise) to any other client and that, if you do, you will notify the major client and give them the same deal. I think these clauses are extremely difficult to enforce once an organisation grows in size (because of the difficulty of tracking the actual deals done by partners in every location), so they are worth resisting on that basis alone. If the clause must be conceded, then having a proper loyalty/KAM scheme makes it easier to keep track of deals for major clients and to say that the price match will only occur with a client who is providing you with the same type and volume of work. For example, a client who sends you twice as much work (or work of a higher value type) may have a better deal than that given to the client with the most favoured nation deal. Additionally, this should start you thinking about what extras you should give to your best KAM clients based upon their value to you. In creating these extra benefits it is important to think about what the client values, but is low or zero cost to you. For example, if you have city centre offices, clients may find it valuable to be offered the opportunity to use your offices for meetings. You might find it low cost to host a client's team meetings but that might be highly valued by the client. It's well worth a brainstorming session to create these options. In other words, look at the type of added value that airlines give to their top-level 'Gold' clients and think about what you could provide to your best clients that would be similarly valued by them.

Pricing by the client – in acceptable ways

Much has been written about the skills involved in pricing 'by the client', but that makes me nervous. It takes me back to the conversation I had with a plumber who said that he priced his jobs based upon the length of the drive leading to the front door. The longer the drive, the more the client could afford to pay. That doesn't seem fair and appropriate. It would be like writing a book and then selling it at a different price depending upon the buyer's earnings in the preceding 12 months. So the crucial issue when charging clients different prices is to make sure that the difference is justifiable. Let's look at some real-life examples.

Airlines, and also flight search websites, are able to map and model passenger price sensitivities and therefore exploit the price sensitivity of individual passengers to better maximise the profit on each seat. The airline may use some or all of the following factors to create 'dynamic pricing' that reacts to actual client demand:

- **Seasonality** – this is demand driven. Those travelling in a high season will expect to pay a higher price, and are therefore less sensitive to the price. Flexibility on dates would often result in lower prices.

- **Priorities** – direct or indirect, time of flight, departure point and destination. The level of inconvenience that the passenger is willing to bear will affect the price paid.

- **Flexibility in ticket** – refundable, changeable tickets will come at a much higher price when compared to a non-refundable fixed one.

- **Class of travel** – airlines have different classes of travel to address the needs, and therefore price sensitivities, of each segment.

You should examine how you could import this type of thinking into your service business. Which clients are the most demanding in terms of service quality and speed? Try to separate out a different, higher priced, service for them which brings them the benefits they need but charges them extra for those benefits. What are the variables around your service?

If you schedule work for months ahead, do you charge the clients for cancellation? If you do then that means that you could offer a 'no cancellation fee' option at the outset at a higher cost. Let's say that clients book training workshops from you, but the reality is that some will cancel with relatively short notice for one reason or another. You may well have standard terms which say that cancellation is free if 10 weeks' notice is given, but incurs between 20% and 75% of the fee for cancellation between 10 weeks and two weeks before delivery, then 100% of the fee if under two weeks' notice is given. That seems reasonable but it also may be somewhat theoretical – in practice, good relationships with clients may mean that you find it difficult to charge cancellation fees. In such a case you could offer 'no fee cancellations' provided that 10% of the cost of the workshop is paid as a 'flexibility' fee. This should represent marginal extra income (especially if you have found it difficult to impose any cancellation fees in practice). You can calculate the necessary additional fee by looking at past experience and you may want to charge more to a client who regularly cancels or reschedules than one who does it rarely. Or you could offer clients a reduced fee for a workshop if 100% is paid in advance and it is inflexible (no refund if the workshop does not take place). This is similar to the airlines fees for flexible tickets as opposed to lower-cost inflexible ones. This neatly brings us into the issue of service add-ons.

ADD-ONS AND AFTERCARE – DOUBLE THE PROFIT

Anyone who has had the pleasure of shopping for electrical goods and appliances will know the hard sell of a salesperson who tries to persuade you to buy an extended warranty for a product that, not 10 minutes previously, they were praising for its build quality and reliability. There is a reason that the salesforce are often given targets for sales of extras and aftercare products like this. This marginal extra income (all of their expenses in running the business are there anyway, whether they sell you an extended warranty or not) can be a very substantial source of extra profit. It is not unusual for the business to *double* their profit on the transaction if they are able to sell add-ons to you at the same time as they sell the primary product.

Let's look at some easy examples. In the past, a fast food outlet might have offered to supersize your meal (or offered you fries if you haven't already ordered them) this is an easy way of substantially increasing the profit on your visit. The idea of 'supersizing' is often credited to David Wallerstein, the manager of a chain of cinemas in the 1960s in the United States who wanted to increase sales of popcorn (and bearing in mind that, at the time, only one size was offered). He found that people were unlikely to buy two bags of popcorn each, but when he offered also a large size, sales increased dramatically. He was then recruited to work at McDonald's and is credited with introducing the supersize offer (although supersize meals ended up being phased out). If you examine the economics, it shows the dramatic difference. If the profit to be made on a $5 meal is $0.50 and the customer supersizes for $0.75 extra, then if the extra ingredients cost $0.25 you just doubled the profit you are making from this transaction. Car dealers are well known for offering optional add-ons and there is no doubt that persuading you to add air conditioning, metallic paint or satellite navigation to your new car can make a very real difference to the total profit that the dealer makes on the sale. In many cases the dealer's profit from add-ons is greater than the entire profit made by selling you the base model of the car.

In addition, there are 'aftercare' products and services which involve you in paying for something which is going to take place after the sale, such as maintenance agreements, extended warranties or the supply of consumables (for example, it is possible to sell you an inkjet printer at a very low price in the knowledge that you will have to pay a lot for the supply of ink cartridges).

How does this play out for a services firm? I have found it useful to think of these extras in two groups: *add-ons*, which enhance the service that will be delivered ('supersize me' or 'do you want fries with that?'), and *aftercare*, which relates to a follow-on service which is sold at the same time as the main service (even though it will be delivered separately and after the main service has ended). They are particularly powerful with larger pieces of work because the initial budget might be able to cover the extra cost, whereas if you try to sell these additional services afterwards you may find that the client has no budget from which to draw the cost.

Let's look at some possible examples. If you are working on a major project with a client then a useful add-on could be that you would lend them a member of your team who would work alongside them and help them to manage their end of the project. This person will be embedded in the client's team and, because of their previous experience, will help to ensure that the project is a great success. For clients who are having their first taste of such a major project, this could be assistance and reassurance that is well worth buying. Or you could offer the client a 'dedicated team' for the duration of a project so that (in return for an additional fee) named members of a core group agree not to take on other work during this client's project.

In other cases you could be the intermediary who benefits by taking a fee from an add-on from another supplier (as is the case when a retailer sells a customer an extended warranty). Estate agents, for example, may earn fees by introducing clients to suppliers of legal services, removal companies, sources of finance, home design or furnishing.

If you are something of a 'deal junkie' who carries out one-off projects for clients, then it can be valuable to step back and think of what happens to the client *after* your involvement in the deal has completed. There may be issues over implementation of the work or important dates and milestones that need to be followed up. These are typically left for the client to handle (the deal junkies by this stage being wholly engaged on their next deal), but it could be valuable to offer the client some support from your own (separate) implementation team. The client may find it possible to add in this expenditure at the outset as part of a global fee, in cases where they would find it impossible to access a budget after completion. If there are key dates and milestones then it should not be difficult to persuade a client to effectively buy some insurance against missing them by having a clear aftercare service from you that will provide timely reminders to them – provided, of course, that you have insured yourself against missing them!

There really shouldn't be any area of your firm where you cannot think of genuinely valuable add-ons and aftercare that could be offered to clients. Similarly, there may be particular methods of working with individual clients to better meet their needs during a major transaction, in which case there are opportunities to offer extra support for an extra fee.

If you are successful in developing a range of add-ons and aftercare services then you now only have one more obstacle to overcome – your own partners! Despite clearly pricing these additional services, within a short time of their being announced some partner will have already offered all of them to a new client for free, with the explanation that it was essential in securing this important new client. There will be a variety of reasons why the partner has done this and some of them do have apparent validity. For example, a potential client may have been genuinely influenced into choosing you by the array of free add-ons, but it is worth challenging this, as I consider that the client's actual choice is more often about the core service.

To get to grips with some of the issues here, it is probably useful to draw an analogy from the car industry. For example, imagine a situation where Ford and General Motors have competing models in a particular market segment, and let's say that they both enjoy a 40% market share. The Ford dealer and the General Motors dealer have a series of different models within the range and also have a number of optional extras which would be an additional cost for the customer on all but the top of the range models, which include items such as satellite navigation, air conditioning, metallic paint, leather seats and so on.

If Ford were now to recruit a services firm partner as a car sales-person, targeted in the same way as the average partner would be (on turnover rather than profit), then they would see a dramatic improvement in their sales. The basic model would soon be being sold with the completely free addition of satellite navigation, air conditioning, leather seats and auto-parking at the very least. This would result in a greater number of sales and the market share of Ford might reach 50% or even 60% before General Motors even understood what was going on. The partner will claim that customers are, time and again, choosing Ford because of these extras.

The only problem with this huge success is that effectively the partner has been making substantial price cuts but disguising them by charging the full price for the basic model (no price cut there), then throwing in the extras. This is really just a variation on price cutting, and cutting prices is very successful until the competitor reacts. The likely end result in the car contest is, of course, that General Motors either adopts the same strategy on its add-ons or effectively does the same by cutting the prices of its basic model. Both Ford and General Motors suffer greatly reduced profits in this area of the marketplace – and any market share gained by Ford would be very short term indeed.

So what is needed are some real controls on the abilities of partners to give away these valuable extras. In one firm that I worked with, this came down to allocating very clear and communicated costs to each add-on and aftercare service, and then circulating lists to all partners where these had been given away. Once again it was a question of using transparency and peer pressure so that partners saw a benefit in selling extras, rather than giving them away.

UNEXPECTED EXTRA COSTS AND PENALTIES

Bjorn Hanson, a clinical professor with the New York University Preston Robert Tisch Center for Hospitality and Tourism, estimated that in 2014 hotels would charge $2.3 billion in additional fees, up from $2.1 billion in the preceding year. Mimicking the airline industry, which had learnt to charge extra for printing a boarding pass or choosing your seat, hotels were adding 'resort fees' (a daily fee for using the facilities at the hotel), and fees for early arrival and late check-out, luggage storage or parcel receipt.

It can be tempting to follow suit, but in terms of fair pricing (sustainable and believed to represent reasonable value by your client) there is a great difference between being offered an opportunity to have a late check-out at 4pm in return for a (reasonable) fee, and being charged a daily resort fee which is not optional and was not made clear it was going to be an additional cost at the time of booking. If I reserve a room at a hotel for £200 a night then it is not appropriate to make that £230 because of a compulsory resort fee, even if that does include free Wi-Fi and a bottle of water.

When you start thinking in terms of extras, they must be truly optional, clearly explained *and fair.* For example: you need to rent a car for a week and you compare prices with two or three major car rental companies before settling upon one that seems to offer a good deal on the car that you want. As usual you buy full collision damage insurance so that you won't have anything to pay in the event of an accident. Several weeks later, you arrive at the rental location to collect your car and you are offered optional collision damage waiver insurance. You explain that you already bought that, only to be told that the collision damage waiver insurance which you bought online when booking the car does not cover the first £2000 worth of damage. The extra cost insurance you are now being offered covers that first £2000. The cost of the extra insurance is 50% of the total cost of the car hire! How does that make you feel? Will you ever use this car rental company again? On paper they just increased their prices and their profit.

So, bear that in mind when creating extra charges.

INSURERS AND THE POOL

It is worth looking at how life insurance developed different prices for different groups of people. Insurance is essentially a pooling of risk so that, in return for a premium, the insured obtains cover against a risk – the greater the number of people in the pool, the safer it is to be able to estimate and average out the risk. Initially this was a simple pool where the risk was averaged based upon age and everyone charged accordingly.

However, some companies decided that if they could actually just insure the good risks, those with a lower than average death rate, then they could offer them lower premium rates and still make a very good profit. For example, they could offer life insurance only to 18 to 60-year-olds, in the knowledge that the mortality rate would be less than if they offered cover to all, including the over-60s. They might additionally use geographic data (because where you live has an impact upon your health and life expectancy) to find those with better than average chances of survival. Having carried out that exercise, the insurer could offer lower rates to their chosen market segment than a competitor who just averaged risks across all. In other words, the good risks will not be subsidising the bad.

In general, service firms tend to be closer to the original broad pool approach in that we put too little effort into distinguishing between the actual amounts of work that different clients cause for apparently similar tasks. I can think of one example from my own experience, where we were carrying out a similar work type for several different banks. However, the way that the banks were organised internally meant that although we were charging all of them the same price per transaction, the actual work involved varied quite dramatically.

Separating the work out into different elements, and looking at the cost to you of carrying out each part of the work, enables you to refine your prices. Clients who choose everything on the menu (or simply cause more work) are offered a higher price (reflecting the greater amount of work, and hence staff you have tied up in carrying out the transactions), but with the option to reduce the price (even to lower than the average) if they change working practices to reduce the amount of work for you.

PRICE MATCHING PROMISES TO (ACCIDENTALLY) STOP COMPETITION

We can all recall examples of situations where companies have launched price promises. These take the form of saying that 'no one will be cheaper than us', or that 'we will match any competitor's prices', or that 'we will check our competitors to make sure that you get the best deal from us' and so on. I am sure that none of these companies ever intended to stop price competition in their sector, although that can be the consequence. These types of campaigns come in two varieties: genuine price matching and partial price matching. I want to examine them separately.

Genuine price matching

Imagine a situation where you have commodity or generic goods (water, fuel, sand, cement) or branded goods (televisions, computers, food). I want to look at petrol first, so you are going to be the owners of a petrol station. You have just two local competitors who have been coexisting with you over many years. There is sufficient local business to keep you all profitable but then one of your competitors is taken over by a national chain. They start a price war. The clear and obvious purpose is that they take market share from you. After all, petrol is petrol and it is going to be very difficult for you to show a valuable differentiation in what is seen as a generic product. If you don't match the price you may find that too much of your business is lost; if you do match the price then you (perhaps also your other competitor) are now both selling fuel at lower prices, so your profit is reduced, if not removed. If you *do* match the competitor's price, maybe they will cut again. You are in a bad place. Your customers are being taught to shop around and start actively checking prices. You are in a race to the bottom.

There is a neat alternative which can stop price competition: that is, to display a large sign at your petrol station announcing a price match promise. So it might say 'The lowest prices in town – we guarantee to match local prices'. Now your customers don't need to shop around and, more to the point, your competitor needs to stop dropping prices, because you have also very effectively signalled to them that whatever price they drop to, you will match it, and so price cutting by them is pointless. It will not win them any extra business (because you will match the lower price), it will just lower their profit. Unless their intention was to drop to uneconomic prices to drive you out of business (and then put up prices now there is less competition – something that most competition regulations forbid), they will stop price cutting. In fact the lesson they will learn is that if they *put prices up* you will follow, with the end result that price competition ends and you both make higher profits. So that is a really interesting side-effect of price matching and the next time you see this, think about whether someone is trying to stop their competitors cutting prices. To work effectively it needs to be communicated loudly, so that the price cutting competitor gets the message that cutting prices will not win them any market share because you will immediately match the cut.

Partial price matching

More recently, I have seen price matching defences (particularly around branded goods) become a bit more sophisticated. A supermarket may guarantee to match a competitor's price on branded goods but say that you have to go online to recover your excess spend, or it might give you vouchers that represent the excess, but you can only use those vouchers on your next visit. They might also work hard with the manufacturers of branded goods to produce slightly different sizes and specifications, so that the ones that you bought fall outside of the promise. In all these cases they are trying to create the impression of lower prices, while relying upon inertia to reduce the actual cost to them – for example, many customers will not actually use the price matching vouchers they were given or bother to go online to claim the reduction. That reduces the total cost for the seller while still trying to persuade its customers that they need not shop around to find the best prices.

This price matching is not a first-line solution for most services firms, but well worth bearing in mind. If you have a 'dumb competitor' – one who is initiating a race to the bottom on price – it can be effective to make public that you will match prices and (in the process) accidentally halt pure price-based competition.

POWER BY THE HOUR – CHANGING THE SUPPLY DYNAMIC

Created by Rolls-Royce in 1962, 'Power by the Hour' was a revolutionary approach to the pricing of aero engines. It meant that instead of buying an engine, an aircraft operator paid by the hour of actual flight time – which aligned the interests of the operator and the manufacturer in having maximum reliability of performance. Later enhancements included providing replacement engines while the originals were being serviced and having continuous monitoring of engines in flight so that peak performance could be maintained. This takes a single, one-off purchase and converts it into a long-term relationship with annual fees. Moreover, the fees are tied to actual usage so that the client can see the value in what is being supplied.

This 'total care' approach is one that can also be used by service firms if they think about the variety of day-to-day dealing that they have with their clients and how that might be converted into a single deal. For example, I was intimately involved in the creation and management of just such an arrangement with a client when I was appointed as client partner to Tyco (the American head-quartered conglomerate) in a 'retainer fee' deal which involved the supply of legal services to the company in more than 30 countries for a single annual fee, replacing (overnight) some 282 existing law firms. If you are thinking of offering a retainer fee, you need to consider the following:

- You need to be careful, because once you have a fixed fee for future services you have created an 'all-you-can-eat buffet'. Having agreed the fee, the client sees that the more use they make of the services, the cheaper those services become. You need to create clear incentives so that the client also benefits from *underuse* of the services by sharing savings (and penalising excesses).

- If you are giving the client a level of certainty on fees then you need to get something in return. For example, if the retainer fee covers Relationship Advice, you might seek to have the opportunity to carry out more profitable Rocket Science work as a clear part of the deal.

- You need to have a very clear arrangement to work on reducing the level of fees by reducing the demand for services. Spend reduction workshops (which will take time and resources on both sides) can enable you to manage spend, producing savings on an annual basis and underpinning a long-term relationship.

Well structured, these retainer fee deals are a real opportunity to tie a client into you on a long-term basis and provide a framework for true partnering between you and the client. This neatly leads us into the next chapter, in which we will examine in more detail the whole topic of saving clients money.

Saving clients money

When you need to make savings for clients, many service firms fear the worst. Partners feel that this is simply about cutting rates and certainly about reducing the annual spend of the client, and think this will have a severe impact upon profit, even on numbers of staff. As a result of thinking this way, partners frequently ignore signals that the client is itself under pressure. They work on the basis that it is better to bury their heads in the sand and to await the call, rather than to approach the client to discuss the issue of making savings. Isn't it better to hold off rather than to be the first service provider to have the conversation and therefore be the first one to face the cuts?

In this chapter I want to examine this conundrum in more detail and then to look at some practical steps that any firm can take which will create valuable savings for its clients without damaging the firm's profitability. These steps typically involve a strong element of collaboration with the client and work best in the area of Relationship Advice. However, partners who are most involved in Routine Work may well have valuable experiences that they can pass on. Techniques that they have had to develop in order to survive in their more cost-sensitive world can be of real value to partners who are facing these issues in Relationship Advice for the first time.

THE PRICING DILEMMA

When teaching pricing on Executive Education courses I will often present the participants with a classic pricing dilemma that they need to resolve as a group. This helps them gain an understanding of all of the options that might be available to them. I describe a scenario of a valuable long-standing client spending millions of pounds a year with their service firm. Mostly this has been Relationship Advice, although in the last year this client has also (through one of their expert partners, Pamela) started to instruct them on some Rocket Science.

I ask them to imagine that they developed a strong personal relationship with the key person in this client (let's call her Debbie), and they consider her to be a friend as well as a client. In the scenario, I ask them to imagine that they are on a panel of firms sharing this client's work – let's say that the client uses 10 firms in total. Even though there is a substantial income from the client there is much more to go for in the future, and Debbie herself is high profile and well regarded in her sector. So far, so good.

One morning, they receive a call from Debbie. She sounds flustered. She starts the conversation by apologising and explains that, in view of the terrible financial results which have just been announced by her company, her CEO has told her that she has to lose two members of her own team and that she must immediately reduce external spend by 15%. She is extremely sorry, but she needs to confirm to her CEO by 4pm that day that her external advisers have agreed to cut their rates (or other method of pricing) by 15% or they must be fired from the panel. Debbie therefore needs confirmation by 4pm that day that this 15% reduction is agreed, failing which they have to be removed from the panel and their work passed to others.

What would you say if you were in this situation? You have a few hours to think about it, anyway. Take some time now and work out exactly what you want to say to Debbie when you phone her at just before 4pm. When presenting this dilemma on an Executive Education course, I want the participants to examine the pros and cons of different answers and to think about all of the options that they might have. I have set out a typical analysis below:

Say no and lose the client	Say yes and drop 15%
If we drop by 15% it makes the whole account unprofitable. That makes the work pointless: it's better to face up to that even if we lose the client.	This has been a long-standing client, we have a relationship and maybe we have to take the rough with the smooth.
This discounted rate could continue indefinitely. In fact what is to stop the client calling again in 12 months' time and requiring another 10% off? Do we now have prices that are linked to our clients' profits so they drop in bad times? This client didn't offer to increase our rates when they were having good times.	Losing the work overnight would leave a big hole in our income this year. It is very unlikely that we could replace that work and keep the existing team busy. It is much better for us in the next 12 months to take a 15% cut than lose millions in income.
If we accept the loss now we can start making efforts to find new work for the affected staff.	We might have to lose staff if we say no.
If word gets out that we collapse when challenged on fees, then every client could call us with the same demand. That could put us out of business.	Let's say yes and then try to work it out afterwards – let's get Debbie through today and then see how it maps out. It may well be temporary.

Say no and lose the client	Say yes and drop 15% (cont.)
It's lower risk for us to lose this one client than to have every client know that we will drop rates as soon as challenged.	Maybe we could offer to give the discount, but only for six months or perhaps one year.
We don't believe they will pull all our work immediately. Who will they give it to? It's not like our competitors have spare staff standing by to take on the extra work. We don't believe they will pull Pamela off their Rocket Science work. She's the best person for an important matter. That may swing things in our favour. If they want Pamela they will have to negotiate on their demands on the rest of the work.	We could say yes but lay down some conditions. For example, we could ask to increase the volume of work, break into new areas of work, ask Debbie to make some valuable introductions and win some more work by way of referral.
Let's say no and then negotiate after that. We will be in a stronger position to reach a solution once the client knows that we are prepared to say no to their demands.	Yes, let's try adding lots of conditions, although we would withdraw them if it means coming off the panel and losing the work today.
This is a 'relationship client'. It has taken us many years to build up that relationship and now is the time to get payback. Debbie can't just throw that away and blackmail us into concessions.	We are worried about what we say to Pamela. She is a Rocket Scientist and will not be happy if we just cut her rates (but then maybe she has to suffer alongside us). Or maybe we can exclude Pamela for the 15% reduction and just say yes to the other work being on reduced rates.

Let's dispose of the 'no's' first. There are some good points here, but Debbie may feel (her bluff having been called by their refusal) that she must carry out her threat to fire the firm from the panel for two reasons. First, because if the other service firms on her panel have reluctantly said yes to her demand for an immediate 15% reduction, it seems unfair that she exempts one firm (what if the others found out?). Secondly, is she willing to tell her CEO at the end of the day that she has been unable to achieve the task he or she set? Doesn't that reflect badly on her own position, at a very difficult time for the company? Maybe the

CEO would find the additional saving by firing Debbie. Although I think that the no's are 'right' (and in particular may be right in excluding the Rocket Science work of Pamela, which even Debbie may concede should be best left where it is), let's assume for now that 'no' is the wrong answer and turn to examine the 'yes' column.

Partners are generally more comfortable in this column. The doomsday threat has been removed, they know that Debbie's company is going to stay as a client, but they may have some issues to deal with around profitability. Usually a consensus emerges in the yes camp that they should negotiate. While saying yes to 15% they should look for swaps in return. This is a classic negotiation technique ('trade, don't just concede'), and when I ran this exercise with a mixed group of service firms and their clients the result was that that *all* of those on the client side expected the firms to agree to the 15% discount but to negotiate on other terms (i.e. not one of them saw this type of ultimatum as 'take it or leave it', but rather as a robust start to a negotiation), which is itself interesting.

Let's look at the type of swaps for which you could ask, while still agreeing to give 15% off, starting today:

- You could limit the period of the discount. If it is being given to help the company during a difficult period then you could limit it to one year (even better, to six months), and agree that you do not have to negotiate at the end of the period but that your rates will revert to normal (and normal at that time, not just frozen at today's level).

- You can look for more work in existing areas (a higher percentage of the available spend) or to ask for an introduction to new areas of work.

- Debbie is an industry figure. It would not take much effort for her to introduce you to other potential clients, even to recommend you to them.

- You may be able to exclude Pamela. If she is handling a matter of extreme importance to the client then you may just draw the line and refuse any reduction.

- You might offer that Pamela is prepared to drop by 15%, provided that she is offered a success fee uplift of 30% if certain specified outcomes are achieved.

- You may start locking in alternative fees, annual retainer fees to cover specific areas of work, and a move to value-based fees in Relationship Advice.

In fact, once partners put effort into this they will find that there are some truly valuable swaps that could be obtained in return for the 15% concession.

The only problem is that they cannot have *any* of them. It's just too late. Debbie has to conclude the exercise by 4pm, so it's absolutely impossible for her to trade these concessions to all 10 service firms on her panel. That would be ridiculous. How can she agree that you will all receive *more* work when the purpose of the exercise is to make savings? How can she give you all valuable referrals – she would have to spend all her time working on that. Debbie might accept the concession being limited, but wouldn't do so if the other firms on her panel hadn't also insisted on that. Why should she just give that concession to one firm?

The purpose of this whole scenario is to show you what can happen if you decide to be reactive rather than proactive in terms of saving your clients money. Rerun this scenario, but this time six months before Debbie made this call and, conscious that you are supposed to have a strong relationship, you had visited her and sat down to discuss how you might go about saving her some money. Here you would have been much more in control. You could have had free run at all the possible swaps that you have created, plus no doubt some that you hadn't even imagined. The prize goes to the first firm that is proactive and helpful.

A recent experience from a niche US firm with which I consult on pricing issues gives a great example of proactivity. That firm was advising a corporation that had become caught up in a highly publicised controversy and was featuring on the front pages, day after day. The niche US firm simply sent two of its senior team members to work alongside their client for free, and told them, 'We understand that you must be struggling to cope at the moment, you must be exhausted, we are here to help'. That really is the meaning of 'relationship': his client was contacting me to say that their corporate client had been overjoyed by this reaction, and had already sent them extra work and insisted on paying for the support that had been offered so far.

There is an important lesson here. If you are working in the Relationship Advice space with a client then that includes being sensitive to their need to manage spend, to their changing needs, to be seen to create efficiencies for their organisation, and to help your client to show that part of the value that your client brings to their organisation is to reduce spend where that is possible, without damaging the necessary level of service.

KEY PERFORMANCE INDICATORS EXERCISE

As service providers, we can become so involved with organising the delivery by our team that we spend insufficient time gaining a deep understanding of the pressures on our clients, what they have to deliver to their organisation and how they will (personally) be measured when it comes to an annual performance review. Unpacking this allows to you to create some Key Performance Indicators (KPIs) that will align your interests and your client's so that your performance is more tightly aligned with the client's targets. In doing so you are creating a more valuable service for your client and increasing your differentiation from competitors, both of which allow for higher prices. Let's look at some practical examples.

Alignment with corporate objectives

Clients often complain that they are so busy that they end up dealing with whatever is in their inbox, rather than dealing with the most important work. What is most important? It is the work that helps the client to achieve its corporate objectives. A simple exercise for you to carry out (see 'Hidden resources and how to use them' below for where you find the time for this) is to have your team help the client's team to create a grid which analyses how your client's activities, the work in its department, supports key corporate objectives, as shown in the table below:

Corporate objective	Supporting activity	Measures (KPIs)
To ensure that growth in South America runs at 10%+ each year.	Work with sales force to create standard templates and to cut cycle time.	Reduce the days from sales note to completed contract (currently 15 days).
To reduce operating costs by 5%.	Create standard templates to reduce the cost of external advice.	External spend on contracts reducing month-on-month up to target of 5%.
To ensure compliance with US regulatory framework.	Roll out online training programme for front-line staff.	Number of staff trained each month and percentage of total staff now covered.

The huge benefit to your client is that this type of approach enables them to prioritise their work and to decide what they will do and, crucially, what work they will stop doing because it is not supporting the achievement of their organisation's corporate objectives. It also helps them to create a series of projects that will, across each year, have a clear impact in helping to achieve these objectives. You might wonder what is in this for you in terms of pricing. There are two benefits.

First, if you are providing Relationship Advice then you need to make sure you have a relationship – otherwise you are just a 'supplier' like everyone else and so can be played off on price and forced downwards by procurement. Activities like this clearly separate you from those who are supplying the basic service, and what could be more valuable than a service firm that helps the client achieve their own annual performance appraisal objectives?

Secondly, you can envisage a fourth column in the table above – one which asks what *you* could do to help the client to achieve each objective. This is an exercise in drivers of value as discussed in Chapter 8. It helps you to understand what activities you could perform that would have the greatest impact (and so be worth more). It is an excellent exercise in better understanding the pressure on your clients and how you can stop being a generic supplier of services (where the client knows that they can get pretty much the same service from any of your key competitors).

Client satisfaction surveys

A well-run services business must gather feedback from clients on their level of satisfaction with the actual service that they received. The intangible nature of services and the fact that they are actually supplied after (often well after) the actual agreement for their provision means that making very regular checks on clients' satisfaction levels is crucial for success. This is so that you can spot any delivery issues as soon as possible (and take action to correct them) and also as a method of justifying and feeling confident about your prices.

These surveys do not need to be overly complex or expensive (although they may cost more than you anticipate because the gathering and collation of feedback does take time and effort). However, they are like gold in terms of their impact on your prices.

Savings achieved

When an organisation is under cost pressure (and this is now the norm), any service firm that helps its clients demonstrate (to their board, for example) how they are contributing to that initiative is clearly adding value above and beyond its core service. This can be an essential KPI for the client and, once again, the first service firm to volunteer to help the client to create and monitor savings will have a differential value. Examples of how actual savings can be created and what valuable swaps may be earned in return are set out below.

Managing service providers

What data can you help your client create that can show how it is managing all of its service firms? What are the trends quarter by quarter; what is the average cost of each firm; how do they compare in satisfaction surveys; and so on? Clients cannot effectively manage their service firm providers unless they collect and review performance data. As a service firm you should be in the perfect position to help clients to use the right measures (i.e. not just the price) that will help them to compare one firm with another. As you do this you will also learn about your own performance and how it compares with others. This is a great opportunity for you to learn about what your client values and how you can get ahead of the competition in delivering that value, and so justify higher prices than them.

Of course there may be areas where you come up short, where your performance lags behind that of a competitor. This is bad news, but isn't it better that you find out and then address this rather than only finding out when your work starts to dry up? Working closely with clients on projects that enable them to create comparison data on their service firm providers puts you in the leading position to learn from and then capitalise upon that information, while at the same time helping your client to choose between different service firms and to be able to show that they are proactively managing spend.

SPEND REDUCTION PROJECTS

This instinctively sounds like bad news. A project which helps the client to spend less will reduce your income. However, the reality for your client is that they are very likely to be under pressure to reduce costs, so it may be a question of whether you are going to help them develop a solution that works for both of you, or have one imposed upon you. Luckily you have some useful tools developed throughout Chapter 8 which enable you to look for ways that you can reduce the components part of your service in return for a lower price. That maintains the profit (per hour) but would lead to fewer hours being worked – a drop in your firm's income (all other things being equal). So what can you get in return? There are a number of options that you can discuss with your client:

- You could be paid a percentage of the saving. For example, you reduce spend in an area of work from £100,000 to £80,000 and are paid 50% of the saving, leading to extra income of £10,000. Bear in mind that the saving does not need to come from you, or wholly from you. So you might use value engineering to reduce the work and cost in an area where you have one-third of the available work, but you are paid 50% of the saving made across all three service firms.

- You could be rewarded with a greater share of the work. For example, if you currently have one-third of the available work, increasing your share to 40% or 50% (while still keeping the other service firms) would probably be a great reward. Bear in mind that you have not reduced, by even a penny, the charge per hour. You have used value engineering to reduce the total work needed per matter (see below for the opposite situation – consolidation – and its dangers).

- You can ask the client for referrals to similar clients inside or outside that organisation. To be introduced as 'This is the firm that has just saved me 10% on my annual spend, I wonder if they could do the same for you?' is really powerful. Who wouldn't want to investigate the possibility that you could save them money, when introduced by someone that they trust?

Clients will understand that you need to earn something in return for creating savings, and it is quite acceptable to ask them for their suggestions about how they might help your service business cover the costs of a spend reduction project. The important thing, in relationship terms, is that you have put effort into creating savings for the client and, as a result, will have differentiated yourself from your competitors – provided that you were the first one to do this. I cannot overemphasise this point. It is the most proactive service firm that reaps the reward and will often end up truly working jointly with the client across all of their service firm providers to create savings. In this way you will have much greater control and opportunity – or would you prefer that it was one of your closest competitors who launched this project with your client?

TARGETED REDUCTIONS

The starting point for most clients who want to make savings is to create a percentage target. So you might hear that there is a desire to reduce spend by 10% or to cut 25% off the relevant budget. The partner receiving this news tends to translate that into the equivalent drop in demand (and starts to reduce their forecasts for income that year), but it is worth pausing to think how those people *who supply us* would react if we were to declare such a target to them. Let's see what it is like when the boot is on the other foot.

Let's say that I sit down with my gas bill and decide that I am spending far too much on gas to heat my home. I am going to give myself a target to reduce my monthly spend by 15% so I contact my gas supplier with this demand. How do they react? Well, there will be talk about improving the insulation at my home (spend some extra money now to save money in the future); suggestions that I turn down the thermostat on my heating to a lower temperature; a look at whether I need a new boiler which is more efficient (spend now, save later); an offer to switch me to a tariff which locks in current prices for the next 12 months; or an offer to reduce costs by 1.5% if I buy both my gas and my electricity from them.

It is important that your own reaction to targeted reduction requests from your clients is along similar lines. It isn't about supplying exactly the same as you did last year, but this time for 15% less money. My own first reaction to a client who has mandated a reduction in spend is to look at ways that demand can be reduced (the equivalent of turning down the room thermostat by a couple of degrees). With this logic in mind, it is worth running a workshop with the client that examines the causes of demand for your services and examines what could be done to reduce that demand. This sounds counterintuitive ('I am going to help you to need me less in the future'), but it is really about creating a closer and more sustainable relationship and looking for the reward in terms of valuable swaps, as we did in the spend reduction projects above.

In one example, I recall working with a client on business disputes and we discovered that, of the eight regions involved, one region accounted for 12% of their business but for 47% of their disputes work. Something was wrong here. Our project became one of examining what was different in this region and correcting it. As a result, the necessary savings were achieved and not a single penny taken out of our prices.

In another case we looked at the division between the work that the client did in-house and that which was passed out to service firms like ours. We agreed that if the target for reductions was going to be achieved, the in-house team needed to take on more of the work themselves: we transferred a member of our staff to work full-time at the client and as a result, reduce their spend. What did we get in return? We signed a long-term contract guaranteeing us the remaining work for the next five years.

Other solutions included creating a level of self-service for the client so that standard advice could be automated (spend now, save later) and running process improvement workshops, where every stage in the work between us and the client was critically examined over a two-day event in order to find shortcuts and cut out work, and hence time and cost.

Given any realistic target, I would be surprised if the necessary savings could not be achieved using a combination of these techniques. If the target is too high, then it is part of your role to point that out and look at alternative solutions. For example, can you restrict your involvement to certain stages only, with other parts being given to much lower cost service firms, perhaps offshore?

CONSOLIDATION AND ITS DANGERS

Pretty much a first port of call when clients want to make savings is to swap savings for a greater share of the work. This is logical and natural: bigger clients expect better rates, and if a client is spreading the available work across too many firms then it may not be receiving the best available terms. So, a client who has a £400,000 spend across four firms equally may not want to move all work to one firm (there may be concerns that this stops inter-firm competition and increases risk) but it could move to two firms, offering each of them a higher share of spend in return for a discount. In addition, knowing that two firms are about to lose £100,000 of work will make all of the firms compete to offer the best deal and win the prize of becoming one of the two chosen firms.

Not only is the client thinking that consolidating the work into fewer suppliers will save money, but the service firms are thinking along the same lines. If the client wants to save 10% on spend, then that is acceptable in return for a substantial increase in the volume of work. The problem with this thinking is that it is actually much more beneficial for the client than for the 'winning' service firms.

In broad terms (for the moment ignoring any economies of scale), achieving a reasonable saving for the client may come at a very high price for the service firm. By way of example, a firm that currently has £100,000 of work at a profit of 30% will see that giving 10% discount in return for an increase to £200,000 has a surprising effect as shown in the table below:

	Before deal	After deal
Income	£100,000	£200,000
Less discount	£0	£20,000
Net income	£100,000	£180,000
Overheads	£70,000	£140,000
Profit (%)	£30,000 (30%)	£40,000 (22%)

The service firm is carrying out twice as much work after the deal, meaning it has to recruit, train and retain twice the number of people, will need twice the working capital and perhaps an investment in equipment and premises – so business risk is increased, in return for a small increase in cash profit and a drop in percentage profit (so that the firm now receives £40,000 profit on its increased income of £180,000 which is 22%).

Now, there will be *some* economies of scale in a typical service firm, but they may be much less than you think. Economies of scale, in the above example, means that the overheads will not double if you are carrying out twice as much work. If they become £135,000 rather than £140,000 then that £5,000 will fall to the profit line. I would caution that you work out actual economies of scale before offering discounts for volume.

Moreover, there is a better way, which was described in 'Spend reduction projects' above. It is quite different if you use a project to reduce *the amount of work involved* and create a corresponding reduction in price, and then use that as the basis for the client giving you a greater share of work. Compare those economics where, in return for reducing costs and price by 10%, doubles the work it gives to you, as shown in the following table:

	Before deal	After deal
Income	£100,000	£200,000
Less discount	£0	£20,000
Net income	£100,000	£180,000
Overheads	£70,000	£126,000 (£140,000 less 10%)
Profit (%)	£30,000 (30%)	£54,000 (30%)

In this second example we have earned extra turnover from this client by creating a 10% saving from efficiencies and maintained our profit at 30%, even assuming that there are zero economies of scale (and if there are some, then profit and percentage profit are increased).

CREATING AND SHARING SAVINGS

You may find yourself facing a client who has been mandated to achieve savings and who is clear that they will not 'spend to save' – for example by paying you to develop new services that are more efficient and cost less. In those cases it is possible to create money out of thin air by agreeing to work on such a project but to limit your fee to a percentage of actual savings achieved.

This creates a no-risk project for the client which is very clearly aimed at achieving their cost saving objective, but which can also pay you for the work involved. If a client is spending £250,000 a year with you and wants to reduce that to £200,000 (all other things being equal, i.e. for the same volume of work), then you might say that you will put a team to work on that project and will charge 50% of the actual savings achieved in the first year. This means that if the project actually costs you £25,000 or less to achieve the required savings, then you have been paid a proper amount for your work.

Of course, you cannot guarantee to create this type of efficiency saving, but it is a reasonable project. You should ask for a high percentage of the saving in year one, because the savings should be locked in (without any charge from you) for all sub-sequent years. Also although the result of the exercise is that you have lowered your total income (but should have preserved your overall profitability), you can look for other rewards from this client, such as a greater share of their spend or referrals to other potential clients.

If you find that you have a group of people in your service firm who are underutilised perhaps because of a sudden downturn in demand, then this is a good way of keeping them busy – for them to visit clients and potential clients and offer to run projects that only bill a percentage of actual savings achieved. Let's look at that in more detail in terms of projects for the underutilised.

HIDDEN RESOURCES AND HOW TO USE THEM

It is a rare service firm that neatly runs at 100% utilisation every day in every type of work. If you have managed to pull off this trick then you are indeed fortunate and I expect you will be using some clever methods of capacity planning and resourcing.

For everyone else, there is a reality that any available time which was not billed is lost forever. It can't be carried forward, and it represents waste. A great way of using that unused time is to invest in projects of the type explored in this chapter. This might be entirely internally focussed, where teams look at your existing pro-cesses and seek out more efficient ways of doing the work. That is standard practice in Routine Work, where the typical fixed fee means that all efficiencies fall to the profit line of the service firm – and this positions the firm for regular price conversations with clients who continually seek more for less. A good starting point for Relationship Advice is to look at those areas of work where there are regular write-offs of time: time that you cannot bill to a client because it was outside of the fee estimate for project-based costing, or where you allowed scope creep without obtaining per-mission for a higher fee. In those cases, efficiency gains are for your benefit in reducing write-offs.

If you have areas of your business that are quiet then it is a great use of the available time to have people sit at clients' offices and look for ways of improving service and reducing costs. For example, if you have a team of five people who are 70% utilised then you could take one person out (increasing the utilisation of the others to over 85%), and have a 'free' person spend a month (or three) embedded with the client in order to look for efficiencies and savings. If you weren't going to fire this person (to reduce overheads), then it is much better to have them working on relationship-enhancing projects onsite with the client than for them to be helping to further lower the utilisation levels in their team.

If you have read through the projects in this chapter but doubted your ability to put them into action, then using these hidden resources is a great way of actually seeing some results.

ROCKET SCIENCE

When a client needs a Rocket Scientist it is pretty rare for them to then tell the Rocket Scientist how to carry out the work. In fact there would be dangers in that. By definition, the client has called in a real specialist so they are likely to allow them to carry out their work in the way they think best. When going into a difficult operation in hospital, it would be strange to see a patient arguing with the surgeon about how many nurses or anaesthetists are going to be in theatre (in order to try to save some money), or what methods the surgeon should use.

However, there has been a trend in some areas of services for clients to expect some disaggregation: simply meaning that the Rocket Scientist will focus upon the most difficult parts of the task, but if there are relatively straightforward parts then they will be passed to less specialist (and less expensive) staff. They could be different staff within the main service firm, they could be passed out to a separate part of the firm (on- or offshore) that specialises in the more routine aspects of work, or outsourced to a specialist provider.

It can enhance the reputation of a Rocket Scientist that they clearly have such disaggregation services set up and in place, especially if their direct competitors have done so. However, other than that, I would not expect there to be much talk of saving money (other than in terms of achieving a great result for the client) in Rocket Science work.

ROUTINE WORK

At the other extreme, clients are very keen to hear that money can be saved on Routine Work and in fact may demand year-on-year reductions on the (usually fixed) price. Clients want to hear about clever use of technology, outsourced services and efficiency. The problem is that there must come a point where the price approaches zero (although never reaches it because of the exponential curve effect). For example, if a client expects to achieve savings of 10% at each two-yearly review of service firms, then across 10 years the price drops from £100 to £59. Factor in even modest inflation of 3% per year in overheads and 34% will have been added to them across the 10-year period. Given the typically low percentage returns on Routine Work, it takes little time for profit to disappear.

As a result, it is those who are involved day-to-day in delivering Routine Work that will have most experience in process improvement or the more radical business process re-engineering, which looks to take a fresh look at the whole process from start to finish, examine the outputs and see if there are very different ways of achieving those. This is in contrast to a more traditional process improvement approach which may seek, for example, to computerise existing manual processes. As I have explained, it is important for those involved in Routine Work to focus not just on the cost of delivering the service, but also upon the results achieved and to create data around that, or they will end up with a one-dimensional conversation around price. However, without doubt, the greatest experience in managing process and cost lies with those involved in Routine Work, and they can be very valuable in helping those in Relationship Advice to rethink how they deliver their service. If you don't have such people within your own service firm, then it can be worth asking a client if you can borrow one of theirs, and to create a joint project with their Routine Work expert and your Relationship Advice people to see what they can learn. As any improvements are likely to feed through into that client's bills they can be very willing to help out and, once again, achieving savings with one client is a great way to attract other clients.

WHEN TO SAY NO

What happens if a client needs you to reduce prices and cannot offer you any acceptable swaps? What if the client just needs a service that is cheaper than the one you can provide (even after you have stripped out as much as possible)? What if the client has found a very low-cost supplier and either wants you to match that price or accept that you are going to lose this work?

This is becoming an increasingly common situation and one which demands a strategic answer – do you really want to keep this client or not? Partners often seek to hold onto these clients, typically offering some price reductions and convincing themselves that they will, now, change the way the work is done in order to decrease its production cost. However, no one has time to make substantive changes to working practices so all that is achieved is the price drop.

The key question is whether you need to provide this (lower value) work to this client. If it is the only work that the client gives you then you have a straightforward decision. You could find ways of lowering your costs of production sufficiently that you can lower your price and still maintain an acceptable margin of profit. Is it worth it? Is this client part of a trend? Could you just let the client go? To keep the client may mean investing in nearshore or offshore teams, structured with higher leverage, and investing in technology. It can be much better for your business to accept that there is a bottom end to your current work which could be handled more cost-effectively by lower level competitors – perhaps firms which focus entirely on that work, or are much smaller than you or have developed systems, processes and economies of scale that you may find difficult to match.

Frequently, partners are faced with a client that delivers a range of work to their firm and the immediate threat is the loss of the bottom end of the work. The partner will typically aver that, if the lower end is lost, then it won't be long before all of the work is lost. That might be true but you should ask the client if that is the case. If a low-cost competitor has come into your market and segmented the low-end work as its target market, it may not have the skills to take on the high-end work. It would be quite different if this was a mainstream competitor that covered the same range of services as you, but then those competitors are less likely to be able to (sustainably) undercut you.

So, bear in mind that a very good alternative where the work is at the bottom of your range is to let it go, and to focus your efforts on winning higher-end work where the margins will be higher as well. It is OK to say no if you have thought it through and made a considered decision.

CLIENTS WHO ALWAYS WANT TO SAVE MONEY

Pricing experts are quick to identify those clients that are *always* looking to save money. They are often called 'price buyers' because they have a habit of negotiating very hard over price in the area of Relationship Advice (whereas it would be expected in Routine Work). You need to beware of these clients, as it is often true that your lowest price client is your highest maintenance client. There can often be cultural issues here – the client may work in an organisation where savings have become the norm. If you have created your service business using the 'Cost leadership strategy' (we provide pretty much the same service as our competitors but at a lower cost), then your business will be structured to cope well with this type of client.

However, if you are the more typical service firm, pursuing a differentiated service strategy, these clients can be a real danger because they can tie up resources out of proportion to their worth. In Chapter 8 we looked at how you might cope with these clients by developing a minimum level of service, and that should be your first response. Lower price must mean lower level of service. If the client cannot be contained by service reductions then at some point you are going to need to say 'no' to them, so it is important that you develop a replacement strategy which puts real time and effort into winning new clients that are more focussed upon the value that you deliver. By gradually increasing these, you will have more confidence in your ability to say no to the problem client.

In fact, having identified these price buyers, it can be very satisfying to pass them on to your competitors. It means that you have stood your ground and maintained your pricing in the face of continued pressure, and have accepted that you cannot please all of the people, all of the time. In your service firm, you need to avoid being in a situation where you are totally reliant on these types of clients, or they will certainly take advantage of that fact to the detriment of your prices and your profit. Think back to our discussion of market positioning and how a hotel would accept that there is a segment of the market which they can serve, and others that they cannot. You don't have a pricing strategy if it collapses in the face of a persistent price buyer.

FINALLY – WHEN DID YOU LAST SAVE A CLIENT MONEY?

Here's my key lesson on this topic. I have found that, in practice, only one service firm gets close enough to the client to run the cost-saving exercises described above with them and to help the client to analyse its spend across all of its service providers.

The investment of time by the client usually means that they can only realistically run this with one firm, and they then impose the results upon all firms.

Being proactive about helping clients to save money can therefore have a big payoff, and can result in you truly partnering with them to look at how they can be more efficient and how you can help. That help is often at the expense of competitor firms, and that is the incentive for you to be the one who opens up these conversations with clients – or would you rather that your closest competitor did this, so that they were the one making suggestions to the client about how they might save money in the future?

Let's now move from the topic of saving money into our final chapter, which examines two topics. First, how you can manage pricing within a service firm so that there are sensible controls on the prices that can be agreed with individual clients. Secondly, how service firms can truly embrace pricing as a key capability of the organisation which is as important as finance or marketing, and is given the resources to make maximum impact on the success and profitability of the firm.

11

Pricing controls and capabilities

BUILDING PRICING CONTROLS

When we come to implementing better pricing in service firms, paying attention to the most basic sales and delivery behaviours can have a substantial impact upon the prices that can be achieved and the profit returned. This may be due to the high human involvement in the design and delivery of services – it's not like running a production line for physical goods where uniformity is more easily implemented. The fact is that remuneration policies in service firms are usually targeted on increasing income through sales, rather than maintaining prices. A great starting point is to tackle these systemic issues, and then to use that as a foundation for developing true pricing capabilities which will enable the firm to create the right services and to reap the full rewards for its efforts.

When consulting in service firms, I usually ask at board level to set a profit improvement target of at least 5% across a two-year period. I show them that achieving this would dramatically improve cash returns. For example, a firm with a turnover of £10 million gains £500,000 *in profit each year*, and one with £1 billion can expect an extra £50 million *in profit* because these improvements can go straight to the bottom line without increasing costs (for simplicity I am assuming no customer attrition). If these projects failed to achieve the target and delivered only 2% this would still mean a £200,000 or £20 million increase in profit, which is not a bad reward for failure.

Let us begin by looking at what should be some of the easy wins of the pricing world. We'll then move on to explore how pricing can become a strategic capability for service firms, just as relevant and important as finance or marketing and worthy of talented resources and the attention of boards.

UTILISATION

The income and profitability of any firm is as much linked to utilisation – what percentage of available saleable hours are sold each month – as they are linked to the prices charged. Even if you are selling fixed price services, there is a huge difference between people who have enough work to be busy all of the time, or just enough for half of their time.

The equation is shown by Figure 11.1.

Of course, the drive to sell the available time is a sensible one. Whatever time is not sold each day is lost forever. It cannot be

Figure 11.1 **Calculation of net utilisation**

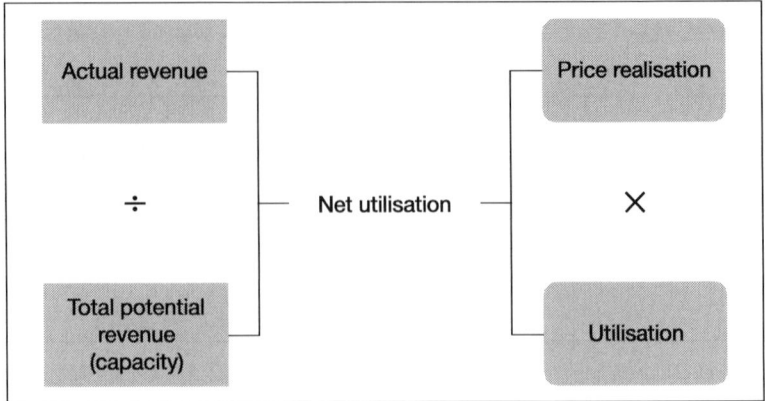

carried forward. The important issue is to understand that it not *always* the right answer to base your actions upon maximising utilisation in the short term, as that can lead to very damaging pricing outcomes over time. It is similar to the actions that you see when firms target a growth in percentage market share and then do whatever it takes to reach that share. Whatever it takes usually means discounting until growth targets are met (to the great detriment of total profit).

Improving utilisation by dropping prices is undeniably a rational thing to do in terms of growing income in the short term. This partly explains why partners are quick to drop prices to keep their team busy (although it is also because teams that are quiet are hard to keep together and are well-motivated). Let's look at the maths to see the dramatic effect: I will use the example of a team that is budgeted to achieve income of £200,000 a month and has overheads of £160,000, giving a monthly target for profit of £40,000 (20% margin). In January and February income has been running at £150,000 and that is also the anticipated income in March. However, the partner in charge he/she is given the opportunity to win an additional piece of work that should be priced at £100,000, but he/she can only win it if he/she offers to do it at half price. He/she does this and the work is carried out and billed in March, so that total income in March lifts from £150,000 to £200,000.

	January	February	March
Income	£150,000	£150,000	£200,000
Overheads	£160,000	£160,000	£160,000
Profit (loss)	(£10,000)	(£10,000)	£40,000

As we can see, this clever partner has more than made up for the £10,000 of losses in each of January and February, and the profit for that year is (all other things being equal) going to be £50,000 higher than if the partner had turned down the half-price piece of work. At the margin, extra income falls 100% into profit (or into reducing losses). This is often referred to as *marginal pricing*.

However, this sugar rush of relief to an underutilised team has some very unfortunate side-effects. At the client level it teaches them that amazing discounts are available when you ask for them (so, of course, they will absolutely ask again), and it can be very difficult to obtain good prices on services delivered to that client in the future. More worryingly, the client may tell others about their good fortune and that could lead to other clients and prospective clients expecting similar discounts (or being unhappy that they did not receive this reward in the past). So your most loyal clients start to be at risk. This behaviour is also likely to stimulate your competitors to react – and that can only trigger a race to the bottom on fees. If every client paid 50% of 'normal fee levels' in the example above, then income would drop to £100,000 a month, which is £60,000 less than monthly overheads. The special offer forces some clients to effectively subsidise other clients – not a recipe for success. Finally, the partner might actually perceive the outcome as a good result and reach for this tactic again in the future. After all, hasn't the team's monthly loss turned into a profit again? However, this is a failure to see the potential impact over time, and what if every partner adopted the same tactic? Are these risks and blind spots enough to stop an individual partner offering special deals when they and their team are not busy? Perhaps not, which is why effective control of pricing is needed at both departmental and firm level; quite simply, pricing decisions should not be left *exclusively* to the individual client-facing partner. We will look at that in more detail below.

A much better approach is to take people out of the under-utilised team and transfer them to busier parts of the firm or send them to work inside a client for a period for free or at low cost. That's an investment in building relationships and goodwill in a way that does not violate your pricing policies.

THE RATE CARD

If I were to walk into a car showroom and approach a salesperson to enquire about the price of a particular car, I would be surprised if I found out that the price quoted to me depended upon which sales-person I had asked. The complexity of services pricing is not just because the scope of work is often uncertain (just like the specification and cost of fitting a new kitchen in a given property could vary immensely), but because even the price of individual workers in the firm is usually very flexible, and no two people will necessarily perform the service in the same way. Seemingly identical partners or associates will be charged at different rates to very similar clients. The typical situation where you are charging for time spent (not on a fixed fee) is too flexible and uncertain, too open to individual negotiation.

In one firm where I was working, the partners discovered that clients had started shopping around *within that firm* because the clients had discovered that if they rang three different partners and asked for a quote, they would receive three very different figures!

The foundation of good pricing is that it must be *fair and equitable.* Fairness is about not taking advantage of clients and always being able to explain and justify your prices openly. Equitability is about ensuring that similar clients are paying similar prices for similar services. If you want to understand the importance of this, imagine that a hacker gained access to your systems and sent every client a list of the prices being charged to all your other clients. Would that be OK?

Imagining this worst-case scenario can be useful in persuading partners that you need to pay attention to your baseline pricing (this is your rate card), to your discounting policy and to your approach to deals that fall outside one or both of these (for example, when signing multi-year service agreements).

In constructing your rate card you need to stand in your clients' shoes and consider the value that they receive from the individuals that will be delivering the service, particularly because firms are surprisingly egalitarian when it comes to individual rates. This means that some firms set rates according to grade/level (e.g. partner or manager) without differentiating by depth of expertise. This is a very simple error. It almost goes without saying that most clients would prefer a partner with 20 years' experience to another with two years'. Giving both these people the same price leads to overwork at the senior end and a younger partner struggling to establish their practice. Similarly, the shape of the pyramid underneath a partner, the extent to which they are able to leverage their team with more junior staff who are also able to charge for their time, is also an indicator of the required hourly rate. A true Rocket

Scientist may have only one or two other people in their team and that requires that they all charge at hourly rates that are higher to reflect their specialism and expertise, while those carrying out Relationship Advice with much larger teams would justify lower rates.

After taking these factors into account you are then able to create a list of rates for each level of fee earner in the business. These rates need to be informed, but not set, by your costs. Remember that cost-plus pricing is suboptimal, but will enable you to set minimum rates that deliver a minimum level of profitability. The actual rates will also be affected by your current rates of charge (what clients believe is the 'going rate'), what your key competitors are charging and your business strategy (type of work, type of client, rate of growth, perception of the brand and so on).

Now to the key issue. Having set your rate card, do you allow discounts from it, by whom and by how much? You need to take great care that you do not end up creating a discount policy as opposed to a pricing policy. Let me explain the difference. It is very common for organisations to have a rate card and then to have layers of discounts that can be provided to clients which require increasing levels of sign-off. So, the front-line salesperson may have the right to give up to 10%, a divisional head can add another 5%, a regional director another 5% or 10% and so on. Add to this structure a sales incentive (often through the chain) that rewards income rather than profit, and the way ahead is clear. Clients will be offered whatever it takes to seal the deal, safe in the knowledge that there is simply an administrative process that will (in most cases) rubber-stamp the deal. Such discount structures are particularly generous when they meet strong-arm, heavily procured purchasing procedures. A soft process meets a tough one and there is no doubt who wins.

A pricing policy, on the other hand, allows for discounts but those discounts need to be justifiable incentives for desired client behaviours. That is the difference – they are incentives, not price cuts. The front-line partner should have an ability to give a discount up to a certain amount, but only against agreed parameters, and after receiving something valuable in return. For example, a maximum of 10% might be allowable against factors such as a minimum annual level of spend, a commitment to (sole sourced) future projects, flexibility on the speed of response. You can also assume that, being on the front line, these pricing defences will be relatively weak and that in very many cases, for one 'good' reason or another, the 10% discount will be given. Your rate card needs to be built upon that assumption (to spell this out, the rate card must start at prices which assume 10% will definitely be given away).

After that 10% any greater discount needs to be thoroughly justified – so that a value engineering exercise is carried out on the basis that a changed price would mean a changed specification. In other words, discounts above the discretionary 10% need to be reflected in changes to what is going to be delivered. If the argument is around hourly rates then you need to hold the line. Negotiations should be around, 'I can't get you more than 10% off the rates, but if you spend more than £250,000 then I could look at some added value', rather than, 'I will have to get my regional manager to sign off the discount of 15%'. If you find this difficult, then I recommend some professional training in negotiation skills as we all tend to be rather weak when negotiating on our own behalf, as opposed to a client's.

WRITE-OFFS

There can be many reasons why you need to write off time or work on a matter. You may have agreed a fixed fee but carried out more work than budgeted; you might have given a project-based fee and some elements of the work took longer or involved more people than anticipated; you might have decided that you cannot charge some work to a client because (even to you) it looks superfluous or excessive in scope. Given that the key management systems of firms tend to rely upon tracking activity levels and (very often) recorded time, there have to be controls in place to prevent people simply being able to write off time or money after the event (or worse, understate time during the event), or your accounting systems will not stand up to audit. Profits can prove to be illusory or overstated.

It may come as some surprise that the typical controls are often paper-thin in that they may require a sign-off from other partners, but those same partners are more than happy to counter-sign these because they will require the same treatment on their own write-offs. So a culture grows where partners soon learn who will sign write-offs without raising too many questions, and are then happy to return that favour. Better controls are needed, in the first instance to challenge the write-offs and test if these can be negotiated with the client, but also so that the firm can learn from its overruns and partners feel under a real obligation to avoid them if possible. Partners need to learn the skills of accurate quoting, scoping (and re-scoping when needed) and efficient delivery, and they won't do that if they can just 'carry on as normal' and write off their mistakes.

When I am consulting into firms, one solution I often suggest is for the firm's finance team (separate from the partners) to circulate their top 10 write-offs each month, showing the amount written off, the partner requesting the write-off and the name of the partner who signed it off. Peer pressure does the rest.

ANALYSIS OF CURRENT CLIENTS

Entire volumes have been written about the financial aspects of service businesses, but I have found two relatively simple tools that can help to prioritise action and identify individual strategies for each major client. Before using them there is a very simple listing that you can create that will make you think hard about which are your most valuable clients.

That is, to take your top 100 clients (or whatever number is relevant for your business) and create two lists. In the first list you rank them, in the very typical fashion, by turnover. Next to this you create a list of the same clients but ordered by profit: i.e. the client that earns you the most profit is number one, rather than the one that has the largest turnover. Every time I have seen this done, the lists are very different and it will make you realise that it is the clients who top the profit list that are the really valuable ones for your business.

Let's now look at two analytical tools that can be used with pretty much any service business. The first of these is called a waterfall diagram, and shows the different steps (down) that have taken place from your full rate card price to the actual payment rate you receive. The example in Figure 11.2 illustrates how simple and effective this can be. It needs to be conducted on a client-by-client basis (and may run across reporting periods) to get an accurate picture.

This example uses a rate card rate of £400 for a partner, and then a cost-plus calculation to show the breakeven point of £250 an hour. The waterfall shows that:

■ Against a starting rate per hour of £400, the client has been given a £50 discount (12.5%) so that the client has a contractual rate of £350 an hour.

| Figure 11.2 | Waterfall diagram |

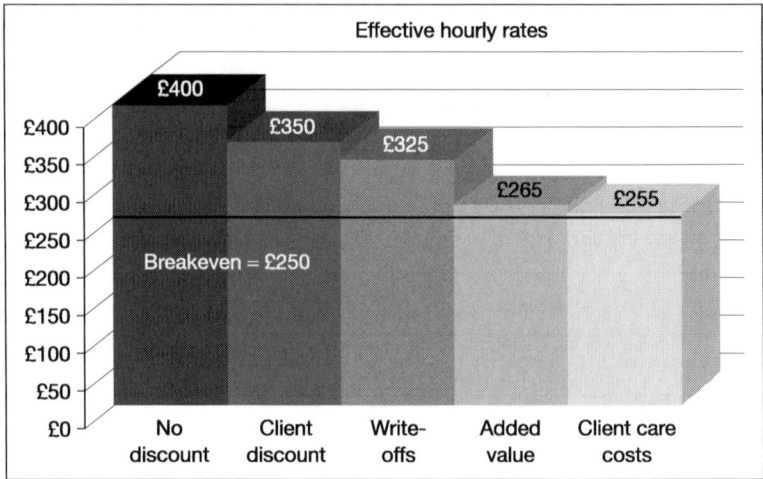

Effective hourly rates

- Looking back over (for example) the last 12 months of bills, the average write-off on bills (irrecoverable recorded time) equates to another discount of £25. You would calculate this by seeing the total value of write-offs and then converting that by averaging its cost across the total of hours worked.

- Next, calculate the total cost to you of all the added value (e.g. uncharged work, benefits in kind and the like) given to the client and average that over the recorded hours which, in this example, creates another discount of £60 an hour.

- Finally there are client care costs – this could be the cost of regular review meetings with the client, entertaining, preparing and analysing performance data and so on. In this example that equates to an average discount of £10 per hour. For simplicity the example is using chargeable rates for this time on that the assumption the partner could have served another client.

- The end result of all of these steps in the waterfall is that the effective recovered rate from this client is £255 an hour, only marginally above the breakeven point.

You need to examine your own business to work out what the actual stages are in your business' waterfall, and then take your largest clients and perform this analysis to create a unique waterfall for each client. The main purpose is for you to work out what actions would have the greatest impact on the profitability of that client. In the example above there are two major areas of concern: the initial discount looks high at 12.5% and the added value is clearly a

Pricing scattergram

Figure 11.3

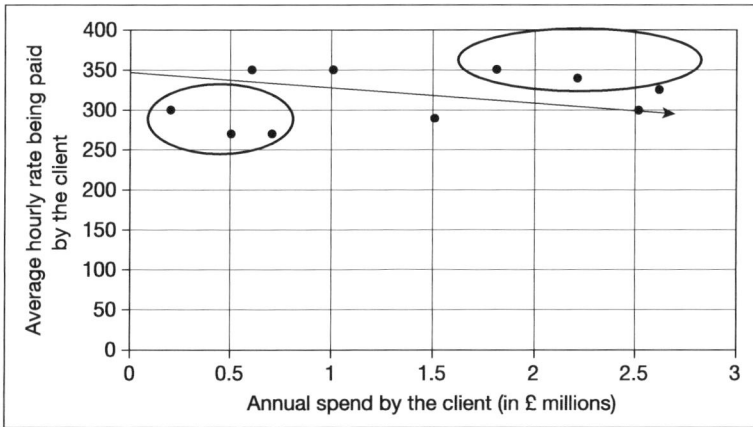

real issue here, knocking an effective £60 an hour from the effective rate. So you need to concentrate your efforts there. It's a simple and very visual way of identifying the right strategy on a client-by-client basis.

The second analysis is a scattergram and it shows which clients have good deals and which have poor deals on fees. It compares their average rates and the volume of business they conduct with you against similar clients. Here we accept the normal business assumption that larger clients will expect to be on better (lower) rates than small clients, and it works irrespective of whether you are charging by time taken or on fixed fees. In the example shown in Figure 11.3 I have used average hourly rates of charge and compared that with annual spend for a selection of similar clients (such as by type of work or geographies served). The line shows the gentle slope that you would expect (and so would the client) that the more they spend, the better average rate they would be given.

In the scattergram, the line shows the anticipated drop in average hourly rate as volume of business increases across the x-axis on the bottom line – dropping from £350 an hour to say £300 an hour from minimal spend to £3 million. What this reveals in the highlighted area on the left is a group of clients that have a low annual spend *and* a low average rate. This is a relatively easy starting point. These clients need to have it explained that they need to pay an increased rate of charge or they need to deliver a lot more business. They are enjoying lower rates than much larger clients.

On the right you can see a group of large clients paying rates that are above the expected level. The task here is to deliver real added value to these clients (rather than simply dropping the rates) so that you can show that they are receiving fair value for money. This is your protection against these clients being approached by a competitor who offers them a lower rate (closer to or below the line), because you are then able to respond to show that the competitor may be offering lower rates, but without all of the added value which you provide. That may, of itself, end the matter but if not, the line provides a guide for reducing the price against a reduction in the added value that you are providing.

In this section I have briefly looked at the fundamental control issues that should be useful to any service firm. Without these in place, it is not possible or realistic to excel at pricing.

Now it's time to turn to this final topic. How does a firm look beyond controls and seek to achieve competitive advantage from its pricing capability? I am greatly indebted to Robert Browne for writing the following section. Robert has over 20 years' experience helping companies around the world develop and execute pricing and sales strategies that drive growth. He is a partner in KPMG and leads their pricing practice in the United Kingdom.

BUILDING PRICING CAPABILITIES
BY ROBERT BROWNE

Let's start with an important lesson from many years working with service firms. What we find is that most think about pricing as a tactical lever to drive sales: if you lower prices, your win rate and volume will increase, and if you increase prices it will have the opposite effect. In practice, more often than not, these firms set their prices based on cost plus a margin or relative to perceived competitor prices. Most of the firms we encounter have not invested in pricing as a strategic capability and have not developed and embedded pricing policies, processes, roles or training. In contrast, purchasing departments have made vast improvements in capabilities over the last two decades and have been very successful in driving prices and margins lower in many service categories. A recent conversation with a chief purchasing officer from a large European bank drove this point home (what he said is echoed by other purchasing professionals): service firms and particularly professional service firms, are easy targets for purchasing departments. They are typically not well prepared or disciplined in price negotiations and, given the fixed nature of their cost base (the marginal pricing problem), are quick to give up price and margin to secure sales.

In the absence of strong pricing capabilities, a number of service sectors have been (or are) in the process of driving down long-term profitability either quickly through 'price wars' or a slow, gradual decline in prices through over-discounting or added value (i.e. adding valuable features or performing services without changing prices). As prices and margins slide, it's unsurprising we now hear more and more executives and managing partners of firms talk about their need to protect or improve pricing. Easy to say but hard to do of course, particularly when we look inside these organisations and see little or no pricing capability.

THE ROLE OF PRICING IN THE ORGANISATION

The first step for any firm is to make the decision to build a pricing capability: this must be visibly and consistently sponsored by executive management. The second step is then to define the role of pricing in the organisation, and we believe this must be completed *before* deciding what the pricing organisation will actually look like or be responsible for. We believe this sequence is necessary, simply because we have seen a lot of pricing organisations become marginalised and ineffective because their role was not defined clearly in the first place, and they defaulted to roles others didn't want to play or for which they did not have resources. We see the role of pricing defined by two dimensions: the role in pricing decisions and the role in pricing processes. The combination of these two dimensions produces four distinct roles (see Figure 11.4) and it's critically important to choose one role only and build the pricing capability around this purpose, recognising that the role may evolve over time. Naturally, the service sector (its maturity, competitiveness, growth, etc.) and business type (size, client mix, offer range, etc.) matter a lot. Businesses with large and complex contracts are likely to want pricing to lead the bid management process. Businesses with a high frequency of transactions will want pricing to set guidelines, or rules for tactical execution of pricing decisions. Businesses with new or fast-changing offers may want expert pricing resources to advise as and when needed. Businesses with

| Figure 11.4 | Role of pricing in the organisation |

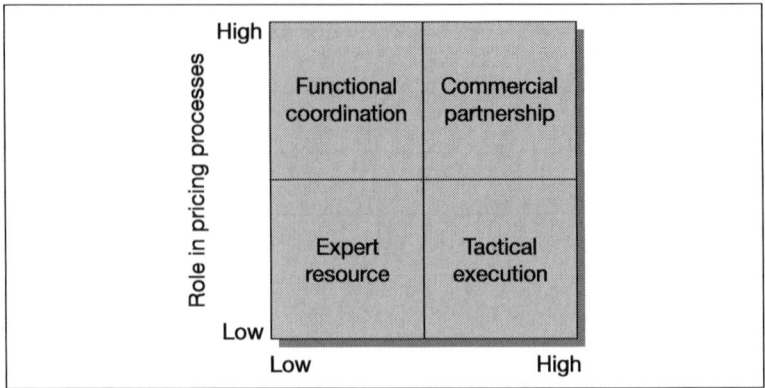

frequent, complex transactions will require pricing to play leading roles on both dimensions. While appealing in some ways, we would advise most firms not to start with Commercial Partnership as their pricing purpose if they have little or no capability today. We had this experience recently with a client providing services to the telecom sector. They wisely defined the pricing role as Functional Coordination first, with an ambition to migrate to a Commercial Partnership role over time. Our experience with successful pricing organisations is that they typically started with one of the other three roles and evolved it over time.

DEFINING PRICING CAPABILITY

Once the role of pricing has been agreed, the next step is to define and develop an effective pricing capability. There are three overall elements to the pricing capability – Strategic, Tactical and Supporting (see Figure 11.5) – and within each there are distinct capabilities and a range of phases of maturity. Among the best firms we have worked with, their strategic, tactical and supporting capabilities are aligned and drive pricing decisions that are integrated with the overall business strategy.

At the strategic level, pricing decisions should be based on an understanding of value created for clients, as well as the cost and risk to provide the service (pricing should be set based on value, but with cost plus target margin as an important sense-check). Examples of strategic pricing decisions include the definition of the offer

Pricing skills pyramid

Figure 11.5

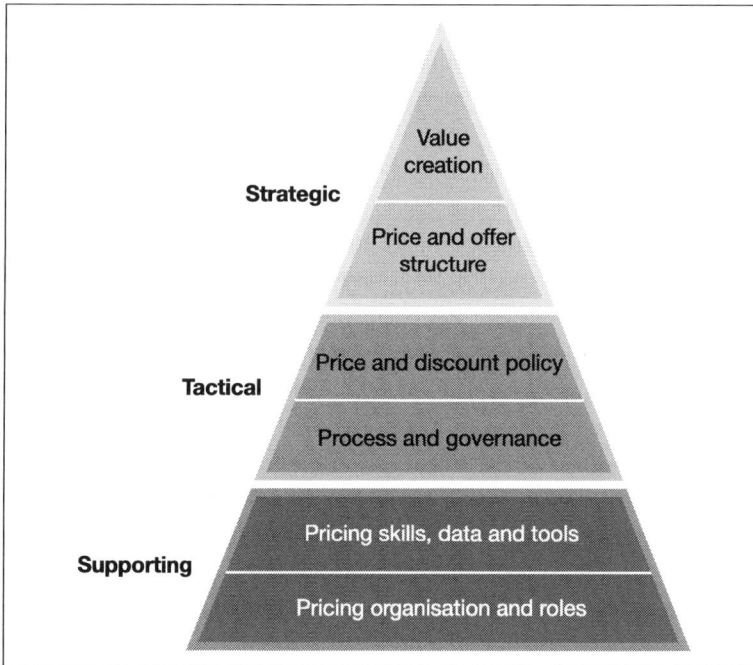

(services, bundles, solutions and so on), segmentation of clients (offer and price structure by segment), price model (fixed fee, performance-based fees, subscription-based fees and so on), but also how pricing changes over time (to account for changes in costs and demand). These strategic pricing decisions must be clearly articulated and understood across the business, and executive management must commit to the strategy and walk away from work that does not fit with it. To illustrate, we spent time with the CEO of a printing service to move him away from a volume-based pricing strategy (his declared ambition to 'fill the machines') to a value-based pricing strategy that reflected the value of their higher quality service and flexibility, as well as the effect of seasonal changes in demand.

At the tactical level, the price and discount policy must align with the pricing strategy, and pricing processes and controls around the policy need to be clearly defined. Perhaps most importantly, how pricing decisions (particularly the difficult ones) will be made should be clearly articulated and relevant responsibilities assigned. We are no longer surprised when we see firms make pricing decisions at the last minute, in the final days leading up to the pitch or possibly in the taxi on the way to the client. While intuition and experience will always play a role in pricing decisions, the best-performing firms we have worked with use data and analysis far more than intuition in pricing decisions. For example, a client of ours that provides scientific testing services was faced with a difficult price negotiation with their largest client. To prepare for this negotiation, the management team created a data pack (the history of past prices paid by the client benchmarked against other large clients, analysis of the client's realistic alternative sources of testing and so on), and a range of price negotiation options with supporting financial models. Having clear, data-driven pricing processes and controls allows pricing decisions to be made consistently and effectively. It also creates a disciplined and proactive approach that helps an organisation move away from being reactive (typically with insufficient time or data) to competitor and client tactics.

Finally, it is the supporting capabilities – the right pricing organisation, skills, data and tools – that drive and sustain successful pricing strategies and tactics. As mentioned earlier, we find that most firms have not developed the supporting capabilities that will deliver consistent, high-quality pricing decisions.

In the table below, we give examples of pricing capabilities from our work with clients and an indication of what leading practice for these capabilities would represent.

Capability	Example	Leading practice
Strategic	Pricing strategy is based on value created for clients.	■ Value-based segmentation of the market is defined and value creation relative to competitors is understood and measured. ■ Pricing decisions are based on value balanced with a thorough understanding of costs and risks. ■ Innovative price and performance-based metrics are used to align price with value created.
	Pricing strategy is clearly defined and integrated in the business strategy.	■ Pricing strategy is clearly articulated and supported by senior management. ■ Functional and business unit budgets explicitly include the pricing strategy. ■ Incentives are aligned with the pricing strategy, in particular the sales function. ■ Pricing Key Performance Indicators (KPIs) are tracked and reported to senior management.

Capability	Example	Leading practice (cont.)
Tactical	Price and discount policy and decision authority are clearly defined and communicated.	■ List and floor prices by client segment and criteria for discount eligibility are articulated and communicated. ■ Decision authority and escalation procedures (e.g. for higher discounts) are clearly defined. ■ Deal board (or pricing council) exists to review and agree pricing of important bids.
	Prices are regularly reviewed and refreshed.	■ Embedded process to review pricing relative to policy and refresh based on updated information on clients, competitors and costs.
Supporting	Routine collection and analysis of relevant pricing data.	■ Systematic approach to gather pricing data and perform analysis. ■ Relevant price sensitivity data is available at the segment/service level. ■ Proactive use of modelling to support key decisions, e.g. new service introductions, price changes, etc. ■ Cost and profitability data by service, by client and at transaction level.
	Pricing specialist roles exist and are engaged across the business.	■ Pricing specialists support commercial decisions. ■ Specialist negotiation team for large deals. ■ Negotiation training for salespeople.
	Pricing tools and solutions support pricing decisions.	■ Pricing or quoting tools embed pricing processes and policy. ■ Modularised database of standard services and respective pricing is available.

Leading capabilities cannot be created overnight, and for most businesses this list will represent a substantial shift in capabilities and mind set. Successful businesses that have developed leading pricing capabilities have taken a phased approach. Once there is alignment on the role of pricing in the organisation, their first step is to get clarity and consensus on the target capabilities required for executing this role. The second step is then to assess and agree on the gap between existing capabilities, and the final step is to define the action plan and responsibilities for delivering the changes required.

Not all capabilities can or should be addressed at the same time. We recently worked with the pricing function for a client and helped them to identify and describe each of the individual capabilities they wanted to build, and then rank them against two dimensions. The first dimension – 'Enabling' – allowed them to evaluate the degree to which each capability supports other functions in the organisation; and the second – 'Impact' – measured the degree to which each capability will put them on the path to top quartile performance in their industry. This helped the client to develop a priority shortlist of capabilities and develop an action plan for each. Over time, other capabilities can be added and existing capabilities can be reviewed and refreshed.

PRICING NEEDS A HOME

In small firms, the owner or managing partner will be heavily involved in and responsible for pricing decisions, and we believe this is a good use of their time. However, in large and more complex organisations, it is likely that many functions will want to play a role in pricing. This is where problems can start: not only does everyone want to be involved in key pricing decisions, but most people feel entitled to or simply have worked in the business long enough to 'have their say'. The issue is that ownership for pricing is not clearly articulated in most service firms, and this can produce lengthy 'internal negotiations' as well as bad pricing outcomes.

There are two information challenges, one internal and one external, at the heart of the ownership issue. Looking internally first, sales partners and associates will claim they should own pricing because they are closest to the client and competitors, and have the best insight on what is a competitive price in the market. Operations, on the other hand, are able to look across the business (for example at utilisation levels) and know when capacity is more or less valuable. Finally, finance will have the best understanding of the cost base and the impact that pricing decisions (particularly poor ones) have on profitability. The challenge is that all three have a role to play, but none have all the information needed to make the best pricing decisions. The second, external, challenge relates to clients and competitors. In terms of clients, what we want to know is how (and ideally how much) they value our services and solutions compared to competitors, which will help our understanding of their willingness to pay. In terms of competitors, we would like to know how they will price when we compete against them.

Given the complexity of these two challenges but also the critical impact that pricing has on sales and margins, we believe every firm should have a pricing organisation. This may be just one individual or a full pricing team, but every firm needs one, and if we accept the need for a pricing organisation, three questions arise: what should it be responsible for, where should it report in the organisation, and how should it be structured?

What should the pricing organisation be responsible for?

The answer to this question will be defined for the most part by the role of pricing in the organisation. Along the two dimensions (pricing processes and pricing decisions), there is a continuum of responsibility which we have already discussed above. For example, the scientific testing services client mentioned earlier has recently created a two-person pricing team with responsibility for working with locations to define their pricing plan for the next financial year, and then measuring their performance against plan. Another area of responsibility for the pricing organisation should be managing relevant pricing data and tools. Most firms have more data than they know what to do with, and this is acute in the case of pricing. Historical transaction and win–loss data are often a treasure trove for the pricing team to analyse pricing trends and consistency by client and by salesperson. Simple analysis of past pricing decisions can illuminate poor pricing controls, and sources of value leakage and more sophisticated price sensitivity analysis can identify opportunities to increase or decrease prices to drive sales. However, the truth is that most firms today don't actually know how price sensitive or insensitive their clients are, and as a consequence are far more likely to reduce – or at best maintain – prices and shy away from any thoughts of price increases.

Developing and maintaining pricing tools and systems should be assigned to the pricing organisation. Almost every firm will have some form of pricing tool, and these vary from spreadsheets to sophisticated software. The nature of one's business (high versus low transaction volume; complex versus standard solutions) will determine the tools or system requirements, but the accuracy, effectiveness and consistent use of these tools is critical to good pricing decisions. Recently we worked with a data services client to build a new quoting tool that embedded a revised rate card and new rules about discounting and escalating price decisions for approval, and this is what we expect pricing organisations should be capable of delivering. However, there are some limits to the use of tools and we would caution against 'black box' pricing tools or pricing organisations defaulting to be a 'modelling team' for pricing decisions. We have seen many pricing tools end up on the scrap heap because they have either become too complex, or no longer reflect the reality of prices in the market.

A further area of responsibility for the pricing organisation should be reviewing and reporting on pricing performance. We have found that good pricing metrics have been overlooked by most firms. There are a few simple metrics which can be highly effective in driving better pricing outcomes (such as adherence to pricing policy, number of pricing decisions escalated and turnaround time for pricing decisions); but there are also some more complex metrics that start to get at the question of whether one's prices are successful in the market (for example, when sales growth is separated into price-driven and volume-driven growth). We have also found that most firms do not put adequate effort into defining the role of pricing in the budgeting cycle. We see a lot of firms make simple, inflation-driven price assumptions for next year's budget, whereas a more accurate and action-based approach (so that results can be tied back to actions) can be a key responsibility of the pricing organisation. This is exactly what our testing services client implemented for their most recent budget, and not surprisingly what is agreed in the budget must be delivered and attracts the attention it deserves. The client used past transaction data to assess the level of pricing performance (e.g. list price adherence), identified and quantified a number of areas for improvement and used this information to set a price uplift target in the budget. They defined a set of metrics to monitor the execution and reported progress to the senior management team on a quarterly basis.

A final area of responsibility for the pricing team, but perhaps the most important of all, should be to help the organisation to define its pricing strategy. This may be by practice or service line or by location, but every firm needs to have a clear pricing strategy and it needs to be understood and executed by every function.

Where should pricing report in the organisation?

Among the firms that have a pricing capability, there is a surprising amount of variation in the answer to this question. We recently conducted a benchmarking study of pricing capabilities for a client and found that each of the five firms we reviewed had pricing reporting to different functions. Typically, however, most pricing organisations report to either sales and marketing or finance, and there are arguments for and against both. On a few occasions, we have seen pricing report to operations or strategy, and we have yet to find a firm where the pricing organisation is a stand-alone function with a chief pricing officer and a seat among the executive team. The debate over where pricing reports is based on three key criteria: insights, incentives and independence. It's not surprising that the rationale for locating pricing in sales is to keep it close to insights and reality around clients and competitors, and there is a lot of merit to this argument. On the other hand, the incentives in the sales organisation are typically weighted towards sales volumes or income, and hence prices and margins are often sacrificed to drive sales.

The rationale for locating pricing in the finance function is usually because their incentive is to see both sales and profits grow, and they are independent of sales (who want to drive volumes and serve clients better) and operations (who want to keep costs down and increase delivery effectiveness). However, finance will always lack the client and market insights required for pricing decisions. Locating pricing in finance is often a convenient match of capabilities (access to data, analytical skills), but our experience is that it works only if the processes and decision authority are very clearly established and the pricing organisation is a true commercial partner to the sales team. One of our clients has made this work. The pricing team (sitting in finance) run the bid management process and they also have veto rights to stop deals that are below an agreed profit threshold. However, what doesn't work is when finance acts as a gate keeper for pricing decisions or becomes a modelling resource for the sales team without a role in pricing decisions. We have seen most success when pricing is a stand-alone function reporting to the Profit and Loss owner (e.g. managing partner for small firms or practice leader or Chief Operating Officer for large firms). Moving pricing away from the exclusive domain of the front-line sales team creates the necessary independence to avoid marginal pricing and, when it works well, the pricing team can provide support and coaching to the selling partners, particularly when dealing with high-stakes negotiations.

How should the pricing organisation be structured?

Interestingly, this is also a question with many answers in practice. The spectrum of options is based on two dimensions – the level of centralisation and the level of collaboration – and the choice of structure will be determined by the business type, size or culture (complexity of business, speed of pricing decisions required, volume of transactions, regional, national or global clients and so on). We have identified four organisation archetypes (see Figure 11.6) while obviously recognising that there are many hybrid versions possible. The centre of scale option is typical for organisations with a high volume of standard products and services, such as a quoting or trading desk. The centre of excellence is more typical for firms that have fewer but more complex transactions where the pricing team can get involved in all aspects of the deal, including preparing for rounds of negotiation, or firms that have high volumes but have decided to deploy light-touch pricing support in the form of pricing 'fly-in' support or a pricing helpdesk (similar to what both our data services and testing services clients employ). The remaining two archetypes are more typical for larger, and more decentralised, firms that operate many business units across many sectors and markets. They are similar in that pricing resources are local to pricing decisions and can therefore provide support quickly when needed. These two archetypes differ only in that the networked support model creates a virtual pricing community across the entire firm to share training, tools, best practices and experience. Typically

| Figure 11.6 | Pricing organisation archetypes |

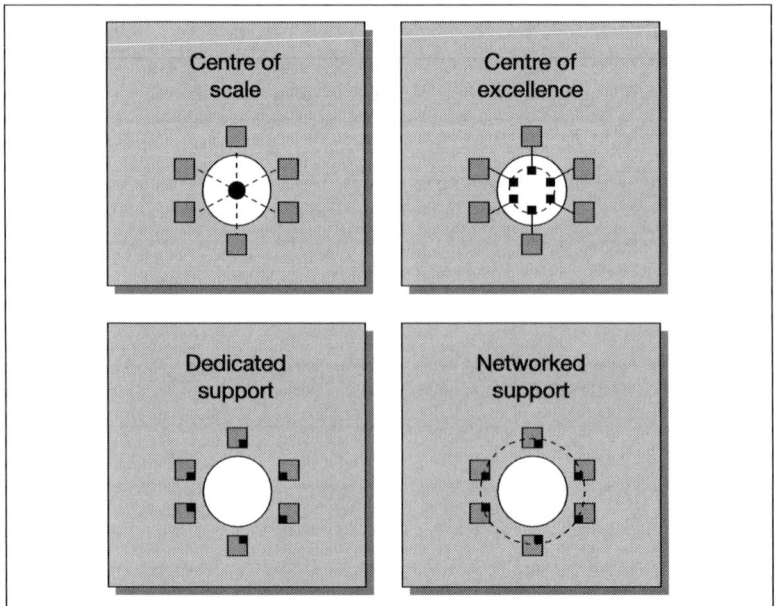

the networked model is a superior approach, but does create additional cost in terms of maintaining a community across the firm, and works best when sharing best practice is relevant from one part of the firm to another. We have seen clients where the business units are so different that the potential for learning is limited. However, one of the challenges with pricing resources dedicated in business units or markets is whether they can maintain the overall pricing role. We have seen clients where one pricing person in each market gets isolated and becomes an analytical research resource for the local management team.

A successful hybrid model we have seen at another data services client is a mix of centre of excellence and networked support. They have a global centre of excellence reporting to strategy in the corporate centre as well as dedicated pricing resources in their key business units. The centre of excellence performs and guides 'special projects' where required as well as guiding local projects and sharing best practice. There are no hard rules as to which archetype fits any given firm, but the business type, size and culture as well as the nature and volume of the pricing decisions will determine what is most appropriate.

Two further considerations for the pricing organisation will be the size of the team and the seniority of the sponsorship. The team size will be a factor of the volume of deals and complexity of pricing decisions and, to a degree, the speed of pricing decisions required (although speed can be managed by better pricing tools). We have seen a number of clients separating their pricing roles into 'bespoke pricing', where individual deals are priced and negotiated, and 'standard pricing', where standardised products and services are priced and promoted and updated periodically. The data, tools and time frames for pricing decisions vary considerably between 'bespoke' and 'standard' pricing decision support. The second consideration, senior sponsorship for pricing, is critical to sustaining pricing capabilities over time and delivering the benefits. Without senior sponsorship, pricing processes and decisions can get 'stuck' and once that starts to happen, the perception of pricing's role and effectiveness can be negatively affected. We strongly believe that a sponsor for pricing on the senior management team is a key success factor for pricing capabilities. This could be the head of sales or finance director or, better still, the managing partner. In our experience, we only see firms with senior sponsorship for pricing as 'price leaders' and realising the most benefits from effective pricing.

SUMMARY

Firms that are world-class in pricing focus on three key areas. First, they invest in understanding value. They analyse and quantify how their services create value for clients compared to competitors, and this requires that they have a detailed understanding of where and how value is created from the client's perspective, by segment, to inform better propositions and pricing decisions. Second, they leverage relevant and timely data to inform decision making. For example, most have access to accurate profitability by client and service. Analysing past transaction data for consistency is critical and analysing price sensitivity data can be invaluable. However, what pricing leaders all certainly do, is trust pricing analytics to inform pricing over intuition and anecdote. Finally, these firms are investing in and developing their pricing capabilities. We see the leading firms focussed on continuously improving their pricing processes and controls. Clear pricing strategies and policies are standard for pricing leaders, as are effective pricing metrics and Executive sponsorship.

Index

Do you want your people to be the very best at what they do?

Talk to us about how we can help.

As the world's leading learning company, we know a lot about what your people need in order to be better at what they do.

Whatever subject or skills you've got in mind (from presenting or persuasion to coaching or communication skills), and at whatever level (from new-starters through to top executives) we can help you deliver tried-and-tested, essential learning straight to your workforce – whatever they need, whenever they need it and wherever they are.

Talk to us today about how we can:

- Complement and support your existing learning and development programmes
- Enhance and augment your people's learning experience
- Match your needs to the best of our content
- Customise, brand and change it to make a better fit
- Deliver cost-effective, great value learning content that's proven to work.

Contact us today:
corporate.enquiries@pearson.com

Printed in Great Britain
by Amazon